THE BATTLE FOR BERMONDSEY

PETER TATCHELL

THE BATTLE FOR BERMONDSEY

preface by
TONY BENN

heretic books

First published October 1983 by Heretic Books,
P O Box 247, London N15 6RW
World copyright ©1983 Peter Tatchell
Preface world copyright ©1983 Tony Benn

 British Library Cataloguing in Publication Data

Tatchell, Peter
   The battle for Bermondsey.
   1. Great Britain, *Parliament*—Elections;
   1983 (February)
   2. Elections—London—Bermondsey—20th century
   I. Title
   329'.023'421640858   JN956

   ISBN 0-946097-11-9
   ISBN 0-946097-10-0 Pbk

Cover photograph reproduced by courtesy of the *Morning Star*

Cover by Aubrey Walter
Photoset by Shanta Thawani, 25 Natal Road, London N11 2HU
Printed and bound by Book Plan (Billing & Sons Ltd), Worcester

Preface

This book, in my considered judgement, is one of the most important political documents to have been published about the Labour Party since the war, and will remain a classic text long after the events in Bermondsey have faded from the public memory. For what Peter Tatchell has done is to write a detailed account of those events, and to do so with a meticulous attention to detail, without ever losing sight of the larger issues raised which concern everyone in the party.

The high drama of the story commands attention from the very first page, but in retelling it he has been absolutely fair and accurate, certainly insofar as I have knowledge of what actually happened. That, in itself, is a considerable achievement, given the fact that Tatchell himself was subjected to more abuse, distortion, misrepresentation and personal harassment than any other Labour figure during the period of eighteen months that stretched from his selection as candidate in 1981 to his defeat in the by-election of February 1983.

He bore himself throughout with great dignity and restraint, and has not allowed his own feelings to blunt his judgement about what occurred and why. Although it was right and proper for him to refer to his own personal background and nature, since the press made this central to their campaign against him, these matters are kept secondary to the political issues which should command the attention of the movement if it is to learn from them for the future.

Everyone will recognise in his account of the Bermondsey party and its decline from pre-war idealism and activity to the depths of decay and bureaucratic manipulation, one of the major causes of the fall in public support for the party itself, locally and nationally, over the last thirty years. The arrogance and self-isolating elitism which overcame the Bermondsey councillors under the old regime can be seen in many other municipalities which Labour has controlled for a similar period. We can also recognise in the personalities who ran that machine the very same characteristics which marked the SDP defectors who left the PLP.

Any serious student of the Labour Party who wants to understand the reasons why the party has had to undergo a period of renewal will have to read this book, for it sets out the frustrations of decent members when they honestly attempted to work with the old guard. The Bermondsey story is the story of the recovery of the party achieved by many thousands of party members who got together and consciously decided that they were not prepared to see the party die just for the lack of trying to save it. Some learned this in the cabinet, as I did, but most learned it in their ward meetings.

No one reading this account with an open mind could believe for a moment that those who undertook this campaign of renewal were, or are, enemies of democracy or were plotting to take away the liberties of the people — indeed the truth was, and is, that they were working to win back the democratic rights of the citizens — and the party — which had been filched by a clique of careerists who had forgotten why they were there. But in addition to learning the true nature and aspirations of this new generation of democrats and socialists who began their work at grassroots level during the Wilson and Callaghan years, we also learn a great deal about the counter-attack to which they were subjected, especially after 1981, when it became clear that they had won a majority support from the conference. This counter-attack took various forms, of which the most highly publicised were the defections to the SDP. But an even larger number stayed inside the party and conducted their campaigns from the front bench, or by organising to take over the NEC with the help of very senior figures in the PLP and the trade unions, which they succeeded in doing over a two-year period. Thus by the time that Peter Tatchell was adopted the machine was ready and waiting to deal with him, with Bermondsey and with any other constituency party that showed any signs of wanting to carry the renewal process through.

The witchhunt against Militant which also drew a lot of press comment was almost entirely irrelevant to what was happening, since Militant was not the prime mover, and as this book clearly shows was no part of the majority in Bermondsey; indeed it was not at all supportive of Peter Tatchell himself, at a time when he needed all the support he could get. But the attacks on Militant were important to the right for a very different reason, namely they allowed the counter-attack to be presented in such a way as to suggest that what was at stake was the maintenance of parliamentary democracy itself, and gave the media a licence to denounce everyone who wanted any sort of reform as a bloodstained revolutionary. This was never true of Militant, nor of any of the others who had their reputations blackened by the same process, and the net effect of it all was to suggest to the electors that the leadership of the party actually believed the party at local level was deeply infiltrated by a group of dangerous men and women who were plotting to destroy their hard-won freedoms.

I believe that this campaign played a large part in Labour's defeat in the general election, and it certainly played the decisive role in the crushing defeat which the party suffered in Bermondsey itself. For not only did the right-wing majority on the NEC spend most of the last eighteen months before the general election discussing how to deal with the Bermondsey situation, Militant and the application of Tariq Ali to join the party, but it also spent hours and hours of time on enquiries into very similar situations in other cities where local Labour Groups were fighting to maintain their power against the same sort of renewal campaigns as had occurred in Bermondsey.

There is a great deal about the media in this book, and the detailed description of how individual journalists behaved merits a special study since it shows quite clearly that, if democracy is ever destroyed in Britain, the media — including the so-called heavies and the BBC and ITN — will bear a very great responsibility for having deliberately corrupted the information system for their own reasons. I can confirm from my own experience, over the years, how frightening it is to be made an outlaw by Fleet Street and Broadcasting House, and how this process of harassment can affect someone's personal life and act as a standing invitation to others to send death threats or abusive and obscene letters. But unpleasant as that is, it is more than compensated for by the enormous warmth from far more people who will write supportive letters or just come up in the street or on a train or bus and clutch you by the arm with a word of encouragement, which more than makes up for the violent language of the well-paid hit-men who are hired by the proprietors to do their work for them.

The real danger of the media lies in the way that they work on the party leadership, and offer them a sort of exemption from attack if they will do the attacking themselves. Therein lies the real tragedy of Michael Foot's unhappy period as leader, for he was chosen by a right-wing PLP because the majority actually thought that with his left-wing past he was the only man who could defeat this new move to reform the party, and it was to that prime task that he turned his attention, giving it the top priority while he was there. He opposed the electoral college, tried to prevent it from being used, intervened directly in shadow cabinet elections and in re-selection conferences, denounced Peter Tatchell in the House of Commons on the advice of Bob Mellish and to placate the right, and then at the end, after demanding the expulsion of Militant, found that despite all his efforts to please them, and the media, they were both conspiring to get rid of him too before the general election.

No one on the left wants to see a leadership of their own choice use this influence to do down the right, because we recognise that whoever leads the party has a clear job of keeping us all together. But we do expect that any leader will respect the right of the party at every level to use the democracy of the party to choose who they want to represent them and who to admit as members, and will never accept a situation where a party leader uses the media to attack the party itself, even if he or she believes that by doing so they themselves can buy media support, which as we now know is not available while the party remains a socialist party linked to the trade unions.

These then are some of the lessons this important book can teach us, and our success in building up our strength in the future, when the British people need us so desperately, will depend on whether we learn them in time.

TONY BENN

Dedicated to my comrades in the Bermondsey Labour Party
and to the memory of Ada and Alfred Salter
who first began Labour's 'Battle for Bermondsey'
75 years ago.

Chapter One

From Radicalism to Right-Wing Decay

In the House of Commons on 3 December 1981, during Prime Minister's question time, there was an exchange involving James Wellbeloved, a Social-Democrat MP, Margaret Thatcher, the Prime Minister, and Michael Foot, the leader of the Labour Party. That brief exchange was to affect my personal and political life irrevocably. It was to plunge myself and the Labour Party into a maelstrom of controversy and internal strife that culminated in the loss of Bermondsey to the Liberals in the notorious by-election of February 1983. For the next eighteen months, Bermondsey was destined to play a prominent part in the disastrous scenario that led up to the defeat of the Labour Party in the 1983 general election.

Wellbeloved, a Labour defector to the SDP and a baiter of the left, asked Thatcher whether she had seen the statement by the Labour prospective parliamentary candidate for Bermondsey advocating extra-parliamentary action to challenge the government's right to rule. He went on to ask whether she agreed that such an 'irresponsible demand should be condemned by all those who hold precious parliamentary democracy and should not be condoned by craven silence'. Thatcher made some nebulous reply, knowing that the real target of the question was sitting exactly opposite her. Michael Foot duly obliged and got to his feet to reply to the question initially directed at the Prime Minister: 'Since the matter has been raised, can I say Mr Speaker, that the individual concerned is not an endorsed member...the individual concerned is not an endorsed member of the Labour Party, and as far as I am concerned, never will be.' Foot went on to make a party political scoring point against the Tories about not needing instructions from 'skin-deep' democrats about sustaining parliamentary democracy. Later that evening he issued a statement amending his comments from 'not an endorsed member' to 'not an endorsed candidate'. The Bermondsey Labour candidate referred to was me - Peter Tatchell.

From Michael Foot's unprecedented statement in the House of Commons to the Bermondsey by-election fifteen months later was one of

the most intense periods in the battle for Labour's soul. It was a period of
right-wing offensive against the left which ended with the party's defeat
in the 1983 election. Throughout those months, Bermondsey was at the
centre stage of Labour and national politics. Not that we were special.
Bermondsey was simply a microcosm of the changes that were taking
place in the Labour Party up and down the country. Through our struggle
to win the right to choose our own parliamentary candidate, Bermondsey
came to symbolise the struggle of the left and mirror the aspirations of
countless local constituency parties and grassroots activists all over
Britain. To understand the 'Battle for Bermondsey', it is necessary to go
back in time and examine the background of that struggle.

Family, Political Beginnings and Coming to Bermondsey

I moved to Bermondsey from Hornsey late in 1978, being offered a hard-
to-let single person's flat on the delapidated Rockingham Estate near the
Elephant and Castle. The estate had seen better days. It was a vast, mock-
Georgian, brown-brick London County Council estate with over a
thousand flats. Hailed as a 'people's palace' when it was built in the 1930s,
it had since fallen into decay and become another typical South London
working-class slum. Later, our political opponents seriously claimed that
I and others had moved into Bermondsey as part of an organised left-
wing conspiracy to take over the local party. Wild claims like these were
typical of the last-ditch attempts of an out-of-touch local leadership to
protect their rotting political base. When I moved into Bermondsey, I
knew hardly anyone in the area and I had no plans to take over anything
apart from my modest flat.

Bermondsey was a long way from Melbourne, Australia, where I was
born in 1952. But the poverty that still exists in Bermondsey today
reminded me of the circumstances in which I grew up all those thousands
of miles away. In September 1982, when the press were intensifying their
campaign to get me ditched as the candidate, the *Sun* ran a story about the
'Middle-Class Past of Working-Class Hero'. The sub-headline to the
article was 'Tatchell Had an Easy Life in the Leafy Suburbs'. The story,
and it *was* fiction, went on to say: 'Australian Tatchell was not reared in a
tough dockland area of Melbourne as he claimed. He grew up in the
comfort of a solidly middle-class home in the city's tree-lined residential
suburb of Mount Waverley. The young Tatchell wanted for nothing...'
The *Sun* had gone to the expense of hiring one Suzanne Chapple in
Melbourne to unearth these 'facts' about me. The story illustrates the
gross lies that the right-wing press will invent to down an opponent.

My father was a lathe operator and my stepfather variously employed
as a gardener, factory cleaner and taxi driver — my parents had been
divorced when I was four. My mother last worked as a packer and

storeperson in a local biscuit factory. For the first few years of my life, I grew up in the inner-city West Melbourne docks area. Later, when I was ten, our family moved out to Mount Waverley which was then dirt roads and open paddocks. Throughout my childhood my mother suffered from chronic asthma. With my mother's sickness, it fell to me as the eldest child to take on much of the responsibility for bringing up my younger brother and two sisters. There being no National Health Service in Australia, much of our family income went on medical bills. It made us exceptionally poor, even by working-class standards. We had to put up with patched and darned clothes, second-hand school textbooks and sandwich lunches because my parents could not afford meals from the school canteen. Family holidays were rare, and by comparison with other kids, our Christmas and birthday presents were modest. I remember thinking, even at an early age, how wrong it was that anyone should have to endure such hardships because a member of their family happened to be born with the misfortune of bad health. I was determined that one day I would do something to ensure that neither myself nor others would have to suffer such indignities.

To earn extra money, from the age of eight I sold newspapers on street corners to commuters driving home to the suburbs after work, receiving 1p for every six sold. Together with my brother, I also collected old newspapers door-to-door which we then sold for ½p per pound weight to local butchers' and chip shops. In the summer we went into parks to collect discarded soft drink bottles which, on returning them to shops to get the deposit, earned us five shillings on a good day.

I was educated at the Australian equivalent of a comprehensive, Mount Waverley High School. It was there I got my first experience of elected responsibilities, being chosen by fellow pupils as secretary of the Students Representative Council, and in my final year, as school captain. It was also my first beginnings in 'politics' when a group of us started an underground school magazine and embryonic students' union in the days when such things were strictly forbidden and grounds for expulsion. But it was raising money through sponsored walks to help Aborigines on reserves to continue at school that created the biggest furore and led to the headmaster denouncing me as being manipulated by 'communists' — the first of many smears!

Though I did well at athletics and my studies, I was reluctantly forced to leave school at the minimum age of 16 because my parents could not afford to keep me there. For the first few years I did carpentry, painting, decorating and display and worked in a big department store. At the age of 17, I realised that I was gay. Initially, because of my strict Protestant upbringing, I was resistant to accepting my homosexuality. But then I met a very special man. It seemed so natural. Over a period of months we grew to love each other very much and we ended up sharing a most wonderful relationship together.

At that time, in Australia, homosexuality was still completely illegal. It was punishable by long prison sentences and enforced psychiatric treatment. With virtual impunity the police regularly beat up and occasionally murdered homosexuals. I grew to despise the judges, police and psychiatrists and ceased to have much respect for the law. Democracy and human rights were a myth for gay people; just as the 'lucky country' was a myth for poor families like mine.

After leaving school, I became very active in the anti-draft and anti-Vietnam War movements. During 1970-71, I was elected to the committee of the Vietnam Moratorium Campaign. This involvement in the anti-war protests was a further radicalising influence. A ban on leafleting in the streets and savage and unprovoked police violence against the 'Stop the War' demonstrations shocked me. It made supposed freedom of speech seem such a sham.

I soon started questioning everything that I had previously taken for granted. Gradually I began to see how the hardships we had experienced as a working-class family were not an isolated individual problem. They were part and parcel of a huge web of injustices against lots of different people. From my initial experience in politics, I quickly came to realise that those in power were prepared to go to extraordinary lengths to perpetuate their system and suppress anyone who challenged it.

Along with many other Australians, I was passionately opposed to the American and Australian intervention in the Vietnam War and to conscription of young Australians to fight in that war of aggression. I had no intention of being drafted to fight in a totally immoral war to prop up a brutal and corrupt dictatorship in Saigon which was notorious for the torture and execution of political opponents. The war had nothing to do with the defence of democracy as the Americans claimed. It was about the defence of American financial and political influence in South-East Asia. It was blatant imperialist interference in the affairs of a tiny country thousands of miles away, which did not threaten America, Australia or anyone else. Johnson, Nixon and Kissinger were war criminals to be ranked with the worst in history and I was not going to be part of their war machine to napalm and massacre innocent Vietnamese people with whom I had no quarrel.

Faced with the 'choice' of joining the army or two years imprisonment, I left my family, friends, job and all my possessions in Australia and arrived in London with a single suitcase in 1971. A planned temporary stay until the war was over eventually became permanent. Later, in the by-election, our opponents were to make much of my 'draft-dodging' and 'refusal to defend my country'. I stand by what I did then. However, if Britain were ever again attacked, as we were in the Second World War, I would be prepared to fight in a war of self-defence to defend our civil liberties, trade-union freedom and our right to self-determination.

When I arrrived in Britain in 1971, I settled in West London. I began catching up on the education I had missed by leaving school early. I studied A-levels at evening classes and eventually took a degree in social sciences at the Polytechnic of North London. Afterwards I got a part-time job working at the North Lambeth Day Centre for the single homeless at Waterloo and became active in campaigning for the rights of homeless people.

Soon after my arrival in London, I renewed my involvement in the movement against the American intervention in Vietnam, and also against Britain's war in Ireland. My early political commitment also included the Gay Liberation Front, and later, the National Union of Students' Gay Rights Campaign.

Despite Russia's undoubted economic achievements and the debt we owe its people for their heroic sacrifices during the last war, the Soviet 'barbed-wire socialist community' has never been a model for the kind of radical but democratic socialist Britain which I envisaged. Hence my early involvement in campaigns supporting left-wing dissidents in Eastern Europe such as Rudolf Bahro who were fighting for political liberty and free trade-unionism.

In the late 1970s I went out to Malawi to investigate and expose child labour, starvation wages and the repression of trade-union rights on British-owned tea estates. Subsequently, efforts to improve conditions were organised through the World Development Movement, the European Socialist Group and international trade unions.

In 1978, I successfully joined the Hornsey Labour Party in North London. Earlier, in 1972, I had applied to join the North Hammersmith Labour Party but received no reply to my application — an all too familiar complaint from people who have tried to join the party and found the bureaucratic machinery so creaky that their application is never followed up.

The Decrepit Mellish-O'Grady Political Machine

After moving later that year to the Chaucer ward of the Bermondsey constituency, I immediately applied to transfer my membership to the local Labour Party. The 'old guard' of the Bermondsey party were still in charge then. They were the right-wing followers of the MP, Bob Mellish, and the Southwark council leader, John O'Grady, who had run the party machine in Bermondsey for thirty years or more. By 1978 it was a very ramshackle machine indeed. Membership of the party had dropped to below 400 which was disgracefully low for a Labour stronghold such as Bermondsey. This was a far cry from the pre-war Bermondsey party which had boasted 3,000 members and full-time paid organisers. By 1978, in some wards less than half a dozen people, mainly elderly, attended monthly ward meetings. They were mostly either councillors or ward officers and often both! Perhaps it was not so surprising that so few members attended. In the right-wing wards, 'dissenters' sometimes did not receive notices of meetings and found difficulty in renewing their subscriptions.

It took several 'reminders' on my part before I was accepted as a member in Bermondsey. I claim no special treatment in this, because at the time it was notoriously difficult to join the Bermondsey Labour Party. New members were seemingly not welcome. Some people speak of having made repeated applications and waiting over a year before they were admitted into membership. Heaven only knows how many less determined applicants gave up in desperation and were lost to the party for good!

Charitably, perhaps it was partly a case of inefficiency and incompetence. But it is also true that the right wing who were in charge, some of whom subsequently defected to the SDP or otherwise left the party, were basically not interested in increasing the membership and repeatedly mislaid new applications. The constituency party held little or no political debate. It seemed to exist to re-elect local worthies to Southwark council (which covers the Bermondsey area) and to re-elect Mellish to Parliament. The party talked a lot about dustbins and memorial funds to retiring party workers, but very little else. Contact with the local community was practically nil. The General Committee (GC), which is the decision-making body of the constituency party, never challenged the policies of the Labour-controlled Southwark council. The council was a gerontocracy, the average age of councillors being well over 60. One was nearly 90 and virtually immobile. Some had sat on the council continuously for over forty years. Undoubtedly, years ago some of them had given great service to the party. But now they were collectively so incompetent that in the 1978 borough council elections, the Labour manifesto was not issued until three weeks after the election! The party's attitude to Bob 'I'm the son of an 1889 docker' Mellish was deferential. Mellish ran Bermondsey as his personal fiefdom and brooked no opposition; not that there was much in the flaccid ranks of the right wing. Reg Goodwin, an honourable man, was Greater London Council member. Councillors held most of the key party officerships. The whole party revolved round Mellish, Goodwin, O'Grady and the councillors. Like a dynasty, this handful of ruling families, often related by marriage, used their positions to perpetuate their rule and sit on any burgeoning opposition.

The stories about the dirty tricks of the right were legion. It was these that led to their being referred to openly in Southwark political circles as the 'Bermondsey mafia'. Some of the delegates to the GC were fairly dubious, in the sense that certain trade-union branches affiliated to the constituency party without their members' knowledge, and there were even delegates whose occupation bore no relation to the union they purportedly represented. Typically, a teacher was signed up as a delegate from a TGWU road transport branch. The right wing's voting strength was also augmented by retired union delegates. Since these were no longer active in their branches, it was doubtful whether they genuinely represented their members. These manoeuvres had for years helped ensure an impregnable right-wing majority. The failure of the party officers to provide the GC with a list of delegates and the union branches they represented only served to heighten our suspicions that the GC was being packed by the right.

Not that such fiddles were confined to the unions. Right-wing dominated wards, where only three or four people attended branch meetings, sent large numbers of delegates to the GC. They had more delegates than their actual members entitled them to, but this was obscured by the fact that officers never disclosed ward membership and subscription lists. Our suspicions of 'bogus' delegates seemed confirmed when some of the more contentious ones suddenly disappeared just before the 1980 AGM.

During the reign of the old guard, party members found it difficult to obtain copies of the constitution and standing orders. So far as the right were concerned, the less we knew about them, the less likely we would be able to challenge the status quo. When we did actually get copies, our objections to infringements were then overridden on the grounds of 'custom and practice'. This pretext was used, for example, to rebuke a party member who had circulated a letter to ward branches. We perceived this as an attempt by the party hierarchy to stifle free communication between members. For a while, they even led us to believe there was a separate rule book which superseded the constitution and standing orders and which, of course, only the right wing possessed. Frequently, the chair ruled out of order matters that were disagreeable or controversial, and the right would also filibuster to avoid sticky subjects. This was particularly the case with motions regarding the debts owed by the Labour Club.

The administration of the GC was lamentable. Delegates would sometimes receive their agendas late, or not at all. The Post Office always got the blame. Minutes were often inaccurate or incomplete, and handed out on the night of the meeting, when their approval could be rushed through before delegates had time to read them. The officers were less than efficient at carrying out GC instructions that they disliked. On more than one occasion important letters addressed to the party were not communicated to the GC, and duly submitted motions were either not placed on the agenda or were ruled out of order.

Several long-standing members of the party also expressed their unease at the laxity with which credentials were checked at meetings to choose candidates for the local council elections. Old age pensioners who had not been seen for the previous four years would be wheeled into the selection meetings to vote back the same old councillors. The right also had interesting ways of counting votes. This was usually done outside the meeting room in a dark hallway, by scrutineers who were nearly always friends of the officers and councillors.

Downstairs in the Bermondsey Labour Party headquarters in Lower Road, there was a Labour Club with a bar, pool table and fruit machine. Though Bob Mellish was president, like so many clubs round the country it had slipped completely out of the hands of the party and become a law unto itself. It was supposed to be open to all party members, but it was in essence a right-wing social club. If you weren't on the hard right of the party it was extremely difficult to join. Labour Party members were refused on the spurious pretext that the club was 'full up', although talk at the bar suggested that more than a few Tory and National Front supporters had found their way in. In the late 1970s there was a scandal when Lenny Mayers, a local black trade-unionist and Labour Party member, was refused membership of the club. The finances of the club also gave cause for concern. In the early 1970s, despite a roaring trade, thousands of pounds had piled up in debts to the Labour Party. Not only did the club refuse to make financial contributions to the party, it even refused to pay its share of the rates and electricity bills. It was bleeding the Labour Party dry.

It was a tragedy that some formerly good party members and elected representatives had grown flabby under a system of one-party rule. They took the voters for granted and rested on the laurels of the past. Indeed, the old guard used to boast that if you put up a monkey on a Labour ticket in Bermondsey, it would get elected. Even in 1978, with rising disenchantment in the local electorate, that was clearly not the case.

This then was the constituency party I joined in 1978. I found new comrades in Chaucer ward and in the other branches, many of whom were seething with discontent at the mafia's arrogant disregard of the party's constitution and their contempt for the electorate. The right-wing faction had wielded unchallenged control for so long that they had not only become complacent and inefficient but corrupt too. By that I do not mean to imply that there was financial corruption in the sense of illegal bribes and other such practices. Their corruption was the corruption that prolonged and unaccountable control of a political machine inevitably brings. A ruling elite of councillors and party bureaucrats looked on local politics as their personal preserve and were ready to repel any challenging intruders.

Rebellion had already broken out before I joined. Older, long-standing party members had broken the right-wing dynasties in three of the eight wards — Cathedral, Riverside and Chaucer. However, at this stage, the left's nascent struggle was fragmented and isolated in the separate wards. During this early period, whenever I went to see Mellish to take up matters on behalf of our tenants' association, he made the most friendly of overtures. He positively encouraged me to get involved in the party; he said 'new young blood' was desperately needed and a lot of the 'old dead wood' had to be cleared away. He conceded that the Bermondsey party was very inefficient and that membership had fallen alarmingly low. When Mellish heard that Chaucer ward were planning a newsletter and recruitment drive, he expressed approval and delight. But what surprised me most was his scathing criticism of the old councillors. It was their complacency and incompetence which he blamed for the huge number of housing complaints he received at his constituents' advice surgeries.

Dr Salter and the Pre-War Radical Tradition

Yet the Bermondsey Labour Party had not always been so moribund and undemocratic. It had a proud history of left-wing socialism in the pre-war period when Dr Salter was the Labour MP for the area. For many older rank-and-file party members Salter's radical socialism was still an inspiration, though the right poured scorn on his memory. But much as they sought to deny it, the authentic Labour tradition *was* one of radicalism and militancy, rather than the 'moderation' of Wilson, Callaghan and Mellish. Since the early 1970s, the left has merely sought to revive this tradition. To me, the Salter era was both an inspiration and a textbook for the changes we sought.

Bermondsey was typical of many parties around the country in the pre-war period. The Bermondsey Labour Party was founded by Ada and Alfred Salter in 1910. Alfred Salter was not born in Bermondsey. He first came to the area as a doctor at the turn of the century. Radicalised by the terrible poverty he witnessed, Dr Salter joined the Liberal Party which was then the main political opposition to the Tories. At about this time, Salter was imprisoned in Wandsworth on six different occasions. As a matter of conscience he had refused to pay his rate bill in protest against the state subsidy of church schools.

Salter soon became disillusioned with the Liberals' failure to relieve the misery of the working class. He gave up a promising career in Liberal politics to form a branch of the Independent Labour Party in 1908. Out of the ILP, the Bermondsey Labour Party was established two years later. Within a few months of the party's formation, its radical reputation was firmly established when Ada Salter was elected as London's first woman councillor. A year later in 1911, party members played a prominent role in the Bermondsey General Strike. Though the strike began in Surrey

Docks, it quickly spread throughout the riverside. At the Pink's jam factory, women workers draped the building with a giant banner: 'We are not white slaves, we are Pink's'. Women workers and young girls employed at the jam, cocoa and tin box factories played a crucial role in the strike's astonishing success in securing higher wages and mass unionisation among the Bermondsey working class.

In 1913, a Labour Cooperative bakery was established to produce cheap, good quality bread for local people. Eventually it grew in size to employ over one hundred workers. Feeding much of south-east London, it raised thousands of pounds to finance the Bermondsey Labour magazine with a monthly circulation of over 15,000.

At the outbreak of the 1914-18 war, Salter wrote a now famous anti-war treatise in the ILP paper, *Labour Leader*. The article was reprinted as a leaflet and 1½ million copies were distributed throughout the UK. Later it was translated and distributed world-wide. It was banned in many countries. In Australia, New Zealand and South Africa, people caught distributing it were arrested and sentenced to long terms in gaol. By 1916, nineteen members of the Bermondsey Labour Party had been imprisoned and tortured as conscientious objectors. They refused to slaughter workers of other lands in an imperialist war to fatten the pockets of the rich bankers and industrialists.

Such radicalism did not always endear Salter and Labour to the local electors. It took 14 years of unsuccessful attempts before Salter was eventually elected Bermondsey's first Labour MP in 1922. His maiden speech in Parliament very nearly secured the establishment of a legal minimum wage to end the exploitation and hardship experienced by low-paid workers. Later Salter scandalised the House of Commons, including the Labour leadership, by his outspoken criticism of drunkenness and extravagance among MPs and the abuse of their privileged office for personal gain. Predictably, Salter was pilloried in the press and his own party as a 'trouble-maker' and 'left-wing rebel'.

Also in 1922, Labour won control of the Bermondsey borough council for the first time. The red flag was flown from the Town Hall to the outrage of high society. In keeping with Labour's feminist beginnings, Ada Salter became London's first woman mayor. As an act of humility and a token of her identification with the 'common people', she defied tradition by refusing to wear the mayoral robes or chain of office.

In the early 1920s Bermondsey teemed with tiny, damp and over-crowded dwellings, many of them dating back to the 1700s. So, despite opposition and threats from the Tory government, a direct labour organisation was set up by the new Labour council to clear the slums and create local jobs. Under Salter's guidance, Labour's plan was to turn Bermondsey into a garden city of cottage houses. Work had hardly begun before the Conservative government intervened to block Labour's plans, forcing the council to build fewer houses and more flats instead. Despite this setback, by 1933 Bermondsey's Labour council could proudly boast that it had cleared more slums than all the other London boroughs put together.

The council's wages to direct labour employees were well above union rates and among the highest in the country, as was the level of poor relief to the sick and unemployed. Embarrassed by these achievements of municipal socialism, the government yet again intervened in Bermondsey affairs, ordering reductions in wages and poor relief. For a long time the councillors resisted. But eventually, on union advice, they reluctantly backed down after being threatened with imprisonment and a lifelong ban from public office.

When Labour took power, Bermondsey's 19,000 homes had only 250 baths between them. So the new council built a magnificent public baths in 1927; inlaid with marble, it was reputed to be the finest in Europe. The Tories attacked it as a waste, saying it was too good for the 'mere working classes'.

Poverty and bad housing combined to breed disease. One in three homes had a case of tuberculosis. The death and infant mortality rates were among the highest in London. Labour's answer was to establish a Bermondsey Health Service financed through the rates. Britain's first municipal solarium, convalescent home and mobile health clinic were set up. Long before 1945 and the National Health Service, Bermondsey people had their own health centre where they could see specialists and receive the best treatment either free of charge, or for a nominal fee. In the case of the most desperately ill tuberculosis patients, the council used its rate fund to send them to a Swiss sanitorium for recuperation. As a result of Labour's effort, within a few years the number of tuberculosis cases halved. The infant mortality rate dropped by 60 per cent and the maternal death rate even fell below that of posh Hampstead.

Apart from Southwark Park, there were no open spaces and hardly a blade of grass or single flower to be seen in Bermondsey. The Labour council established a Beautification Committee. It proceeded to turn church graveyards into public parks. Flower beds and trees were planted down every grimy street. In two years, Bermondsey could claim more trees and flowers than any other inner-city borough.

Not surprisingly, visitors came from all over the world — from Europe, America and the Soviet Union — to marvel at Bermondsey's remarkable socialist achievements. But though they had vastly improved the lives of Bermondsey people, Salter and the Labour councillors were constantly smeared in the press as 'extremists' and 'communists'. The Tories attacked them for 'extravagant overspending' and 'frittering away ratepayers' money'. However, the people's judgement was otherwise. In 1934, Bermondsey became the first constituency in the country to have 100 per cent Labour representation — the MP, London County Councillor, Board of Guardians and borough council were all Labour. The party's membership swelled to over 3,000, which amounted to 25 per cent of those who voted in the constituency.

The new Labour council managed to engender a tremendous sense of working-class solidarity. During the 1926 General Strike, the council suspended itself and delegated its power to an Emergency Committee. This committee liaised with the trade-union Council of Action. It put the Town Hall at the strikers' disposal. For much of the strike Bermondsey was a 'no go' area for the police and army; it was barricaded off with roadblocks controlled by the Council of Action. Power passed out of the hands of government and into the hands of local people. For nine days, the working class administered all of Bermondsey. It was under workers' control!

Despite their own deprivations during the strike, Bermondsey people showed enormous generosity and sacrifice in aiding the striking miners in the Welsh village of Blaina, Ebbw Vale, They collected over £7,000 and Salter donated all of his MP's salary for the seven months they were out on strike.

Throughout the 1930s Labour kept its radical tradition alive in Bermondsey. In 1935 the mayor declined an invitation to meet the king in protest against the squalor of the Depression and the pomp and privilege of the monarchy. The council also refused to spend public money on a civic reception to celebrate King George V's Silver Jubilee. Instead the money was spent on helping the elderly and unemployed. Near the mayor's house a huge anti-royalist banner was hung across the street: 'God Save the People!'

Defying even Labour headquarters, the Bermondsey party held secret fund-raising campaigns to buy milk, blankets and medical supplies to aid the Republicans during the Spanish Civil War and the victims of Nazi persecution in Europe. Then, during the 1939–45 war, Bermondsey went through a devastating baptism of fire. After the war was over, Labour's dream was in ruins and many of its pioneers such as Ada and Alfred Salter were dead. Of Bermondsey's 19,000 dwellings, 90 per cent were either damaged or destroyed by the blitz. Nearly 300 factories and warehouses were obliterated, as were half the schools.

The Right-Wing Coup of 1946 and Mellish's Unsavoury Friends

With the post-war merging of the Bermondsey and Rotherhithe constituencies, there also came a dramatic political shift to the right. The newly merged party was packed with right-wing Catholic dockers. On selection night many of them turned up for the very first time. Few were ever seen again. With the block of transport union votes, the Rotherhithe faction won dominance and voted Mellish into power. To maintain right-wing hegemony over the left from the old Bermondsey party, a bureaucratic political machine was established. From this point onwards Bermondsey Labour Party began its slow spiral of decline.

There is a good deal of irony in Mellish's later accusations about 'young rebels' taking over and pushing him out of Bermondsey. When Mellish was first selected as candidate for the Rotherhithe constituency in 1946, there was great uproar about this young 'upstart', Major Mellish, who ousted Dr Gillinson, the long-standing London County Councillor. A couple of years after his selection, the young rebel Mellish was sacked by Attlee as a Parliamentary Private Secretary because he refused to vote with the Labour government on the Ireland Bill.

Mellish won the 1946 selection almost entirely on the basis of TGWU delegates, whose votes Mellish's organisers were able to deliver to him. It was easier in those days for individual unions to tie up constituencies for their own candidates by packing GCs with their delegates. Mellish's control of the Rotherhithe party was dependent on these votes. This began to erode in the early 1970s, but Mellish continued to act in the bullying, string-pulling manner to which he had become accustomed, and which made him such an unpopular Chief Whip during the Wilson years. Mellish's period of serving as the area's MP coincided with the transformation of the local Labour Party from a democratic, campaigning party to an authoritarian and bureaucratic election machine.

After his election to the House of Commons in 1946, Mellish rapidly drifted even further to the right. He was a central figure in the anti-communist witchhunts of the late 1940s. Not only did he brand the 1949 dock strike as a communist conspiracy, Mellish actually handed over details on alleged communist subversion in the docks to the intelligence service MI5. When the government put several dockers on trial in 1951, Mellish backed the government against the unions. Later, he showed unacceptable tolerance to the fascist dictatorships of Franco and Salazar, becoming deputy chair of an Anglo-Spanish parliamentary Group in the 1950s. After a trip to the Portuguese colony of Angola, Mellish returned loudly proclaiming that he saw 'no signs of suppression'. In recognition of his service to the Catholic lobby, the Vatican made Mellish a papal Knight of St Gregory.

In parallel with his rightward political drift, Mellish also developed associations with the corrupt businessmen Oliver Cutts, T. Dan Smith and Sir Eric Miller (who suddenly committed suicide while his financial affairs were under police investigation). The full extent of these associations was dramatically revealed by the *New Statesman* on 6 August 1982. The *Statesman* disclosed that Oliver Cutts was an unscrupulous businessman who had been convicted for handling stolen anthracite in

1945. He went on to make a fortune owning garages and developing property in Bermondsey and Deptford. Cutts had set out to become a millionaire and get himself a knighthood. He looked to Mellish for help. Their friendship began in 1953, and thereafter Cutts claims to have entertained Mellish a couple of times a week at the Savoy Hotel. In 1962 Cutts gave Mellish £4,000 of the £7,000 cost of a large house in spacious grounds in Catford, South London. This coincided with Cutts' attempts to secure a knighthood. Though there is no suggestion that Mellish acted improperly, when the knighthood failed to materialise Cutts demanded and got the money back.

Also in 1962, Cutts paid £280 towards the cost of a birthday party for Mellish's eldest son, Robert. Later he arranged a job with a law firm for Mellish's third son, Michael. The firm subsequently changed its name to Mellish and Harkavy of Mayfair. It was later investigated by the Law Society following its conduct of Cutts' divorce case, which the presiding judge described as making him feel 'most uneasy'.

Another Cutts venture was the International Sports Trust to train Olympic athletes at a house he had bought in Hampshire. The trustees included Cutts, Mellish and Sir Hamilton Kerr, the Tory MP. Then in 1965, after the International Athletes Club had refurbished the property, Cutts closed down the sports centre and later sold it for more than three times the price he had paid for it.

Mellish's recommendation had resulted in the award of an MBE to Cutts; well short of the knighthood he had hoped for. But even that honour was not to last. In 1968, Cutts became the first person to be stripped of an MBE following his conviction for malicious damage, perjury and conspiracy to pervert the course of justice.

Cutts was relatively small fry in comparison with T. Dan Smith. In the 1970s, the Smith and Poulson corruption scandals rocked local councils and even the government at Westminster. Eddie Milne MP claimed that Mellish was one of the key people who blocked his efforts to get an investigation into corruption within the North-Eastern Labour parties and Labour councils. T. Dan Smith, with his Labour connections, had sought to persuade councils to build houses designed by his partner John Poulson and the Open System Building Company which they had founded to promote industrialised building methods. As Minister for Housing, and later Public Building and Works, Mellish was a strong advocate of these methods too, though he now admits that estates and tower blocks built by this system were an 'appalling blunder'. At the suggestion of Andy Cunningham, a Smith lieutenant and Durham councillor who sat on Labour's NEC, Mellish joined the party's Local and Regional Government Advisory Committee, of which Smith was also a member.

The *New Statesman* article also connected Mellish with the Tory MP Paul Williams, with whom Mellish formed a company called Personal

Relations Ltd. Williams later became chair of the right-wing Monday Club within the Tory Party. And according to the *Daily Telegraph*, Mellish was identified in a police intelligence report in 1979 as a close friend of the late Sir Eric Miller. The report prepared by Scotland Yard's C6 Commercial Criminal Intelligence Branch had described Miller as 'a very unpleasant person who would screw anyone for a buck', though Mellish later denied this association.

These were strange friends for the golden-hearted dockers' MP, especially as a government minister. The *New Statesman* article raised several important questions about the career of Bob Mellish. The very fact that these were asked, in the issue of 6 August 1982, may have been a severe embarrassment to the long-serving MP for Bermondsey, who claimed to represent everything good and decent in the Labour Party. Could it have been sufficient reason for him to bow out a few days before the article was due to appear, so that the fuss over his resignation from the Labour Party, and his accompanying emotional theatrics, would divert attention from the exposé?

Despite our disagreements with Mellish, he was the official Labour candidate in the 1979 general election. So we all worked very hard to get him re-elected. Canvassing for Mellish we encountered a great deal of criticism of his recent record as an MP. In some cases we met people who had never seen Mellish or a Labour canvasser for twenty years. There was immense opposition to the policies of Southwark's Labour council, while the Callaghan government, with its attacks on the living standards of working-class people, naturally made it far more difficult to argue convincingly that electors should vote Labour. It was hardly surprising that Mellish was returned with a much reduced majority — 19,000 in 1974 had shrunk to below 12,000. Mellish attacked the unions for the 'winter of discontent' and blamed them for Labour's election defeat. He took revenge on the electorate who had nearly halved his majority by cutting back his constituents' advice surgeries from four to two a month.

After Labour's defeat in the 1979 general election, many activists in constituency parties up and down the country were filled with a sense of betrayal. The Callaghan years had seen the imposition of wage restraint at a time of rising profits, cuts in public expenditure, increased unemployment, sanctions-busting in Rhodesia and Namibia, the secret modernisation of the Polaris nuclear deterrent and a reneging on Labour's commitment to a Freedom of Information Act. The taskmasters were NATO, the IMF and the huge multinationals based in the City. For any socialist, the Callaghan government was a tragic period in the history of Labour politics.

Nothing like those years of Labour rule could ever be allowed to happen again. In Bermondsey many party members shared such feelings and yearned for change. Their feelings were intensified by the appalling record of Southwark council and the absolute unwillingness of the old guard of the Bermondsey Labour Party to engender any political activity. Surely it is only worthwhile belonging to the Labour Party if it is genuinely committed to solve people's hardships and suffering and is actually prepared to enact the radical socialist policies necessary to achieve this end? Who wants to join a party which has become identified with the status quo and the establishment, and all the continuing injustices that implies? Change had to come, and nowhere was it more essential than in Bermondsey.

Chapter Two

Grassroots Resurgence and the Leadership's Resistance

After the disastrous 1979 defeat, as we contemplated the dismal record of the Callaghan government and Southwark council, many party members from both the left and the centre made up their minds that things had to change in the party if Labour was to return to its socialist roots and re-emerge as a campaigning party of working people. Some of the left in Bermondsey initially sought compromise with the right and a path of gradual change. But the old guard were impervious to change. They wouldn't even listen to our arguments, let alone meet us halfway. Those who wanted and sought rapprochement with the right were soon disillusioned. Somewhat reluctantly, we realised that change would have to be total.

Why Total Change Was Necessary

During late 1979, a group of party members began to meet to discuss how best to challenge the control of the right-wing Bermondsey mafia. This caucus was a broad-based coalition of the left and centre that for the first time drew together party members from all wards in the constituency. What primarily brought us together was a profound dissatisfaction with the state of the party as it was. In the wake of the 1979 election defeat, there was great discontent in the party throughout the country. This discontent was compounded in Bermondsey by a lack-lustre local Labour council and a decrepit constituency party. What began to happen in Bermondsey was also happening in many other constituencies as well. Bermondsey was a typical example of what was taking place in the Labour Party at large.

The broad left caucus included party members who were also involved with trade unions, tenants' associations and community groups that were highly critical of Southwark council's policies, particularly on housing and the redevelopment of the huge riverside areas of the constituency. The immediate political aim of the left caucus was to mobilise majority support and take control of the party machinery through democratic means. Unlike the right wing we did everything by the rule book. We wanted more democracy and constitutionality in the party and so we strove to bring about the changes we wanted by democratic and constitutional means. There was a strong feeling that if we stooped to the level of our opponents, we would be off on a similar path and end up just like the right wing. When some of the old-timers suggested lightheartedly that we should resort to dirty tricks, this was flatly rejected. We chose not to adopt the methods of a morally bankrupt opponent to win the battle. In the event, we won control because enough people encompassing all shades of opinion wanted to see change in the Bermondsey Labour Party. They wanted to see the party run according to the rule book and a return to the days of campaigning radical socialism.

Of course, the right were to claim that the 'takeover' in Bermondsey was achieved by an illegitimate conspiracy. This is a laughable charge from those who for years had scorned so many democratic principles and procedures in their desire to keep power. What the right hated, of course, was that we were very well-organised and resisted all attempts to block our progress. When a delegate sympathetic to us was elected to the GC via a trade-union branch, the right would often delay acceptance on the pretext that the letter of appointment had never been received. We would not let this pass. We would question and query relentlessly. No longer could the councillors who dominated the officerships of the GC escape unchallenged when they resorted to such ruses to preserve their power base. Naturally, after years of unquestioning rule the right did not take kindly to the exercise of the party's constitution and pressure from the grassroots. Their antagonism became overt and at some GC meetings they increasingly adopted a belligerent stance.

Much has been said about the supposed influx of middle-class 'trendies' and their subsequent 'hijacking' of the Bermondsey party. According to the press and the right, these middle-class people were all bedsitter entryists; vegetarians who wore sandals, looked like Trotsky, wove their own clothes and drank real ale. Certainly there were more professional middle-class people living in the western part of the constituency than in years gone by. But most of them were the children of working-class parents — beneficiaries of the Labour movement's struggle to win the opportunity of higher education for all. The gentrification that has happened in other parts of London has largely passed Bermondsey by, despite proximity to the West End and the City. The reason for this is primarily that there is so little property to buy in Bermondsey. Most of the population live in council flats. A change in the Bermondsey party was only made possible because a lot of Bermondsey 'born and bred' working-class party members joined with their middle-class comrades to oust the right wing. When it was obvious that a new energy was flowing through the party, these older members united with the younger and newer members around opposition to the council's approval for widespread office development, the plans for a new Southwark Town Hall, and the arbitrary expulsion of left Southwark councillors from the Labour Group by O'Grady.

Those issues were there. People cared about them. We as socialists were vitally concerned. It was absolutely essential that the Labour Party was seen to be in the forefront of community struggles and for local people to have a say in the future of their area. It was a pity that so much of our effort was in opposition to a Labour council. How much better for the party had we been able to cooperate with Southwark council in planning the redevelopment of the area along socialist lines. But the differences between us were so great that we were headed for open conflict with the elected representatives of our own party. None of us wanted that. We owed loyalty to the party. But when our public representatives were turning their backs on socialist principles by co-operating with Tories like Heseltine to implement his cuts before they were even on the statute book and to sell the local community down the river, we could not turn a blind eye to that. We could not toe the line.

The plans to build a new Southwark Town Hall brought the council into open opposition with local people and the left and centre of the party. At the time, the Tory government was forcing massive cutbacks in local services and Southwark tenants were facing large increases in rents and rates. It was indefensible in these circumstances that Labour councillors were planning to spend up to £30 million on a new Town Hall, which included such fripperies as mayoress's boudoirs. Naturally the right were enraged when the rank-and-file members of the party urged them to scrap their plans. Their rage was multiplied when they saw these same party members active in the marches and meetings against the building of the Town Hall. After all, in their view, they were the elected representatives of the party and they had the responsibility to make decisions. When they had, after due consideration, made their decisions, it was up to party members to back up the policies of the council. They were used to a docile, unquestioning party membership. But things were changing rapidly. There was never any real doubt in the minds of the broad left activists that we would inevitably come into head-on conflict with the right-wing council led by O'Grady, who had been a founder member and vice-chair of the Social-Democratic Alliance, the forerunner of the SDP.

Too often the claims of party loyalty had in the past led left-wingers to fall into line behind policies that were directly contrary to socialist principles and opposed by the majority of rank-and-file Labour members. Southwark council was not accountable to the party, just as the Wilson and Callaghan governments seemed to be out of control by the party in the country, making policies and decisions without any real reference to party members. O'Grady and his followers made no real attempt to find out what the party and local people felt about issues such as the Town Hall. When told they did not have our support, they merely ignored us. After all, they knew better. They were the elected representatives. As in the local council, so in the 1974-79 Labour government. No widespread consultation preceded decision-making. Our councillors were cut off from the party, just like many Labour MPs.

When the right were ousted from control in Bermondsey and Southwark, they were fond of saying that it had all happened clandestinely: that they had little idea of the extent of 'infiltration' and our whole 'takeover' had been a closely guarded conspiracy. This is palpable nonsense. Myself and numerous other activists were prominent in all the campaigns on key local issues. These public campaigns attracted a good deal of press attention. The right wing knew opposition was growing against them. But they were powerless to halt the tide, such was the strength of the conviction among the majority of ordinary party members determined to bring about radical changes.

How We Captured Power

The broad left caucus which began meeting in October 1979 was not open to known right-wingers. But its ranks embraced the Bennite left, Fabian reformists and even some centre-right members who loathed the inefficiency and trickery of the old guard. At the time, there were only two Militant supporters out of 400 members in the party. They showed no interest in our plans and did not attend until much later, after the right had been ousted. Entry into these meetings was not difficult; a personal recommendation or just an interest in bringing about change meant that a new name would be added to the list to whom notices of meetings would be sent. The right obviously knew of these meetings from an early stage. Though they later complained loud and long about secret caucus meetings, the old guard had been deciding things in secret cabals for years. The right tied up the GC at pre-meetings in the Labour Club. Behind the doors of the leader's office in the Town Hall, Labour Group and council decisions were pre-determined by O'Grady and his closest council committee chairs.

After the left's victory at the 1980 AGM, when Mellish accused us of holding caucuses and drawing up slates, we never denied it. Of course, Mellish should know about such things because for 21 years, when he was chair of the London Labour Party, he was part of a far more powerful and secret right-wing caucus which elected him chair on its slate. The fact is that ever since people began to join in political parties, small or large groups of like-minded people have met together to discuss issues and organise themselves. The centre-right grouping, Solidarity, is a caucus of a sort. So is the Tribune group in Parliament. The Labour Party is a very broad church. It is inevitable that groups within it will meet together, sometimes in secret, to decide a common view on slates of candidates or political decisions. Indeed, slates and caucuses have always been part of the ritual at Labour's annual conference. Anyone who claims this is not part and parcel of the world of politics is prevaricating. A meeting in someone's house, or even in the St Ermine's Hotel where party and trade-union bosses are prone to gather, is a sort of caucus. The term 'caucus' has recently been used as a term of abuse by the right to smear the organised left. That is exactly how it was used against us. But what happened in Bermondsey has happened in thousands of constituencies up and down the country ever since the Labour Party was formed.

When the broad left came together in Bermondsey we were united on one important issue at least — the need to infuse democracy and a radical vision of socialism back into the Labour Party by toppling the politically corrupt right-wing regime. Beyond that, there were lots of political differences among those who attended the caucus meetings. Although these differences of opinion surfaced from time to time, most of our energies were directed organisationally. We had to ensure the left took over the reins of power. Perhaps what exactly we would do with that power was never sufficiently thrashed out, especially at local council level. At that stage, whenever a contentious political issue came up, comrades tended to say, 'Well, we don't have time to discuss that now.' Inevitably we had to concern ourselves with the more immediate task of winning control of the party machine and subsequently Southwark council. The left, and even the centre-right, were all opposed to O'Grady's support for big business plans to redevelop the south bank of the Thames for the office overspill from the City of London. We wanted the area developed for the benefit of local working-class people, with new housing to replace the pre-war slums and industry to create local employment. We all shared an immense anger at the way in which O'Grady arbitrarily cut the council's grant to the North Southwark Community Development Group, which had criticised the council's pro-office planning policy and become a focus of local dissent. But we never sufficiently discussed within the caucus how we would overcome problems created by Tory quangos such as the London Docklands Development Corporation, or the precise forms of housing decentralisation. We also never adequately planned how we would deal with obstruction and sabotage of Labour's policies by some of the council's chief officers, the local civil service who were patently hostile to the wind of change.

These were some of the issues in 1979-80 when a Southwark-wide left caucus was also established to include members from all the three constituency Labour parties which made up the borough — Bermondsey, Peckham and Dulwich. In retrospect, although we were racing against time and faced an immensely powerful right-wing monolith, perhaps it was a mistake to devote almost all of our energies to discussing how the left were to take power. More time should have been given over to deciding what we would do with that power when it was won. The view that 'everything will be alright once a socialist council or government takes over' was proved wrong-headed. From our experience of the new Southwark council, strategies and policies must be decided in advance; otherwise a vacuum exists when power comes to the party, and vacuums tend to be filled by pragmatic solutions. The next few years in opposition again give the Labour Party the opportunity to work out in detail precisely how we are going to use the reins of power to transform society. The revolutionary left's view of the Labour Party is that the energies of socialists within it are exclusively channelled into capturing control of the party machine and Parliament. This leaves no time or energy to fight the real battles of socialism. Such a view is clearly an exaggerated version of what being a radical socialist within the Labour Party is about. But there is more than a grain of truth in it. Getting into government, whether local or national, is not the be-all and end-all; it's what socialists do when they have control that ultimately matters.

In Bermondsey, then, in the autumn and winter months of 1979-80 the left activists were embroiled in organising for the future transfer of power within the Bermondsey party and in reaching out to the people of the local area, making them aware that a revitalised local Labour party was taking shape. In some wards such as Chaucer, this included major recruitment drives and door-to-door newsletters, which did not draw back from roundly criticising the councillors and outlining our alternative policies. The councillors were deeply unpopular, and only by disassociating ourselves from their actions could we hope to retain public credibility and support for the party. Many members were active in local tenants' associations, union branches and local pressure groups such as the North Southwark Community Development Group. For my part, I was involved in the tenants' association on my estate, eventually being elected chairperson in 1980. Through the association, with Labour support, local tenants started up several new initiatives: English-language classes for Bengali immigrants, Rockingham Against Racism concerts, a pensioners' group, nursery facilities for the children of working mothers and an adventure playground. Adjacent to the estate, derelict Dickens Square had been boarded up with tin hoarding for ten years; yet there were no decent playspaces for local children. So we organised young kids from the estate to campaign for a neighbourhood park on the site. They plastered Dickens Square with slogans: 'OPEN THE TIN AND LET US IN', defying even the warning of the local police. Thirty children aged from five to fifteen marched with placards to County Hall and petitioned Southwark council; eventually we won our fight to convert rubble-strewn Dickens Square into a beautifully landscaped neighbourhood park with garden allotments and a youth club.

By our participation in activities such as these, we were renewing Labour's links with the local community for the first time in many years. We were showing that the Labour Party was at last fighting shoulder to shoulder with the people once again. We were publicly stating that in our view party policies could not be confined to the business of the GC, the administration of the party machine or the committee rooms of the Town Hall. One encouraging aspect of this community-based activity was that membership at ward level was steadily growing. Even lapsed members were rejoining. These new members were not part of the old guard. Indeed they were hostile to it. They were attracted to our new kind of radical campaigning Labour politics. No longer did they identify with the 'stone-age' policies of Southwark council. The new members strengthened our hand by increasing the delegate entitlement of the broad left wards. Many of them got themselves elected as union delegates by their branches. In this way, we increased the forces of the left in preparation for the 1980 annual general meeting of the GC. It was at the AGM that we had to win the vital votes for officerships which would give us control of the party machine.

But just before the AGM, in February 1980, Mellish announced that he was planning to accept Michael Heseltine's invitation to take up the post of vice-chair of the Tory government's new Docklands Urban Development Corporation (later renamed the London Docklands Development Corporation). Since the post was an 'office of profit under the Crown', Mellish's acceptance would normally have required him to resign as MP. However, the Tories were so keen to have him that, when setting up the Corporation, they added a special clause to the Bill to make his position 'non-profit-making', thereby allowing him to continue in Parliament. Despite this clause, Mellish's provisional agreement to be vice-chair was used as a pretext for the London regional officials of the Labour Party to 'freeze' our GC 'for the purposes of parliamentary selection' just one month before the AGM when it was clear that the left might win power in the party. This meant there could be no new delegates appointed and the old right-wing majority would choose the new MP. Regional officials claimed the freeze was carried out on the instructions of the National Executive Committee. However, we later checked this and found it to be untrue. The NEC had never discussed the issue and did not even know the GC was frozen. We were immediately suspicious that the freeze was simply a crude attempt by the right to preempt a left majority and ensure that one of 'their' people succeeded Mellish as MP. At the time it had been rumoured that Mellish would retire to pave the way for Shirley Williams' return to the House of Commons, following her defeat in the 1979 general election when she lost her Stevenage seat. We thought it quite wrong that a right rump — including 'bogus' delegates — which was at the end of its term of office should be artificially maintained in power by a bureaucratic manoeuvre in order to choose the next parliamentary candidate. This freeze was to be the first of many attempts by the right to thwart the normal democratic process and the forward march of the left. It was also our first experience of the way regional and national officials of the party used their authority in a partial and political manner to bolster the right.

Also in the run-up to the AGM, some of the centre and right joined with the left to carry votes at the GC which instructed the party officers to secure the repayment of thousands of pounds owed to the party by the Labour Club. But nothing was ever done. Just before the AGM, the officers' inaction provoked Mellish's former election agent, Bill Musgrave, to resign from the party in disgust. This dramatic split in the right further strengthened our hand on the very eve of the AGM.

In late February 1980 a slate of broad left candidates was drawn up. Our agreed nominations for officer posts included a representative cross-section of the wards and the political spectrum, including a couple of right-wingers. Though we did not agree with them politically, they were honest and decent people. Besides, we wanted to show conciliation. The slate was fairly widely circulated. The right wing under O'Grady must have known about it. The vote was likely to be close. Delegates who had not been part of the caucus meetings, but who were fed up with the antics of the old guard, were gently lobbied with success.

By the time of the AGM, the atmosphere of the GC was poisoned with the venom of right-wingers. For the first time since their own successful coup after the war, they faced the prospect of defeat. Such were the stories of past chicanery, we felt unable to overlook even such 'minor' matters as who the tellers would be to count the ballot papers. Colourful stories of 'creative arithmetic' in past Bermondsey votes under the old regime made us very wary about not only who counted them, but where they were counted. We were to insist that the votes should be counted in the room in front of the delegates with two scrutineers. If the ballot papers were taken into another room we were not absolutely confident that all would be fair and square. If anyone thinks we were being paranoid, consider the lengths the right were to go to later to hold on to the vestiges of their power. Could we safely predict they would count ballot papers fairly if by altering or adding ballot slips or making 'mistakes' they could have defeated the left?

We were well-organised. We left no detail uncovered. Nothing undemocratic or against the rules had been engineered by us. There was nothing the right could object to. By 36 votes to 29 I was elected secretary and the left slate of candidates won every other officership as well. The dynasty was broken. We were jubilant, though we did not make a show of it, preferring even at that stage to hold out an olive branch. The right were shocked and dismayed that we had actually succeeded in overturning nearly forty years of unbroken power. Even after the vote, they showed a marked reluctance to give up what had been unquestioningly theirs for so long. One of the leading right-wingers refused to hand over his keys to the local Bermondsey Labour headquarters and even threatened to assault me when I called at his house to request party files which he was withholding.

At the GC a month later, one of the last he was ever to attend, Bob Mellish referred derisively to the AGM result as a 'palace revolution'. However, for a long time afterwards I saw Mellish regularly when we met to liaise about organising his advice surgeries and constituents' mail. We would often chat about what was happening in the party at local and national level. In these conversations, which continued to be outwardly friendly, he expressed his disquiet about the drift to the left, but also reiterated criticisms of Southwark's Housing Department and the failure of councillors to deal with local tenants' problems.

O'Grady's cries of conspiracy naturally began to circulate after the AGM. But even he could not dispute that there had been a strong will for change in Bermondsey. Comrades could not be led by their noses to vote in a particular way if they did not want to do so. The changes in Bermondsey came through a collective political will. The members wanted to participate in a meaningful way in Labour party decision-making. They wanted their elected representatives to be accountable. They wanted to be consulted by councillors about council policy. They did not want to carry on being treated as donkeys on whose backs councillors and the MP were elected. This mood of unrest in Bermondsey was duplicated in many constituencies elsewhere. It helped to bring about the major changes in the party's constitution at the 1980 annual conference. The party rank and file were in effect saying, the Labour Party belongs to its membership, not to its leaders or its elected representatives. Those people are there to serve us and working people. However, the impression that elitists such as Callaghan and Wilson had given was that the party belonged to them and that we, the rank and file, were there to serve the leadership.

Revitalising the Party and Choosing a New GLC Member

In the heady days after the AGM, there was a surge of party activity, an explosion of 'grassroots community socialism'. Contrary to press claims of a takeover by a tiny left-wing clique, our first priority was to admit all those new members and delegates whose applications had been obstructed by the right. We embarked on the production and distribution of a newsletter to every household in the constituency, together with a mass membership drive. Within a few weeks 120 people were received into the party, and through similar drives over the next eighteen months our membership was doubled to 800. The Women's Section of the party, which had collapsed under the dead weight of jam-making sessions and serving tea and cakes to the male-dominated GC, was re-established with a clear feminist orientation. Appointments to the trustees of local charities were reformed by limiting the number of posts that any one person could hold. This broke the system of patronage monopolised by a handful of right-wingers and enabled more members to participate. Under threat that we would close the Labour Club, the new club committee, which was not involved with past allegations, agreed that they would admit party members into membership and pay off their outstanding debts to the party. We appealed to the NEC against the 'freeze' of our GC. They agreed it was without constitutional justification and lifted it in the summer of 1980. That was our first victory over regional and national officials and it taught us that the powerful party bureaucracy was not invincible.

The enormous effort that had gone into changing the party and overcoming the resistance of the right, plus the surge of activity after the AGM, was not without a personal price to pay. Lots of other interests and pleasures went by the board. Night after night and month after month, I was often up working till 2 or 3 a.m., doing everything from printing agendas to designing leaflets. All of us were novices who had taken over a political machine that had to be fundamentally re-organised; and that proved to involve a lot of very hard work.

Inevitably, the months of strain took their toll. For the first time in my life, I became run down and prone to regular bouts of sickness. It was immensely uplifting the spontaneous way other party members rallied round to care for me during those periods of ill-health.

A major factor which further alienated Mellish and showed him that the left were determined to breathe new life into Bermondsey politics was our choice of candidate for the 1981 Greater London Council elections. The selection was held in July 1980. Reg Goodwin, former leader of the GLC and until that year leader of the Labour opposition, had been the member for many years. Goodwin was 72. Very few of the left felt any antagonism towards him. In fact, he was always meticulous about reporting back to the GC and, unlike Mellish, his manner was not arrogant and elitist. Despite political disagreements, we actually liked him. So it was with no sense of vindictiveness that we voted for George Nicholson rather than Goodwin. Nicholson won the selection vote by 39 votes to 34. George had been a Southwark councillor since 1978. He was one of the 13 'rebel' councillors whom O'Grady expelled from the Labour Group and had been very active in local planning issues. He later became GLC chair of Planning in 1983. At the end of the selection, Goodwin was given a prolonged standing ovation by everybody in the room. The atmosphere was cordial and Reg took his defeat with great dignity. Later we were to make a presentation to mark his years of service to the party and local people.

Goodwin had been an elected representative of the party for 34 years, firstly on the old LCC and then, since 1964, on the GLC. That period of representing the party is by any standards a very long run indeed. It seems absolutely axiomatic that new blood should be pumped into the body politic at frequent intervals, otherwise MPs and councillors who are elected automatically year in and year out become complacent and weary. Goodwin stood head and shoulders above Mellish and the local councillors. However, he was an elderly man who was growing out of step with what was going on at the grassroots of the party. His gentlemanly tactics belonged to an era that had long since past. The Tories were out to destroy every gain the working class had ever made. The GLC was obviously going to be in the front line of the battle to resist Tory dictats. We felt that a younger rebel like George Nicholson was likely to put up a stiffer fight in that situation. Besides, Goodwin would have been nearly 78 by the end of the GLC term of office. He had already had several bites of the cherry. It was time to give someone else, someone younger, a chance. Despite the right's claim that a left-winger would never win in Bermondsey, Nicholson not only won the 1981 GLC election, but he increased Goodwin's majority by 9 per cent. Labour was on the up again in Bermondsey.

The right, of course, claimed that the dropping of Goodwin was a ruthless tactic on our part. Mellish was quoted in the press as saying it was 'unbelievable'. He conveniently forgot that when he was chosen as a candidate in 1946 he was only 34 and defeated a much more senior and experienced Labour candidate in the process. Mellish and O'Grady are the type of politician who think they have an inalienable right to represent the party. To them, they *are* the party. They have never accepted that they are merely representatives of the will of the membership. If important party positions are filled by the same small group of people year after year, then almost inevitably when they are challenged and attempts are made to make them subject to recall and dismissal, this is viewed as 'treason' against the party. Of course, this is perhaps to be expected in a party whose politics have so often revolved round leadership struggles and the personal ambitions of a few leading lights. Tony Benn's dictum of 'swallow your leader' has real relevance to the Labour Party. As we move towards a more presidential style of electioneering, as evidenced in the 1983 campaign when there was greater focus than ever on personalities and party leaders to the detriment of policies, it is progressively more difficult to keep sight of the need to replenish the party's representatives. The cloistered atmosphere of the Commons, with its outmoded rules and fusty rituals, helps to engender an elitist attitude among MPs. And so, on a local level, do council chambers with their pompous flummery and aspirations to ritual. The Labour Party needs leaders, but these leaders must be accountable and they must be men and women who do not perceive their leading positions in the party's hierarchy as a birthright. Too much trust and power concentrated in the hands of a few representatives is always unhealthy. Perhaps we need to be moving towards a more collective style of leadership. Apart from any other argument, a collective leadership would leave Labour leaders such as Foot, Benn and Livingstone less vulnerable to personal attacks which have not only undermined them individually, but the party as a whole.

Thus, in a few months, we had taken over the reins of power in the constituency and then replaced our rather right-wing GLC member with a younger man who belonged to the 'constructive left', according to some press commentators. The bleats of complaint from O'Grady and his adherents, plus Mellish's growing opposition to us, were naturally picked up by the local press and later the nationals. More and more attention started to be focused on our south-east London constituency. Observers began to see that what was happening in Bermondsey, which was after all practically on the doorstep of Parliament across Westminster Bridge, was highly indicative of what was happening in the Labour Party as a whole. Such media attention was never neutral or disinterested news reporting. Even in 1980, the knives were being sharpened in Fleet Street.

The Right's Manoeuvres to Win Back Control

No sooner had we secured the 'unfreezing' of our GC and foiled one right-wing plot than we faced another 'slaveholders' rebellion' by the right. In November 1980, the Bermondsey party had to ward off a systematic attempt by Frank Chapple's union, the EETPU, to flood our GC with 'phony' delegates. In two weeks during November, Bermondsey party officers suddenly received 12 new affiliations from EETPU branches; the figure later rose to 18 and included some pretty obscure branches based miles away from Bermondsey, such as the Lifts and Escalators and Visionhire branches of the union. Many of the affiliations were sent direct from the EETPU headquarters, a few personally signed by Chapple. It turned out that in some cases affiliations were made and delegates chosen on behalf of the branches concerned by EETPU head office, without the knowledge or consent of the membership and even against their wishes.

Two of the delegates nominated to Bermondsey were Charles Sawyer and Joe Lees, both at that time right-wing Southwark councillors. The EETPU had changed its rules so that its head office could directly affiliate branches and appoint delegates over the heads of branch members. Sawyer was appointed an EETPU delegate, even though he was a housing officer with Lewisham council and his work bore no relation to the trades covered by the EETPU. Lees was put forward by head office in the name of the London Central branch of the union, despite the fact that branch members did not want him. They refused to appoint Lees on the grounds that he was a retired member, never attended branch meetings and was totally unrepresentative of their views. We realised that party and union democracy was at stake. If the EETPU succeeded in Bermondsey, we feared that it might well employ such tactics against constituency parties all over the country to shore up the right. For the sake of all the left, we knew we had to stand firm and resist. The party's full-time officials weighed in against us. They insisted we must accept all the EETPU affiliations and delegates. But we had been given wrong advice once by them over the 'freeze' of our GC. We would not be misled again.

So the Bermondsey party appealed to the NEC for a ruling on the EETPU's practice of appointing delegates over the heads of those they are supposed to be representing. The NEC upheld our appeal and ruled that all affiliations and delegates must be elected or approved by the relevant branches in accordance with Clause IX (1) of the rules for CLPs and branches. The EETPU then simply circumvented the NEC's ruling by threatening branch officials with dismissal and dissolution if they did not approve head office nominations. It suspended and eventually dissolved the London Central branch for refusing to appoint Lees. In the end, though the EETPU did succeed in foisting a number of delegates on the party, many of its potential voting-fodder were scared off by the adverse publicity in the local and national press. Some of the right-wingers appointed ultimately had a greater loyalty to the pub than to the party and their attendance tailed off after a while.

Chapple had long been a sworn enemy of the left. This attempt to pack the GC with delegates acceptable to the EETPU head office was a ruthless attempt to manipulate the rules of the union and the party to wield influence within the constituency. The old mafia had lost their power base. Chapple, a notoriously reactionary trade-union leader, who later came out in favour of an SDP candidate during the 1983 election campaign, wanted to wrest back that power base for the right. The EETPU leaders even went so far as to threaten a High Court injunction against the NEC, which had frozen all EETPU affiliations and delegates while a special enquiry was held. Later, at the May 1981 AGM of the Bermondsey party, O'Grady led a walk-out by right-wing delegates after failing to get the meeting declared invalid because of the EETPU delegate dispute.

The EETPU attempt to 'take over' our GC highlights the danger of a trade-union leadership which acts autocratically towards its own members. The whole EETPU affair smacked of mobster-style union leadership, totally dictatorial and undemocratic. If there is any lesson to be learnt from our experience, it is that the battle for democracy which has gone on within the Labour Party must also be carried into the backwater trade unions. And I say that as a trade unionist myself. The EETPU affair also gave us warning, if warning we needed, that the right were now willing to go to extraordinary lengths to win control back from the left in Bermondsey.

On Collision Course with Mellish and the Councillors

After the 1980 AGM, the Bermondsey party was set on collision course with its councillors. The earlier clashes over the new Town Hall were repeated again on several important local issues. On Hay's Wharf, between Tower Bridge and London Bridge, O'Grady supported plans by the Kuwaiti Oil Investment Corporation to redevelop the site with two million square feet of office space — the equivalent of fourteen Centre Point office blocks. Given the predominance of decaying pre-war estates and chronic lack of open spaces, the Bermondsey party opposed these plans. We joined with other local community groups to demand that Hay's Wharf be used for low-rise family housing with gardens, parkland and light industrial units to bring back jobs to an area hard hit by unemployment. Our view was echoed by nearly every tenants' association, trade-union branch and local community group in Bermondsey. At a public forum in St Olave's School to discuss the plans, attended by 200 people, the meeting voted to oppose the office development with only four dissenting voices, three of these being right-wing councillors, including O'Grady. So much for his later claim in the by-election to represent 'real' Labour and 'real' Bermondsey!

Despite party and public opposition, O'Grady and three other Bermondsey councillors voted to approve the Hay's Wharf offices. The party responded by passing a vote of no confidence in them. Such a decision was not taken suddenly or lightly. It was a last resort, an expression of our frustration that we were powerless to influence our own Labour councillors in any way.

Long before Heseltine's cuts had become law, O'Grady and Southwark council were planning how to implement them. Not even a fig-leaf of resistance was offered. When the handful of left-wing councillors sought to commit the Labour Group to carry out national party directives on fighting the cuts, they were mercilessly attacked by the old guard. Heseltine's dictates on rent and rate increases, the sale of council houses and the selling off of council land earmarked for new housing to private developers were all dutifully obeyed by Southwark council. Just before the final passage of Prior's Employment Bill in 1980, the NEC urged all Labour authorities to beat the Bill by quickly concluding union membership agreements with their employees. Southwark council refused and then laid the blame on the municipal unions.

In all these cases, the council flew in the face of party policy. We were treated with absolute contempt, as if the party did not even exist. By the end of 1980, we reluctantly came to the conclusion that the councillors were beyond redemption. They had to be removed.

Despite the widening gulf betwen the party and our councillors, we did not allow these internal clashes to divert us from the vital task of public campaigning. Much of Bermondsey and Southwark was blighted by the closure of the docks and the subsequent speculative schemes to redevelop the area by Tory property sharks. The party was in the forefront of campaigns to oppose the theft of local land. Mellish had said in the past that the docks would close 'over my dead body'. Nevertheless, the docks did close but Mellish was still alive and planning to serve on a Tory development board which was itching to carve up docklands to line the pockets of property developers. The Bermondsey party decided that some direct action was required to publicise local opposition to the office schemes and our demands that Hay's Wharf be developed in the interests of local people. In taking direct action, we wanted to forcibly remind the people of Bermondsey that the Labour Party was a campaigning party, rooted in the community and intent on defending their interests against the encroachment of huge financial institutions in the City of London.

The first thing the party did was help force a public inquiry into the Hay's Wharf plans so that we could put forward the local community's case and outline our alternative proposals. Then, in April 1981, we decided to occupy HMS Belfast which was moored on the Thames right opposite the Hay's Wharf site. An ex-warship converted into a naval museum, HMS Belfast is a well-known local tourist attraction. The action was planned by the party's Fight Unemployment Committee. We went on board disguised as the Watford East Tennis Club, buying a group concession ticket. For one and a half hours we occupied the bridge and draped banners over the side: 'Houses Before Offices, People Before Profits'. The police were quickly called but our eviction was delayed for a long time while they argued among themselves whether the ship was under the jurisdiction of the Metropolitan Police or the Thames Water Police! The occupation and our cause were widely reported in the media and won us a lot of local sympathy. Later in the year, we organised another extra-parliamentary protest, this time to draw attention to the savage Tory cuts in the National Health Service which had forced the closure of in-patient services at St Olave's Hospital in 1979. The Bermondsey party had ever since that time campaigned for its re-opening as a general community hospital. As part of that campaign, on 4 August 1981 we planned a 'stop the traffic' blockade of Lower Road, Rotherhithe outside the hospital. Suddenly, two days beforehand, the Home Secretary reimposed a blanket ban on marches and demonstrations throughout London. Our initial apprehension that this might put people off and impair the success of the demonstration was misplaced. Despite the ban, nearly one hundred local tenants turned out. For two and a half hours we crossed back and forth over the pedestrian crossing holding up the dense early-morning commuter traffic. Leaflets publicising our demands were distributed to drivers and passers-by. Again, Labour was publicly visible in the thick of a local strugle.

The really big break with Mellish came when the London Docklands Development Corporation was finally officially set up and he accepted the post of vice-chair. Clearly the Tories believed it would give the Corporation legitimacy to have Mellish, the sitting MP and a Labour stalwart, serving on it. The Southwark Labour parties — Bermondsey, Peckham and Dulwich — had repeatedly made their total opposition to Tory plans for redeveloping the area absolutely clear. Yet here was our MP taking up a very important position on the board of a Tory body which was bent on handing the former docklands over to property speculators in the teeth of hostility from most local people. The Docklands Corporation was an unelected body, personally appointed by Heseltine and answerable only to him in his capacity of Minister of the Environment. The chair was Nigel Broackes, head of the Trafalgar House business empire. The corporation was completely undemocratic. It took planning powers out of the hands of our elected local councillors. No Labour MP or councillor could possibly serve on the board and retain their credibility as a servant of working-class people. Mellish's excuse was that he would rather be inside holding a senior post on the board and therefore in a position to influence what was decided. He accused the left of wanting to stand on the outside and impotently poke its tongue out at the corporation. Of course, the fact that Mellish was to receive a fat salary of £16,000 as vice-chair when he eventually resigned as MP had nothing to do with his decision to accept the position. Bob, as ever, was claiming to act with the interests of his constituents at heart, boasting that 'the people of the back streets' were behind him.

When Mellish put these arguments at GC meetings, few of us swallowed them. We knew Heseltine would not have him on the board if Mellish was going to be a thorn in the flesh of Tory ministers and businessmen like Nigel Broackes. Mellish was brought in as a tame Labour stooge. It was hoped he would give Tory plundering a respectable face in the Labour-controlled dockland constituencies. And we were right. Very quickly the Tories were claiming that with 'good old Bob Mellish' on the board, Bermondsey people need have no worries. We told Mellish clearly how we thought he was being used by the Tories, but he turned a deaf ear.

It was this issue, more than the replacement of Goodwin by Nicholson, that hastened the severing of his ties with Bermondsey Labour Party. Accustomed to deference and unquestioning obedience, the old authoritarian and bully boy Chief Whip now found himself criticised at monthly GC meetings, not only about his acceptance of the position with the Docklands Corporation, but also on other issues as well. When he was asked how he would vote on the Corrie Abortion Bill, he said he would not be pressurised by anyone: 'I am my own man' he told us. Richard Crossman in his diaries referred to Mellish as very willing to serve whoever was in power at the time. He had paid only the merest of lip-service to political principles and democratic accountability. His decision to accept the Docklands Corporation job against our wishes and the policy of the Greater London Labour Party was quite in character. What was different now was that he had a constituency party which was not prepared to let him get away with such amazing arrogance and contempt for the people who for so many years had gone out on the knocker for 'Uncle Bob' to ensure his re-election with handsome majorities. Now that loyalty had largely gone, even among previous supporters, because he had shown disdain for the opinions of the ordinary people he purported to think so highly of. Of course, Mellish and O'Grady were to claim that those ordinary people had been driven out of the Bermondsey party. This was manifestly untrue. The solid working-class members who were very much part of the process of change in Bermondsey were simply no longer content to stand cap-in-hand and accept the dictates of their elected representatives. The Docklands Corporation was literally the last straw for them. Mellish could not come to terms with the loss of his subservient power base. All his subsequent behaviour must be viewed in that context.

At the 1981 AGM the left consolidated its position. The right crudely tried to disrupt proceedings and get the AGM declared invalid by claiming that some of their delegates had been excluded; in fact their branches had incompetently forgotten to renew their affiliations. When this ploy failed, amid threats of violence against us, a dozen of the right staged a walkout. That left us with a comfortable majority of 50 votes to 12 on most ballots. The right could not have won anyway. Their cherished hope of a comeback had proved a dismal failure. The realisation of this concentrated their minds on revenge and a determination to do the Bermondsey party down.

On 10 July 1981, Mellish announced his intention not to seek re-selection. The week after, he gave an astonishing interview to Patrick Collins of the London *Standard*. Under the headline 'A Bellyful of the Barmy Mob', Mellish said: 'A group of people have turned up on my management committee that I'd never seen or heard of before. Students, NUPE members,people like that.'They want to pick the party leader,they want to decide party policy, they insist on the re-selection of MPs. I told them to stuff it.' Mellish seemed astonished that rank-and-file members should dare to ask for a say in the way the party was run. Perhaps this is not so surprising from someone who had previously gone on record as finding few faults with the Portuguese regime in Angola. He also seemed to think that 'NUPE member' was a term of abuse, which indicated the contempt in which he held the less traditional unions. Mellish was then quoted as saying, 'When Shirley Williams left the party, it broke my heart ...it was terrible to lose someone like that'. At the time, there had been speculation that Shirley Williams might stand in Bermondsey as an SDP candidate in a future by-election. Here was our MP publicly swearing affection and weeping sentimental tears over a possible electoral opponent. In London's only evening newspaper, he went on to publicly attack his own party and drop hints that he might resign in the autumn and force a by-election. His public avowal of Williams, while saying he personally would not defect to the SDP, was a deliberate piece of back-stabbing. Mellish's determination to defeat the new left, who had in his eyes robbed him of his power base, led him to take the first steps towards his final break with Labour and a declaration of outright war on myself and the Bermondsey party.

When Mellish declared that he would not stand again as MP, the Bermondsey party was suddenly forced into a selection process and the quest for a new parliamentary candidate. First to crop up were the names of former MPs who had lost their seats in 1979. But later there arose a strong demand from the older generation of long-standing and working-class members for a 'tried and tested' local candidate who knew the area and the issues. I was one of several local members initially put forward. To begin with, I was very resistant to being nominated. I felt I had not been a member of the party for long enough and perhaps was not sufficiently experienced. My supporters assured me that one of the principal reasons for wanting to nominate me was precisely because I was not the stereotype Labour candidate. Whatever else I might be I was not the product of a political machine. These comrades wanted a new type of MP as far apart as possible from the remote and elitist machine politician that Mellish had been. My administrative and campaigning record stood me in good stead. When it became evident that I had wide support in the party for my candidature, especially among the older working-class members, I decided to consent to nomination. At that stage I thought it highly unlikely I would be chosen as the candidate.

While this was happening, the wards were beginning the process of selecting their candidates for the 1982 borough council elections. The selection of candidates in Riverside ward was to have especially far-reaching effects. It caused great controversy and affected the result of the by-election dramatically. 'Sitting' councillors have no automatic right to stand again as Labour candidates in local elections. They all have to be re-selected by their individual ward branches. First, the wards nominate people to a panel of candidates where they are subject to approval or rejection by the GC. Second, those names approved are put on the panel of candidates. And third, from this panel the wards select their candidates to represent Labour in the election. In Bermondsey, the party executive set up an interviewing committee to vet all party members who had been nominated as potential candidates by the wards. The executive then made recommendations in October 1981 to the GC, approving most nominees, but not John O'Grady and six other sitting councillors. Our decision was endorsed by the Southwark Local Government Committee which represents the three constituency parties in the borough. The other two parties also knocked off a few of their sitting councillors from the approved panel of candidates, though over ninety others were agreed.

The Bermondsey GC, by an average of 46 votes to 14, accepted the executive's recommendation that the nominations of O'Grady and six other councillors should not be approved. This was not a political purge of the right as our opponents claimed. Only seven were not approved by the Bermondsey GC. Thirty-three others were accepted, including several right-wingers. We only refused to ratify the nominations of the sitting councillors for exceptional reasons. Some of them rarely turned up at their advice surgeries or replied to constituents' mail. Some refused to give an undertaking not to defect to the SDP and refused to commit themselves to implement Labour's election manifesto. On the issues, each of them had repeatedly and blatantly ignored party policy in a range of key areas, such as the new Town Hall, Hay's Wharf, the sale of council land, rent increases, St Olave's Hospital, union membership agreements and resistance to Heseltine's cuts.

Our suspicions were confirmed soon afterwards when two of the seven councillors did defect to the SDP. One, Charlie Sawyer, had such a poor reputation as the chair of Housing that even the SDP ditched him and he ended up fighting the 1982 council election as an Independent Social-Democrat. Later, another two councillors left the party.

O'Grady's camp subsequently argued that the GC's refusal to accept the seven was undemocratic because it should be left up to the wards to decide for themselves. However, Labour Party rules lay down that the GC is required to approve or reject possible candidates before their names go to the wards. It was hardly surprising that when faced with having to make such a decision we turned down those sitting councillors who had shown themselves over many years to be so lacking in a minimum level of competence and commitment to carry out party policy.

Parliamentary Selection and a New Style of MP

The Bermondsey parliamentary selection conference was set for 8 November 1981. Six candidates were shortlisted. My platform was based on a strong commitment to implement agreed Labour Party policy and be accountable to the local party and community. I emphasised the importance of extra-parliamentary struggles to carry out a left-wing programme which included withdrawal from the EEC and NATO, troops out of Ireland, extended public ownership under workers' control, a 35-hour week and £80 national minimum wage, opposition to nuclear power, abolition of the House of Lords and private medicine, democratic control of the police, positive action for women and ethnic minorities, repeal of racist immigration laws, unilateral nuclear disarmament and its replacement by a system of territorial defence with a citizens' army, and a new international economic order to secure development and justice for the exploited poor countries of the world.

I was concerned to be a new type of MP and to explore ways of developing a new type of relationship between MP, party and electorate. My initial premise was that an MP is no more than someone who is temporarily loaned the authority to speak and act on behalf of their party and constituents — the voice of local people in Parliament. The right's view, however, is that MPs should be left to exercise their own judgement becaue the intricacies of power endow them with a superior understanding over and above that of mere party members. To challenge such nonsense in practice rather than in theory, I looked forward to working with other Labour colleagues in the House of Commons to evolve a new style of MP and Labour politics with firm local roots. With declining Labour support and increased public disenchantment with politics, it seems more vital than ever to break down the widespread cynicism that 'politicians are all the same' and 'only in it for themselves'. Labour MPs should be different from the rest. But often they are not. The electorate have witnessed the way so many MPs, even Labour ones, have made a comfortable career for themselves in Parliament and repeatedly failed to deliver their promises of a better deal for working-class people. No wonder so many of them are cynical and disillusioned! No wonder they don't bother voting or in frustration and anger at the two main parties decide to give the Liberals or the SDP a try.

Perhaps we might help restore confidence in Labour if more of our MPs were seen to break with the cosy Westminster club. To begin with, it is indefensible for so many MPs to have extra financial interests and jobs as company directors and barristers outside the House of Commons. Though Labour is far from blameless on this score, the Tories are the worst offenders. Half the 1979-83 cabinet were millionaires. Between them, 170 Tory MPs in that parliament shared nearly 500 company directorships. They were only part-time MPs. Some of them seemed more concerned to look after big business than the needs of their electorate. All these external interests create divided loyalties and detract from an MP's real job which is to represent their constituents.

It is also deplorable that a lot of MPs do not bother to live in their own constituencies. Too many of them live in big houses in well-to-do areas such as Chelsea and Pimlico, with farms in Sussex and country cottages by the sea. No wonder so many working-class people deride MPs as living in a different world. Perhaps this attitude might be less prevalent if fewer MPs suddenly moved out of their constituencies and out of council housing as soon as they were elected to public office. If more MPs lived among their electorate in comparable accommodation, it might help them have a better understanding of the problems faced by local constituents through their own direct personal experience. If they lived in council housing they would certainly be likely to fight a lot harder to oppose rent increases and to put an end to the intolerable months, and even years, that council tenants have to wait for repairs. Unfortunately, it is a commonplace view that 'we only see MPs when they want our votes'. Too often after elections, they *do* disappear inside the House of Commons and are not seen again for another five years. We have to change all that.

Just as important as the accountability of our elected representatives to the party is the accountability of the party to the wider electorate. For this reason, MPs need to spend a lot more time outside Parliament, consulting with local tenants' associations, trade unions, churches, youth clubs, pensioners' groups and women's and ethnic organisations. Not only do we have to explain Labour policies to them, but also listen and learn from their ideas and experiences. Rather than work *for* local people, Labour MPs have to work *with* them. There is a subtle difference. It is the difference between an elitist, paternalistic and 'do-gooding' view of politics as a 'calling' practised by people of 'good conscience' as opposed to a more egalitarian and participatory view of politics which sees ordinary people working for their own emancipation and taking a bit of the power for themselves.

To de-mystify and de-glamourise the role of MP and establish a more collective team-work style of politics, in the run-up to my selection I had

considered the idea of splitting the MP's salary and expenses three ways
to employ two assistants who could share secretarial, constituency caseload and party organiser functions with me. Together, it was envisaged
we would operate as a Bermondsey Labour team both in the Commons
and in the constituency. The implementation of this idea would have been
dependent on another aspect of the new style of MP to which I was
committed — the proposition that Labour MPs should accept no more
than the average wage of a skilled worker, plus expenses, and use the rest
of their parliamentary salary for the benefit of the Labour movement and
local community. This is nothing new. It has long been a standing socialist
principle, dating back to the Paris Commune, and is current practice
among a number of left-wing European parties. In the case of French
Communist Party, its deputies hand over their entire salary and in return
are paid a worker's wage and expenses by the party. Even in our own
Bermondsey party we have such a precedent. The pre-war MP for
Bermondsey, Dr Alfred Salter, donated much of his parliamentary
income towards the foundation of municipal health projects for the local
community. For seven months at the time of the General Strike he gave
his entire MP's salary to the Welsh miners.

The proposition of MPs on workers' wages may seem somewhat
paradoxical given the Labour movement's historical struggle for the
payment of MPs to enable working-class representation in the House of
Commons. However, what now places this proposition on the political
agenda is the large increase in parliamentary salaries over recent years.
For the first time, these increases have opened up a large gap between the
incomes of MPs and the average wage-earner. In 1981, MPs' salaries were
increased to £14,000 and secretarial and research allowances to over
£8,000. Two years later, a formula was agreed to raise parliamentarians'
pay to £18,500 over five years. In addition, there are generous allowances
for second homes and travel, free postage and photocopying, plus the
perks of official dinners and trips abroad, and handsome media fees — not
to mention that being an MP can be an opener to sideline activities in
business and journalism.

It is therefore probably fair to estimate that many MPs, even full-
timers with no outside jobs or directorships, have a very substantial
personal income in cash and kind — even after the deduction of expenses.
This objectively places most Labour MPs in a position akin to senior
management, enjoying the earnings and privileges of the very classes
whose power Labour seeks to curtail. By acquiring a standard of living
equivalent to that of the upper middle-class, our MPs inevitably
experience strong pressures towards cooption into that class and
incorporation into the political establishment. Even the most dedicated
left MPs must tend to face the corrosion of their socialist and egalitarian
principles by the poisonous combination of status, 'perks' of office and a

salary well above average. This perhaps partly explains why so many of them start out as radical firebrands and end up drifting to the right.

Nowadays it is very difficult to imagine many Labour MPs having a standard of living or lifestyle comparable with their working-class constituents whom they seek, and claim, to represent. This surely poses the danger that they become out of touch with the lives and experiences of the party's working-class base. Without an intimate and continuing knowledge of the average person's life, our public representatives can easily fall prey to all kinds of misconceptions about the needs and interests of workers and their families. However, if the personal incomes of Labour MPs were closer to the average wage, say £8,000 a year, they would probably have a much keener understanding of the deprivations suffered by working-class people. They would also fight far harder for workers' interests and be less likely to collude with pay restraint, as happened under the Callaghan government. Though Labour MPs undoubtedly work very hard and long hours, no one would want them to make any financial gain by election to public office. But quite a few of them do leave Parliament much better off than when they first entered it.

We are all painfully aware of the number of Labour MPs who have become farm owners, bank directors and such like. This only serves to fuel the popular view that 'all politicians are on the make'. To restore public faith in our Labour MPs and refute this cynicism that they are simply playing the wheels of fame and fortune, we desperately need to make sure that Labour MPs *are* different from those of all other parties. People's trust in the socialist conviction of the Labour Party would most likely be significantly enhanced if they knew that, though our MPs could draw a large salary, as a point of political principle they chose only to take an average skilled worker's wage. As for the uses to which the rest of the MP's parliamentary salary could be put, we are constantly reminded that the party faces a severe financial crisis. Even if 200 Labour MPs donated only £1,000 of their parliamentary salary towards party funds, this would create a regular annual income to the party of £200,000. Another possibility is the funding of full-time secretary/agents to meet the urgent need to re-establish a mass membership and campaigning role for the party at local level.

The proposition of Labour MPs on skilled workers' wages is already practised by some MPs who make generous donations to the movement and incur huge expenses through their dedicated efforts for socialism. For Labour now to adopt their practices as official policy is not to deny the primacy of socialist policies and accountability when judging the record of MPs, but to complement these in a way that is consistent with the party's tradition of egalitarianism. In themselves, of course, these ideas don't guarantee a socialist MP. But by living in the same area, in the same housing and on the same income as their constituents, MPs would be likely to keep in touch and to put up a stiffer fight on behalf of working people because their interests would be one and the same. Certainly, it would make them less likely to become corrupted and tainted by the trappings of power and status that go with being an MP.

It was this 'new style of MP', together with the commitment to left-wing policies and local accountability, that secured my selection as Bermondsey's candidate by 37 votes to 30 over Arthur Latham, the former Paddington MP. Ironically, in view of the later claims by O'Grady and the press propaganda, this victory was delivered by the votes of the party's older, 'born and bred' working class; the younger intellectual and professional members swung behind Latham.

First Rumours of Plots Against Us

In the three weeks after my selection, several prominent articles appeared in the press which portrayed me as an unacceptably extreme left-winger and put pressure on the Labour right to act against me. In the *Daily Mail*, two days after my selection, Mellish expressed 'dismay' that I had been chosen and threatened a 'few surprises' for the left in Bermondsey. Little did we realise at the time exactly how big a surprise he had in store for us. The rest of the *Mail* article was chiefly concerned to project the crude Fleet Street stereotype of the Labour left. I was described as being dressed in 'cords, open-neck shirt and sandals'. Alas, in the accompanying photograph it was clearly visible that I was wearing a tie! It was typical of the many misrepresentations that were to follow.

A week later, an interview with Max Hastings in the *Standard* resulted in the first signs of trouble ahead. The article focused on my commitment to direct action and civil disobedience as legitimate methods of political protest to resist Tory policies. It quoted my criticism of MPs taking the full salary and expenses: 'How can an MP on £14,000 a year really understand the interests and experiences of working-class people?' This implicit condemnation of other Labour MPs provoked quite a stir among the Parliamentary Labour Party. Even some Tribunites were up in arms. A couple of them advised me to 'lay off'. Clearly, I had hit a raw nerve.

It was these ideas which first drew me to the attention of the Labour right and, I believe, played a significant role in singling me out as their first victim in the witchhunt that was to follow. On 26 November, during a late-night House of Commons debate on law and order, James Wellbeloved first raised the issue of my call in *London Labour Briefing* for extra-parliamentary opposition to the Thatcher government. He urged Michael Foot and Roy Hattersley to 'denounce Mr Peter Tatchell and all those who support him'. Wisely, the Labour benches let Wellbeloved's comments pass without responding.

To add to the mounting pressure, on 1 December William Hickey in the *Daily Express* ran a gossip piece headlined 'Roy's Gang Face a Gay Old

Battle Down in Dockland'. Referring to Mellish's threat to resign and the possibility that a future Bermondsey by-election would be contested by Roy Jenkins of the SDP, the *Express* ridiculed my support for gay rights. The next day, just one day before Foot was to make his infamous declaration in the Commons, Ian Aitken made an astonishing claim in the *Guardian*: 'A group of Labour MPs, including some soft left backbenchers, have given notice that they intend to issue an unofficial repudiation of Mr Tatchell if Mr Foot fails to act against him. They believe his extraordinary combination of far left opinion and militant association with gay liberation, together with the fact that he has been a member of the party for only a few years, should disqualify him.' Aitken went on to report that Foot had a 'hard time' at a meeting of the Northern Group of Labour MPs on 1 December. They had threatened to take matters into their own hands unless he acted against 'ultra-left infiltrators'. For months there had been a rash of demands by the right for action against the activities of the trotskyist Militant Tendency and the attempt by the former International Marxist Group leader, Tariq Ali, to join the Labour Party. Already more than twenty Labour MPs had defected to the SDP. There were rumours that another 25 to 30 were poised to follow in protest against the leftward drift of the party. It was in this atmosphere, with threats of mass defections and of mounting pressure from the right for a purge of 'extremists', that Foot rose to make his fateful statement in the House of Commons.

Chapter Three

Repudiated by Foot
and Banned as a Candidate

Those, then, were the circumstances leading up to Michael Foot's repudiation of my candidature on 3 December 1981. I have always had, and still do have, considerable respect for Foot, but his 'will never be endorsed' statement was unprecedented and constituted a major blunder that was to damage the Labour Party in general, and the left in particular, for many months afterwards.

Frank Allaun, the long-serving Tribunite Labour MP, called Foot's statement 'the biggest mistake of his political life'. The verdict of political historians when they come to write the history of the Labour Party during this period may well concur with that judgement. Certainly my advocacy of extra-parliamentary protests which Wellbeloved referred to in his original Commons question would probably have been used by the SDP to beat the Labour Party with. But what gave Wellbeloved's attack real credibility was Foot's response. It was Foot's statement that signalled 'open season' to the media. They jumped at this chance to undermine our electoral chances in Bermondsey and to stoke the fires of an anti-left witchhunt.

What I Actually Wrote About Extra-Parliamentary Action

I had written the article in May 1981 for *London Labour Briefing,* a broad-left monthly magazine for party activists. At the time, I hesitated in submitting it for publication, not because I considered the content too inflammatory, but because I was concerned that it was quite unexceptional and stating the obvious. After all, what I had written was nothing new. It was merely a restatement of ideas long held and practised by countless thousands of Labour members ever since the party was first founded at the turn of the century; namely that the achievement of socialism depends on struggles both inside and outside of Parliament. Nowhere in the world has radical social change ever been accomplished by Parliament or MPs alone. It has always been based on a mass popular movement. There is no reason to believe that Britain will be any different. Our route to democratic socialism will also require mobilisation of millions of ordinary people and the active consent of the electorate in shaping a new society.

It still seems incredible that any member of the Labour Party should be repudiated as a parliamentary candidate for advocating a more spirited opposition to such a reactionary Tory government.

What exactly, then, was this furore-provoking 'extra-parliamentary' article all about? The section of the article that created most controversy was this:

> Labour has long lost the radical and defiant spirit of its early pioneers. We now seem stuck in the rut of an obsessive legalism and parliamentarism. This 'talking-shop' style of committee politics implies that the realisation of socialism can basically be left to a handful of wise and articulate MPs and councillors debating and voting through the committee structures of Parliament and local councils.
>
> Mistakenly it is these leaders, rather than the party's rank-and-file membership and the working class at large, which are seen as crucial to the success of our struggle. Indeed, leadership often becomes a substitute for the masses. Work in committees often overshadows popular struggles. But these are vital, both inside and outside the forums of electoral democracy.˙
>
> Without such a mass popular base consciously demanding and organising for a thoroughgoing socialist transformation of our society, the prospects of electing a radical Labour government look bleak indeed. So do the prospects of halting this Tory government's remorseless attacks on working-class living standards.
>
> No matter how left our MPs and councillors may be, the battle for socialism needs a large and active Labour membership committed to mass campaigns of real resistance to Tory rule. Reliance on the present token and ineffectual parliamentary opposition will advance us nowhere...
>
> Debates and parliamentary divisions are fruitless cosmetic exercises given the Tories' present Commons majority. And if we recognise this, we are either forced to accept Tory edicts as a fait accompli or we must look to new more militant forms of extra-parliamentary opposition which involve mass popular participation and challenge the government's right to rule. Is it not perfectly legitimate to confront and defy the government when its actions so tangibly threaten the essence of our Welfare State, the living standards and trade-union rights of working-class people, and the equality of women and ethnic minorities? Are not some freedoms

so fundamental to the poor and disadvantaged in our society that we actually have an obligation to challenge the government's present attempts to deny these to the people?

Though the party's marches against unemployment have been very worthwhile, surely the gravity of three million jobless justifies bolder protests? Perhaps we should be thinking more in terms of a 'Siege of Parliament' to demand jobs — a march on the House of Commons led by 250 Labour MPs and a thousand Labour mayors and councillors and involving an afternoon's sit-down occupation of the Westminster area.

Or possibly the Labour-controlled GLC could sponsor a 'Tent City' of the unemployed and homeless in the grounds of County Hall and within sight of the House of Commons.

During the riots earlier this year, it seems remiss that neither the NEC nor regional EC held extraordinary meetings in response to the crisis. Shouldn't they have given a lead by calling an emergency mobilisation of the Labour movement around appropriate demands such as 'Jobs and Better Housing for All, Democratic Control of the Police, and Freedom of Assembly and Demonstration'?

In particular, we ought to be defying the Home Secretary's increasing use of blanket bans on political demonstrations which are by stealth undermining our most basic liberties.

We can but try more dramatic and daring forms of protest as an alternative to our present unimaginative passivity. We might even be surprised by the extent to which a more direct challenge to the legitimacy of government policy actually inspires popular support.

The article was immediately dubbed as 'anti-parliamentary' and a challenge to the sovereignty of the House of Commons, both by the popular press and Labour's right wing. The insinuation was that I had advocated violent revolution, though nowhere in the article did I suggest the use of force. What I was arguing, and it is a view widely shared among many ordinary Labour members, is that the party has been reduced to an election machine almost exclusively geared to putting MPs into Parliament — and a none-too-successful one at that! We have fallen into the trap of 'parliamentary cretinism', increasingly seeing the House of Commons as the sole arena of struggle. Even for Labour, political action by ordinary people has virtually been reduced to a five-yearly ballot box ritual.

Judging by the storm of condemnation, one might have been forgiven for thinking that my article had called for the establishment of workers' soviets at the Elephant and Castle or a people's militia in Surrey Docks. Alas, no. My proposed extra-parliamentary action was more modest; a march of the unemployed on Parliament and a tent city of the homeless.

Of course these ideas were not new. Way back in 1925, George Lansbury, who later became leader of the Labour Party, urged the unemployed to march on London and set up a 'tented encampment' outside the British Empire Exhibition at Wembley. On the other side of the Atlantic, in the early 1960s, Martin Luther King led the Poor People's March on Washington which laid 'siege' to the Capitol building with a 'Tent City' demanding justice for the impoverished and racially oppressed peoples of America. Clearly my views were part of an eminently respectable radical tradition.

Denunciation by the Labour Leadership and Fleet Street

It was at 3.40 in the afternoon of 3 December that I first heard the news of Foot's statement in the Commons. A reporter from the *Daily Express* rang me at work to ask my response. My first reaction was of disbelief. Perhaps this was a practical joke in bad taste? Or had the reporter mistaken me for somebody else? Surely if Foot had done such a thing, he would have had the decency to forewarn me? No sooner had I put the phone down than other journalists called requesting interviews. The reality and ramifications of Foot's statement quickly dawned on me. If true, and I still could hardly believe it, I realised that myself and the Bermondsey party were bound to become the objects of major controversy and massive media attention.

I left work and arranged to meet the Bermondsey party officers at my flat to discuss how we should handle the impending media tidal wave. It was only a ten-minute bicycle ride from Waterloo to the Elephant and Castle. But within minutes of my return, reporters and cameramen were surrounding my council flat on the Rockingham Estate. The 'siege of Parliament' I had advocated in *Labour Briefing* had turned into the siege of Rockingham Estate. Like vultures descending on a prey, the hacks and seedy scribes of Grub Street gathered in the courtyard outside.

The Bermondsey officers who came to my flat late that afternoon to discuss our immediate reaction were agreed that we should avoid exacerbating the situation and not directly criticise Foot's statement. It had taken us by surprise and everyone else was as astonished as I was. We realised it was not just about Peter Tatchell or Bermondsey Labour Party. Foot's outburst was an implicit attack on the whole left and had huge ramifications for party democracy and Labour's future political direction.

The press and television were most insistent that I give a press conference there and then. So eventually, together with party officers, I went down into the courtyard outside my flat and gave an impromptu press conference. I refused to comment on what Foot had said until I had an opportunity to meet with him. I limited myelf to defending the legitimacy of extra-parliamentary action. The press goaded me to condemn Foot. But I refused and reiterated support for his leadership. Many of us in the Bermondsey party felt a real sense of loyalty to Foot, not so much because he was party leader, but because of his earlier years of radical socialism which were impossible to negate, even though he had been increasingly coopted into the party establishment since his appointment as Employment Minister under Harold Wilson in 1974. To us the early Foot was a kindred spirit, which made his repudiation all the more painful.

By chance there was a scheduled meeting of the Bermondsey party's executive committee that evening at the local headquarters in Lower Road. Naturally feelings were running high among the twenty-four members of the executive who were present. We were all absolutely shocked that the leader of the party had virtually declared war on us. Almost everybody realised the importance of the day's events not only for the local party, but for the Labour Party nationally. We were puzzled as to why Foot had acted in the way he had. But there was no question of opposing his leadership.

After the executive meeting, we held another press conference for the mass of reporters and television cameras that had been waiting downstairs. Somehow dozens of them, including two live outside broadcasting units, managed to crowd into the small executive meeting-room. It was now a media circus and I knew that whatever I said would reflect on the Labour Party and particularly the left.

A prepared statement was read out. It unanimously declared the Bermondsey party's 'full and total' support for me as their democratically selected parliamentary candidate and urged the party's National Executive Committee to endorse my candidature.

I stated my dismay at Foot's statement and expressed my surprise that he could repudiate me on the basis of one article. After all, he had never met me and I had never been given any opportunity to clarify and defend my views to him. In all probability, my views and political background had been misrepresented to Foot. We felt confident that once he had met me, he would realise that he had been misled and withdraw his opposition. In these circumstances, I was not prepared to make any further comments on Foot's denunciation until I had met with him personally. I went on to say that I was a radical, but democratic socialist, in the tradition of Labour pioneers such as George Lansbury and Dr Alfred Salter. In response to press questioning, I emphasised that I had never been a supporter of Militant.

The media kept returning to the question of Foot's leadership. They realised the furore would increasingly become an issue which would put his leadership on the line. He had, after all, said I would 'never' be an endorsed candidate while he was leader of the Labour Party. That implied it was now a choice between his leadership and my endorsement. Of course, the press were not slow to quiz me along these lines. They clearly wanted me to come out with a straightforward condemnation of Foot in the hope that an irretrievable split would occur. But we did not want that. We wanted to heal the wounds and to avoid further dissension that could only profit Labour's enemies. To publicly criticise Foot at a time when the right's ultimate aim was to unseat him from the leadership would have been counter-productive. Already, Foot was increasingly a prisoner of the right. They never really wanted him as leader, having backed Healey. Once he was elected, the right were only prepared to tolerate him so long as he fell in with their plans to wrest party control away from the left and provide them with a 'left' cover to do this.

As much as we wanted to hit back hard against Foot's totally unjustified comments, for the sake of the party we chose restraint to prevent further damage.

In a bid to convince Foot of his error and secure his change of heart, I arranged to meet him at the House of Commons the following Monday morning, 7 December, before the NEC organisation sub-committee met to consider my endorsement as candidate. Normally this would have been an automatic rubber-stamping of the local party's decision. But in the light of Foot's remarks, the meeting was clearly going to be a dramatic trial of strength between left and right.

Within a few hours of Foot's statement, we were spontaneously deluged with messages of solidarity from people all over the country. I was also sustained in the midst of the madness which had broken around my head, and which was to continue for many months, by the support and comradeship of the Bermondsey party officers and members. Even those members who had not voted for my selection as candidate rallied round in total support. Regardless of their earlier feelings, they knew the Bermondsey party had chosen its candidate according to the rules. What right had the leader of the party to arbitrarily announce to the world that Bermondsey was wrong and I would never be endorsed?

Although I was the particular victim of this attack by the right on the left, what was at stake was the fundamental principle of party democracy — the right of constituency parties to choose their own parliamentary candidates. And we quickly realised that Foot's leadership was at stake as well. Dubbed 'the Tatchell affair' by the press, the issue was much, much wider than whether any one individual became a candidate or not. It was clearly a new attempt by the right to force the left into retreat, after Benn's defeat in the deputy leadership contest and the shift to the right on the NEC at the 1981 annual conference.

The hullabaloo had started, and for the next fifteen months I had to grow accustomed to constant media attention and to endless harassment that would result in numerous complaints to the Press Council about invasion of privacy and deliberate lies and distortions.

I had been sprung to notoriety by a mere twenty words uttered by Michael Foot in the House of Commons on a Thursday afternoon in early December 1981; a notoriety that none of us wanted, but which suddenly changed my life. It led to my living under frequent death threats and continuous vilification, as well as enjoying the support of thousands of ordinary Labour Party members, and even the sympathies of people from opposition parties or no party at all.

The next morning, the papers were full of it. Friday's *Sun* led with 'Furious Foot Disowns Red Pete — Militant Will Never Be an MP, Says Labour Chief'. More sedately, the *Guardian* reported the discussion at the meeting of the Parliamentary Labour Party the previous evening when Foot had justified his action with the claim: 'Parliamentary democracy is at stake. There can be no wavering on that.' Right-wing shadow cabinet ministers weighed in behind Foot. With an amazing disregard for truth or an elementary sense of justice, Peter Shore was quoted as saying that as far as he concerned, it did not matter what I said — 'political perjury is a positive duty of Leninists and Trotskyites'. Merlyn Rees roundly condemned my 'distaste' for Parliament. Even Jeff Rooker, a Tribune MP, was quoted in the *Times* as supporting Foot's action. In the light of the remarks attributed to me, Foot could not remain silent, he said. A few days later, when the Tribune Group met, a majority present condemned or regretted Foot's public disavowal of my candidature. They felt he had handled the incident badly. However, according to the *Times*, many hitherto regarded as on the left believed Foot's objections were tenable and warranted investigation.

While the soft left wavered, others counter-attacked in my defence. Stuart Holland accused Foot of acting unconstitutionally: 'The Labour Party is not a party where the leader has a personal veto on candidates.'

The press were not slow to turn the issue round to a question of Foot's leadership. The *Telegraph* on 4 December proclaimed: 'Mr Foot's stance against Mr Tatchell was seen last night as another attempt to demonstrate his authority as leader as he did recently when he successfully sought to keep the rebellious Mr Wedgewood Benn out of the shadow cabinet. The gamble for him is that he must win to keep his credibility as leader.' The *Standard* headline that evening summed it up even more pointedly: 'Tatchell: Foot on the Spot'. The article commented: 'By declaring that he would not accept Mr Tatchell as a suitable candidate, Mr Foot has staked his authority on the outcome of this issue.' The press were confirming what we had all along surmised was the crux of the affair.

By Saturday morning, 5 December, rumours were rife that Labour headquarters were contemplating disbanding the Bermondsey party. The *Mail* headlined with 'Foot Faces Blacklist Crisis': 'The clash between Michael Foot and left-wing candidate Peter Tatchell is boiling up into one of the most bitter confrontations yet in Labour's internal war. The

likeliest outcome is the disbanding of the Bermondsey Labour Party...'
The *Star* also led with 'Takeover Bid by Labour HQ in Tatchell Row?':
'The Labour leader is planning a party HQ takeover in London's
Bermondsey constituency, to stop the selection of left-wing candidate
Peter Tatchell. It is understood that Mr Foot will deliver a personal
ultimatum to Mr Tatchell in his Commons office on Monday morning.
The gist of it will be "Step down — or we'll select our own moderate
candidate anyway."'

Allegations of Conspiracy

By this time, there was speculation as to the circumstances of Foot's
denunciation in the Commons. Initially, it was put down to a blunder;
that Foot had mistakenly thought Wellbeloved was referring to Peter
Taffe of Militant or Tariq Ali who was then being refused party
membership. Or perhaps he had even mistaken my name for that of Peter
Tapsell? But he already had a seat and was in the wrong party anyway,
being the Conservative MP for Hornchurch. The blunder theory was
quite implausible and we knew it.

Even the press soon began directing their attention to a more
conspiratorial explanation of events. Stan Cohen, MP for Leeds South-
East, was quoted in the *Guardian* as having been persuaded by Foot on 3
December from defecting to the SDP as he had threatened to do in
protest at left-wing extremists within the Labour Party. Speaking of his
meeting with Foot, Cohen said: 'Within two hours, in the House of
Commons he took a firm stand with his remarks about the Bermondsey
candidate, Mr Peter Tatchell. Maybe it had nothing to do with me, but I
would like to believe our discussion might have helped him to take his
stand.' Other papers picked up allegations of a plot which Ian Aitken had
first outlined in his *Guardian* article the day before Foot's statement in
Parliament. James Wightman, writing in the *Telegraph* on 5 December,
claimed that some shadow cabinet members had previously protested to
Foot about my extra-parliamentary article and insisted that he act against
me. Two days later Anthony Bevins reported in the *Times*: 'It was
revealed last night that the Labour leader's outspoken repudiation of Mr
Tatchell had been rehearsed beforehand; that Mr Foot had been warned
that the issue was to be raised on the floor of the House. For MPs on the
left, the centre and right of the party had already decided that Mr
Tatchell's call for extra-parliamentary mobilisation against the
government's right to rule amounted to a watershed challenge to the very
nature of the Labour Party.' These claims certainly fitted in with the
rumours that Wellbeloved had first seen my *Briefing* article when it was
dropped in his pigeon-hole in the Commons in an unmarked brown paper
envelope which he believed emanated from Labour's front bench. The

view that the whole incident was pre-planned is certainly lent credibility by O'Grady's meeting with Foot the very day before his Commons outburst and the fact that Mellish had had a private meeting with him as well a few days earlier.

There was also the extraordinary intervention of Labour headquarters to block the production and distribution of a door-to-door local party newsletter. Following my selection as candidate in early November, and mindful of a possible by-election, we had agreed to produce a newsletter announcing my selection to the electorate. Just a week before Foot's repudiation, the national agent's department intervened. On a spurious pretext of electoral law, they forbade us to mention that I was the prospective candidate and insisted that they approve the newsletter text before it was printed.

It could have all been coincidence, but I doubt it. Further conspiracy speculation was fuelled by Foot's remarks as he left a meeting of the Parliamentary Labour Party on the evening of 3 December. After being castigated by some MPs, he is alleged to have replied that if his critics had seen what he had seen about Peter Tatchell, then they would suport his repudiation of my candidature. What had Foot seen? His remarks led to rumours, even among respected MPs and journalists, that perhaps the security services had handed Foot a fabricated file on my supposed 'extremist' record and 'communist connections' (sic).

There was also the unexplained question of how Fleet Street managed to dig up details of my participation in the World Youth Festival in East Berlin eight years earlier. Within twenty-four hours of Foot's statement in the Commons, the *Sun* had unearthed an 'amazing story' about Peter Tatchell, who was in 1973 a nonentity, from back numbers of an obscure left-wing publication. That is not the kind of information which is normally kept on file by the average newspaper. It is more the type of material on political activists stored away by the Special Branch. Many hundreds of thousands of politically involved people are monitored by the security services. There is plenty of well-documented evidence of phone-tapping and mail interception. The photographing by police of demonstrators on marches and trade unionists during industrial disputes is now fairly commonplace. It would therefore not be out of character for the Special Branch to hold intelligence files on prospective candidates and MPs. Whether such surveillance and intervention into politics goes as far as leaking files and producing 'black' propaganda against people such as myself can only be a matter for conjecture.

First Press Smears, Meeting Foot and Losing at the NEC

Whatever the security services may or may not have done, much of Fleet Street certainly did adopt an overtly propagandist role, discarding any pretence of impartial journalism. The *Sun* nicknamed me 'Pipsqueak Pete' and 'Red Pete — otherwise known as extreme left-winger Peter Tatchell who symbolises everything that is appalling in the Labour Party today' (5 December). Thus the myth of Red Pete was born and added to the pantheon of left-wing bogies such as 'Red Ken' and 'Red Ted'.

This was to become a common feature of the tabloids. Almost without exception, whenever they mentioned my name, it was affixed with descriptions such 'Australian-born', 'draft-dodger', 'gay rights supporter', 'extreme left-winger' and 'militant'. These became the themes repeatedly highlighted by the press over the next year — I was a foreigner, deserter, political extremist and, by innuendo, homosexual.

Despite my clear and unequivocal denial on the very first day of the furore, most of the press were determined to lump me together with the Militant Tendency. The very next morning, the *Daily Mirror* led with its front page 'Militant Won't Be a Candidate'. The Militant smear falsely connecting me with a trotskyite faction of the party which was accused of acting contrary to the constitution and was under threat of expulsion, was to remain a recurring theme in the press onslaught for many months to come. After I made it repeatedly quite clear that I was not a Militant supporter, sections of the press resorted to more subtle innuendo. The *Daily Telegraph* described me as the 'militant-tending' Labour candidate, and under the headline 'Shadowy Group's Support' detailed how I was allegedly backed by the Militant Tendency. It was a real irony given Militant's opposition to my original selection and its later attempts to ditch me as the candidate. Not to be outdone by the *Telegraph*, the *Sun* followed up with references to my 'militant tendencies'. Thus, while the press actually avoided stating I was a member or supporter of the Militant Tendency, they made sure the idea was firmly planted in the reader's mind. Long after other papers had given up claiming I was a Militant member, the *Daily Star* continued to describe me as 'Mr Peter Tatchell of the Militant Tendency'.

From the outset, the press also began the process of trivialisation, ridicule and personalisation of the issues that was to be such a feature of the whole Bermondsey saga. Fleet Stret reporters seemed obsessed with my clothes and appearance. The *Express* depicted me as 'a rather exotic Australian canary who sings some odd songs'. The *Telegraph* wrote: 'Mr Tatchell, who has the habit of drawing himself erect periodically as he talks, and fingering the wide leather belt atop trendy cord jeans and two-tone wine and beige laced shoes, shows considerable irritation at personal questions.' The *Mail* referred to me as wearing 'a symphony in brown'

and devoted its centre pages on 8 December to the vital issue of the
contrast between Michael Foot's apparel and mine with the headline 'The
40 Year Generation Gap that Splits Labour'. After referring to Foot as
'Worzel Gummidge', Shaun Usher, the writer of the article, then wrote:
'Australian Tatchell...has to be the sharpest-dressed fledgling politician
in Rotherhithe.' After dealing with my 'burgundy casual' shoes and my
'knitted' tie, Usher described me as 'rather nattier than the average social
worker in a deprived inner city area.' We could reasonably ask why the
Mail and other papers were giving up so much space to such trivia.
Perhaps it was because I was different from the dull-dressed stereotype of
what an MP is supposed to look like; though my clothes were fairly
typical of my age group. But a more likely explanation is my
homosexuality, which in the eyes of the press made me fair game for
plenty of snide comments about the way I dressed. Normally it is only
women MPs whose appearance is regarded as significant and remarked
upon by the male-dominated media. Apart from the fact that for some of
the more chauvinistic press a homosexual is not a 'real' man, ridiculing
my apparel was just an additional weapon in their armoury to assassinate
the character of a left-wing Labour candidate.

My homosexuality was made into an issue by the tabloids. They
repeatedly and gloatingly focused on it. The fact that I was gay was
implied to newspaper readers by invariably referring to me as a
'supporter of gay rights'. Typically, the opening paragraph of the
Telegraph article on 5 December emphasised that I was a 'draft-dodger
and a supporter of homosexuals'. The *Sun* the same day headlined a story
'My Fight For the Gays — by Red Pete' next to a retouched photograph
which made it look as though I was wearing eye-liner and lipstick. The
article focused on the trip I had made to the World Youth Festival in '73:
'In 1973 Mr Tatchell was involved in a violent scuffle in East Berlin when
he raised a banner calling for solidarity with East German gays. Fellow
members of his student delegation at a world youth rally ripped down the
banner and attacked him, reducing him to tears.' The fiction of 'tears'
was a crude propagandist attempt to pander to the stereotype that all
homosexual men are pathetic, simpering queens. Three days later, the
Sun followed up this story about the rally in 'communist East Berlin'
under the headline 'The Night He Hid Out With Gay Friends':
'Yesterday it was revealed that Tatchell was there as British
representative of the Gay Liberation Front...Australian Red Pete carried
a banner saying: "Homosexual liberation. Revolutionary homosexuals
support Socialism." The banner was torn down by fellow delegates.
Homosexual friends of Mr Tatchell protected him as violence flared. He
was led to safety in tears. The East German sponsors of the rally banned
him from speaking or taking part in the closing march. The amazing trip
was reported in the newspaper of the Socialist Labour League — now the

Workers' Revolutionary Party, which has actress Vanessa Redgrave as leader.' Just to complete the guilt by association message, the *Sun* ran a picture of me above a photograph of Redgrave. Not to be outdone, the *Mail* followed on 9 December with 'Tatchell in Muddle over Gay Rights Past' which included 'kiss and tell' confessions from a former Gay Liberation Front member, Denis Lemon.

From the beginning I was incessantly quizzed by journalists about my support for homosexual equality. There was rarely a press conference or interview without it being raised at least once. What the media sought to do was portray gay rights as a Peter Tatchell issue — a personal crusade. In fact, what I did was no more than advocate Labour's official policy as all our candidates, before and since, are required to do.

In the light of the press coverage, the issue of whether I should come out publicly as gay was discussed informally within the Bermondsey party in the days immediately after Foot's statement. When I was originally selected as the candidate in November, most party members were aware that I was gay. I had never hidden the fact. A good number of party members supported my selection despite my sexuality. They feared it was a 'vulnerability' which Fleet Street could exploit, particularly in a by-election, but felt the 'risk' was worth taking. Following the barrage of press interest in my personal life after Foot's outburst, I met with officers and close comrades in the Bermondsey party to reconsider the question afresh.

In our hearts, most of us felt that to be open and honest about my sexuality was ideally the best policy. However, we were not in an ideal situation. I was a left-wing socialist, loathed by the media and the right, and facing a critical by-election where the incumbent Labour MP was most likely to campaign publicly against me. From discussions with journalists, it was clear that as soon as I put my sexuality on public record, it would then become in the eyes of Fleet Street a matter of legitimate public interest and justification for them to publish the most intimate details about my private life. We feared that in these circumstances, if I did come out, the issue of gay rights would be manipulated by a hostile press to dominate the inevitable by-election and submerge other key Labour policies on jobs and disarmament. Reluctantly, and after considerable soul-searching, we decided that while refusing to discuss my sexuality with the media, I should continue to reiterate my strong support for homosexual equality. It was left up to me how I should handle questions about my sexuality on the doorsteps in Bermondsey. I decided to be straightforward and frank.

The weekend after Foot's denunciation, the Sunday papers raised the first press questioning of whether Foot had chosen the right target in attacking me. The *Sunday Times* editorial had this to say: 'Mr Healey, Mr Shore, Mr Hattersley and any Labour supporters who think like them still believe the party is worth saving from trotskyites, anti-parliament men and other conspirators. Where Mr Tatchell fits into this crowd is not clear. He declares himself a parliamentary democrat and he has not joined the Militant Tendency. Two Militant candidates have already been approved by the Labour NEC, and a third awaits endorsement. Mr Tatchell sounds no worse than them, from the point of view of a democratic socialist. All the same, Mr Shore and others — not to mention Mr Foot himself — are right to feel that these are aliens, just as Mr Benn is an alien. Leaving aside all policy disagreements, people who believe in the supremacy of Parliament cannot make common cause with people who believe in the supremacy of the party.'

The *Sunday Telegraph* editorial accurately predicted: 'The Tatchell affair has all the promise of a long-running farce in three or four acts, guaranteed to humiliate all those who get involved.' Adam Raphael in the *Observer* wrote about the joy Foot's statement had given to the right wing of the Labour Party: 'The noises of approval for Mr Foot's declaration that he would try to topple Mr Tatchell from his Bermondsey perch came from right-wing loonies (they also exist) such as Mr Andrew Faulds. Mr Foot put his credit at stake in a matter in which he had no concern, no locus standi as the lawyers say, in the first place. Even if he does win at the executive sub-committee tomorrow, he will still have behaved both imprudently and wrongly.'

On the eve of the NEC meeting, the five defeated nominees who had been on the short-list for the Bermondsey selection issued a signed statement calling for my endorsement; they stated that I had been selected 'openly, fairly and democratically'. That same evening the Bermondsey party executive met again and reiterated its support for my candidature. We agreed that the acting chair and vice-chair should accompany me to the Commons to put the Bermondsey party's case to Foot the next morning.

Monday morning, 7 December, was to be a very important day for the future of Bermondsey Labour Party. If I had any doubt about that, a glance at the morning's papers reminded me. The *Mirror* editorial was headed 'The Battle Foot Must Win.' But interestingly, it also raised doubts about whether I should have been the prime target for Foot's condemnation of 'extremists': 'There are other Labour candidates who are more deserving of Michael Foot's condemnation than Peter Tatchell... The Battle of Bermondsey is Michael Foot's last ditch stand against the takeover by the hardline intolerant Left... Michael Foot may not have chosen the best case to fight on. But now he has shown he is determined that Labour should remain the party of democratic socialism. If he loses his battle over Tatchell at the party's organisation committee today, and at the National Executive on December 16, he will have lost credibility as leader. The defeat will not be his alone. It will be the Labour Party's.'

The press and television cameras followed me that Monday morning on my way to Westminster to meet Foot. Together with the Bermondsey party officers, I caught a number 12 bus to the Commons which is a ten-minute ride from the Elephant and Castle. It was strange to experience instant recognition from the people on the bus and I was cheered by the encouraging advice of several passengers to 'keep on fighting' and 'don't let them put you down'.

Arriving at Westminster, and forcing our way through the throng of reporters, we were received in Foot's office. I explained to Tom McCaffrey, Foot's private secretary, that I wanted the party officers to be present at the meeting with Foot. He was adamant that Foot would have a short meeting with me and no one else. This perhaps is illustrative of how the Parliamentary Labour Party sees itself as separate from the rank and file in the country. What possible harm could it have done to allow two officers to be present at the meeting as representatives of the Bermondsey party? What principle or power base was being threatened?

Foot seemed very ill at ease and anxious during my brief meeting with him. He rarely looked me straight in the face. He sat with his chair at right angles to mine so that he was looking away from me most of the time. Uncharacteristically, Foot was distant and acted like a paternalistic grandfather admonishing an errant child. He spoke at length and gave me little chance to reply or state my case. He said my *Briefing* article was clearly 'anti-parliamentary'. It was inflammatory in tone and had shown a lack of judgement on my part. He said that the article would be used by the SDP against Labour, not only in the Bermondsey by-election, but in others elsewhere round the country as well. The SDP would 'hang it round our necks' and do enormous damage to the party's electoral prospects. Foot made quite clear his feeling that if I were the candidate, Labour would lose the Bermondsey by-election to the SDP and that such a loss was unacceptable. He went on to say that he had nothing against me personally, which I took to be code for saying that he did not object to my homosexuality. Foot concluded by asking me to stand down as candidate 'for the good of the party' and to ensure that a 'reasonable and acceptable' candidate was chosen in my place. He also asked me to use my 'undoubted influence' in the Bermondsey party to ensure that long-serving councillors such as John O'Grady were put back on the approved list of candidates for the borough council elections in May 1982. Such a request clearly confirmed that the right wing in Bermondsey had direct access to Foot and had informed him in detail of local party internal politics. For my part, when Foot allowed me to speak, I put the case in defence of extra-parliamentary struggles and spoke of the Bermondsey party's success in increasing membership and organising local campaigns. Foot seemed generally uninterested in what I had to say and preoccupied with exacting my agreement to resign as prospective parliamentary candidate.

Our parting at the end of the meeting could be described at best as 'coldly polite'. I left to face the ranks of the waiting press and television, but decided to tell them very little until I had a chance to mull over what Foot had said and discuss our next move with other Bermondsey members.

That afternoon my comrades and I waited anxiously in my flat for the news of the vote on my endorsement at the NEC organisation sub-committee. Eventually the news came through that the committee had voted 12 to 7 in favour of a motion of non-endorsement proposed by John Golding and seconded by Dennis Healey. Tony Benn, Frank Allaun, Eric Heffer, Les Huckfield, Joan Maynard, Jo Richardson and Dennis Skinner stood by the principle of a constituency party's right to choose its own candidate. The rest of the committee backed Michael Foot; some of them out of personal loyalty and because his leadership was at stake, others because they favoured my non-endorsement as part of a generalised attack on the left.

John Golding summed up Foot's arguments when he spoke to the press after the meeting: 'Mr Tatchell is anti-parliamentary. Mr Foot asked for his non-endorsement on two grounds. The first was that on the basis of discussions he had this morning with Mr Tatchell, he thought he would be an electoral disaster. The second was that he feared the SDP would use material about Mr Tatchell throughout the country which would cause Labour not only to lose Bermondsey but other seats as well.' Betty Boothroyd, who voted against my endorsement, commented with candour after the meeting: 'This was not just about one man. It was about the direction of the Labour Party.'

I had become a symbol of extremism within Labour's ranks. A *Times* editorial stated: 'There are many Tatchells around in the Labour Party these days, some of them with a lethal sting. To block one man who has recommended more militant forms of extra-parliamentary opposition to challenge the government's right to rule would, it is true, be an important symbolic success. It would be a warning to the hard left, and an encouragement not only to the right but to the traditional left as well.'

Clearly, the loss of the vote was a sad blow to us, but my spirits were kept high by the continued enormous support of comrades in the Bermondsey party and many others round the country. That evening the officers of the Bermondsey party issued a press statement deploring the decision of the sub-committee to reject me as Labour candidate for the constituency and reiterating their 'total and unqualified' support.

The statement pointed out that the selection procedure had been carried out fully in accord with the party's constitution. Despite the sub-committee's decision, the Bermondsey party would seek to reverse it at the meeting of the full NEC on 16 December and would continue to fight for the right of all constituency parties to select their candidates 'without outside interference'.

The papers the next day weighed in with delight. The *Star* had the headlines 'Red Pete Gets the Boot' and 'Foot Shows He's Boss'. These headlines characterised the comic-book manner in which Fleet Street dealt with the important issues involved in the controversy. Under a sub-heading 'Red Guerrillas Destroying Labour', the *Sun* led with 'Foot Crushes Red Pete!' Most of the papers emphasised that I was either an 'electoral disaster' or a 'walking disaster'. Only the *Mail* captured our defiant and determined spirit with its front page headline 'Tatchell — We Will Fight On'. The *Guardian* broadened the argument in its editorial: 'If Mr Tatchell is unacceptable, how can the executive accept the Militant Mr Pat Wall at Bradford North — or any of the other Militants recently chosen by constituency parties, some already endorsed? If an overriding fidelity to parliamentary democracy is to be the test, then not just Tariq Ali, but hundreds of other recent converts to Labour will have no place in the party.' In other words, my non-endorsement was merely the opening of the floodgates to a widespread purge of the left.

The *Times* report dealt with the arguments within the committee itself: 'The sum of the debate ranged from the hard left arguing that there was nothing wrong with extra-parliamentary activity, to saying that someone who was against Parliament would hardly put himself up for election. Mr Wedgewood Benn said he had misgivings about any candidate being asked to give assurances about his views.'

Why Extra-Parliamentary Action Is Justified

My conviction that we needed a more vigorous extra-parliamentary opposition to the Tories has not changed since I wrote that original article. How much more pressing is the need, now that we face another four or five years of Thatcherite monetarist rule. Already, four years of Conservative government has plunged Britain into deep recession, devastating our industry and social services. Manufacturing output has fallen by a fifth, causing the loss of a million industrial jobs and a rate of industrial collapse nearly twice as great as the crash of 1929-31. With the lifting of exchange controls, over £20,000 million which could have been used to restructure our industry and create new employment has flooded out of the country. As a result unemployment has nearly trebled to well over four million, while the number of job vacancies is the lowest ever recorded. Mrs Thatcher stands condemned as the only Prime Minister who can claim to have destroyed more of Britain's industry than all of Hitler's bombs during the last war.

By axing £18,000 million from public expenditure, the Tories have torn the heart out of the Welfare State. Over one hundred hospitals have been totally or partially closed since May 1979, with the tragic effect of at least a thousand kidney and heart patients dying on the waiting-list for operations every year. The lives of hundreds of new-born babies are being lost through inadequate hospital staffing and intensive care facilities. By 1984, the government will have slashed housing expenditure by 48 per cent — £2,500 million. It has already more than doubled council rents and brought new council house-building to a virtual standstill. Yet there are 1.5 million households on council waiting-lists. A million people live in dwellings unfit for human habitation or lacking basic amenities such as baths. Every night, 100,000 homeless people sleep rough on the streets of our major cities, or in squalid emergency night-shelters and overcrowded hostels.

In all, eight million Britons are living on or below the official poverty line, and another six million are only just above it. What a damning indictment of the capitalist economic and political system! There is clearly a desperate need for a massive expansion of the Welfare State to solve these enormous social problems. But instead, the government has cut back public expenditure and condemned to idleness on the dole queue the nurses, teachers and building workers who could be nursing the sick, teaching our children and building new houses. Furthermore, in the midst of all this poverty and deprivation, the Tories announced the obscene expenditure of £10,000 million on the new generation of Trident nuclear missiles, plus thousands of millions more on the South Atlantic war and the Fortress Falklands folly.

Not only does Mrs Thatcher show little sense of moral values or priorities, she hard-facedly pursues policies without a clear electoral mandate. Where in her 1979 manifesto did she promise to deny millions of citizens their most basic rights — the right to a job on a living wage and to adequate housing, education and health care? When did she swear to close old people's homes, double VAT and increase prescription charges six-fold? In fact, Mrs Thatcher promised the exact opposite! What further proof does Foot or anyone else require to convince them? If the government exceeds its mandate and refuses to listen to the people, then extra-parliamentary action is absolutely justified to pressure it to change course. It is the only way we can defend the poorer and weaker members of society from a government deaf to reason and blind to compassion. The real 'crime' is not the extra-parliamentary protests which I advocated, but the immense suffering created by the policies of the Tory government. Instead of concentrating their fire on me, Labour's right would have done better to attack the Conservative policies which first provoked my call for direct action. Perhaps they should also have shown more concern about the extra-parliamentarism of the far right. Few of us can recall them making such strident attacks on the IMF in 1976 when it undermined the last Labour government by insisting on cuts in public expenditure, nor on the behind-the-scenes machinations of the multinational corporations, Stock Exchange, Law Lords and senior

Treasury and Civil Service officials. Did not the 'extra-parliamentary' NATO generals and EEC commissioners intervene to dictate pro-business and pro-American policy decisions to the Callaghan cabinet? Where was the Labour leadership's condemnation of extra-parliamentary action then?

The extra-parliamentarism which I called for is nothing new. It has been part and parcel of the whole history of the Labour movement. In fact, it has been the key to every major working-class struggle and socialist advance dating right back to the Peasants' Revolt and the Levellers. At times, the forward march of Labour was even dependent on the illegal and clandestine trade unions which were formed to defend the interests of workers, contrary to the Combination Acts. To win our cherished rights of freedom of speech, assembly and association, thousands of women and men acted outside the law at the risk of imprisonment and transportation, such as befell the Tolpuddle Martyrs. At Peterloo, some even paid with their lives.

It was only through struggle against Parliament as it was then constituted that the Chartists and Suffragettes won the franchise. Later, in response to the threats of longer hours, wage cuts and lockouts in the mines, the 1926 General Strike brought organised labour into direct confrontation with the elected government. Only a decade ago, free and independent trade unionism was preserved at the cost of workers refusing to recognise the Industrial Relations Act. The AUEW incurred huge fines and five dockers were imprisoned in Pentonville for contempt of court. Their release, and the eventual defeat of the Act, was only won through a campaign of non-compliance with the law and the threat of a general strike. At about the same time, the Upper Clyde Shipbuilders occupied the shipyards and organised a work-in to demand government cash to save their jobs. In 1972, a mass picket of miners won a great victory over the Coal Board and the partisan forces of law and order when they closed down a Midlands coal depot in the 'Battle of Saltley Gate'. Two years later, the National Union of Mineworkers forced a general election and brought about the defeat of the Heath government. Far from condemning the strike, the Labour movement applauded and took advantage of it to secure a victory at the polls. Perhaps the best recent example of extra-parliamentary action has been the Greenham Common peace camp. Those women, more than all Labour's fine speeches in Parliament, have succeeded in focusing public attention and the public conscience on nuclear disarmament as a major political issue.

Michael Foot in his radical past was the extra-parliamentarian par excellence. When he wasn't marching with the people in the streets, he frequently voiced his own doubts about leaving everything to Parliament: 'I'm not saying that anyone should choose only Westminster as a battleground — God forbid. Westminster would be an absolutely fruitless place if there weren't battles going on outside. No left MP can be effective if there are no mass movements outside.' This was Foot speaking in 1966; but by the end of 1981, the expression of similar views by myself became the pretext for his repudiating my parliamentary candidature. Aneurin Bevan, Foot's great mentor, frequently disparaged Parliament. In 1938, he expressed this view: 'From Parliament itself nothing can be expected. It is jaded, tired and cynical. It can be stirred from outside and only from outside.' Another quote from the future Foreign Secretary was recalled in a *Sunday Telegraph* cartoon on 6 December 1981, which depicted the ghost of Nye Bevan towering over Foot and saying: 'Parliamentary institutions have not been destroyed because the left was too vigorous; they have been destroyed because the left was too inert.'

A week later, on 14 December, the *Times* quoted from a book by Clement Attlee published by the Left Book Club in 1937:

> While, as I have stated, the Labour Party is steadily opposed to tactics of revolutionary action and violence, and has always pinned its faith to constitutional action, it has never ignored the possibility that occasions may arise when extra-parliamentary action may become necessary. If Labour cannot obtain a majority, it must as a minority accept the will of the majority. It may seek to influence that majority and those to whom it has entrusted power, by other lawful means, but to try and enforce its will on a majority by violence is contrary to this democratic faith. Stated thus, the proposition seems simple, but in fact there are borderline cases which require more examination... It may be that the government which has received a mandate from the electors deliberately goes against or beyond the wishes of those from whom it has derived its power... Thus, a government might, in defiance of its election pledges, take action which amounted to aggression leading to a war. It may be, then, right and necessary for a minority to take action, but it must be recognised that at that stage the method of constitutional action has been abandoned. A revolutionary situation may result.

It seemed that with almost every passing day quotes to back up the respectability of extra-parliamentary action were being offered from past pillars of the Labour establishment.

In turning his back on extra-parliamentary struggles, Foot was refusing to face up to the dilemma which arises from the relative powerlessness of the Parliamentary Labour Party given the Tories' majority. The Labour opposition in the House of Commons may win debates in terms of economic and political argument. It certainly has the moral victory. But it simply does not have the votes to carry the day. However, this does not mean that the rest of the Labour movement can do nothing but despair and meekly await the election of the next Labour government. Both within and without Parliament, we should seek to persuade and pressure the Tories to change course. This bringing of the popular will to bear on the government is precisely what extra-parliamentary action is all about. It does not supersede or usurp Parliament, but complements and invigorates the Labour opposition inside the House of Commons.

By unifying the parliamentary and non-parliamentary wings of the Labour movement in a common and simultaneous struggle, extra-parliamentary action strengthens and enriches the political process. It draws vast numbers of people into political struggles in defence of their own interests through trade unions, tenants' associations, the women's and gay movements, and ethnic and youth organisations. Though the right may wish otherwise, all over the country millions of people are daily engaging in extra-parliamentary demonstrations, lobbies, petitions, deputations, strikes, pickets and work-ins. Through such activities, countless hitherto cynical and passive people can share a meaningful involvement in a political process which they otherwise often regard as distant, and sometimes even irrelevant to their needs. Without such extra-parliamentary action, from one election to the next the political process would be a largely unaccountable and elitist charade conducted by 650 highly privileged individuals. Democracy would be reduced to a five-yearly ritual of putting a cross on a ballot paper, with each individual exercising a sum total of about twelve crosses in their lifetime.

Thus, far from posing a mortal threat to parliamentary democracy, extra-parliamentary activity is an intrinsic part of democratic politics — the sign of a healthy, vigorous democracy. Indeed, the right of people to organise outside of Parliament and challenge government decisions is what defines democracy and distinguishes it from the totalitarian states of Eastern Europe and Latin America where no such rights exist.

Support, Threats and Hate Mail

If the right thought that defeat at the organisation sub-committee would demoralise us, they were wrong. It only served to strengthen our resolve and spurred others round the country to come to our aid. The Bermondsey party headquarters was inundated with hundreds of letters of support from constituency parties and well-wishers from all over the country. Much of the personal mail I received was very supportive and cheering. A fair proportion of it, however, was hate mail (and obscene phone calls) of the vilest kind. Already, soon after Foot's statement and the attendant adverse publicity, I was subject to almost daily abuse and threats. It seemed that in particular my much publicised 'support for gay rights' brought out the worst in some people. They felt compelled to unburden themselves in obscene letters. With obvious relish, their letters ranted at length against the sexual practices they pretended to abhor. It very much seemed as though they were struggling with a repressed homosexual longing in themselves which, to disguise their own deep self-loathing, could only surface in the form of an intense hatred of homosexuals:

Dear Peter,

It should now be clear to you that the people of Bermondsey have no intention of electing a cock-sucking arse-fucking communist poof as their MP. You should therefore confine yourself to doing what you appear to be good at. You may be excellent at pulling cocks but you certainly cannot pull the votes. I have been a life long member of the Labour Party but I resigned when I heard that trash like you can become official candidates. For the sake of the Labour movement — fuck off — we don't want fairies.

Does Mr Tatchell as a known homosexual service all the Bermondsey Labour Party? That's why you all voted for him.

Dear Mr Tatchell,

When I lived in Bermondsey, until my family were bombed out while I was fighting to protect this country from outside evils, we had a saying, Bermondsey was a place where men were men and women counted as 'manholes' and members of the 'Middlesex Regiment' would not be tolerated. So why don't you piss off back to where you come from and leave the decent people of that once great borough alone. This country is in enough trouble without the likes of you and Tariq Ali etc stirring it up. Anyway what is wrong with that land of sunshine Australia, that you want to leave it, is it because you have to work for your living out there?

Sir,

As an ex-docker, and a lifelong member of the Labour Party — the son and grandson of dockers of the same opinion — I am disgusted that you should nominate an Antipodean Marxist QUEER as the next Labour Member for the Borough. Shame on you. We went through the blitz, and my two brothers died for their King and Country — one at Anzio and one at Arnhem. Yet you pick a yellow livered coward to represent these men of great courage as an MP. At the age of 64 with a heart complaint and therefore little to lose, I would be prepared to go to prison for the murder of this creep — don't imagine I'm a crank — far from it. If the IRA can kill with impunity and get away with it, I will certainly have a go! That folly of your choice can only be described as tragic. The Bastard Tatchell, a foreigner who ran away from his Country rather than fight for it, together with the nigger Tariq Ali from India who we educated and he overstayed his time here, and the half breed nigger Peter Hain who was involved in the murder at the airport in South Africa will never turn this country into a Marxist State while I live. If that is what they want let them go to Russia or Poland and stand in the queues for hours for a loaf of bread.

By the way how did a single homosexual get a council flat to begin with? Good luck to Michael Foot for rejecting him and if you persist — you know what to expect!

A Real Labour Member

Tatchell,

It has been noticed by many British people that you somehow got yourself into our Country from Australia in 1971 and worked at honourable jobs as a painter, carpenter and odd job man until 1979. You then found it much easier to take on less strenuous work as a 'social worker' cum Left-wing agitator and would-be politician. Very soon you jockeyed yourself into secretarial work which no one else had time for, and suddenly, in your own mind you became an IMPORTANT PERSON. Forget it boy. We do not want you in Great Britain. You have backed the wrong horse (Lord Stansgate-Benn). This millionaire Aristo has succeeded in splitting the Socialist Party right down the middle. Brilliant. Perhaps the finest double-agent ever... You had better go back to carpentering and painting in Australia. It might be harder work than talking political clap-trap which you are not able to understand properly, but it is all you may be any good for. The 'pretty boy' image does not last long in our country, and from what I know of your countrymen they do not go for it much either. Could this be why they hoofed you out? Does anyone want you (except Lord Stansgate-Benn)? Get lost before you are run over by a grass snake.

Copies to M. Foot MP
A. Benn MP
S. Williams MP
Scotland Yard C.I.D. (for check on possible treasonable activities and funding)
Australian High Commissioner (for check on right of P. Tatchell to remain in this country)

To counter the impression that my mail consisted mainly of garbage such as this, the following extract typifies how ordinary people were seeing our struggle:

> Dear Comrade,
> For what it is worth to you, you have my full support. I have just read your statement in the *Labour Weekly* and you have put into words what I and a lot of my grass roots comrades have been feeling. Please stay in there fighting and stick to your principles and if there is anything I can do to help just let me know. It is now the time for all good socialists to stand up and be counted, it is a shame that Mr Foot did not have the guts. I am a 58 year old granny, I have been Labour all my life and no one will ever get me out of our Labour Party. I will still read *Militant* and fight anyone who attacks our Young Socialists. I shall be very glad when all the Tory MPs have left our Labour Party. I will settle for quality rather than quantity. Good luck and God bless.

The day after the sub-committee vote, left-wing MPs led by Tony Benn wrote to every local Labour party in Britain urging them to flood the NEC with resolutions demanding my reinstatement. The next day, the sub-committee reconvened and decided to set up an inquiry into the Militant Tendency and its activities in particular areas, including Bermondsey. This showed just how clouded the waters of debate had become. My case, and that of the Bermondsey party, had become merged with the issue of Militant. It only served to show how far the right had deluded itself; in Bermondsey, there were a mere four Militant supporters out of 800 members and none of them held any position of responsibility in the party.

If Foot's denunciation of me had hoped to stop further defections to the SDP, clearly it had not worked. On the 12th, two more Labour MPs went over — Jeffrey Thomas and Bruce Douglas-Mann.

By Sunday 13 December, there were more revelations of alleged plots. Adam Raphael in the *Observer* wrote: 'That Mr Foot should have felt compelled to lash out in this wholly uncharacteristic way can only be understood by reference to the pressure on him. Manifesto Group MPs on the right of the party had bluntly warned him that, unless he took decisive action, not only would there be mass defections to the SDP, but they would provoke a by-election in which a Labour right-winger would stand against an official left-wing Labour candidate.' If this were true, and that threat had been put to Foot, here was the right wing threatening to do then what they eventually did fifteen months later when O'Grady stood against me in the by-election.

In the same edition of the *Observer*, Alan Watkins, in an article headed 'Lynch Law Trial of Mr Peter Tatchell' said:

> There has been a disposition in some quarters to lump the case of Mr Tatchell with the inquiry into the Militant Tendency which was

announced last week. According to this view of events, Mr Tatchell and the Militants are much the same in terms of real politics... But the cases of Mr Tatchell and the Militant Tendency are quite different and must be considered separately... Mr Tatchell was properly selected by his local party. In 1971 the executive resolved (perhaps misguidedly, but this is not the point) not to investigate political views in giving endorsements. In any event, Mr Tatchell is not a member of the Militant Tendency. Yet already five Militants have been adopted and endorsed as parliamentary candidates. This, as Mr Foot admits, is awkward. He will meet the problem as he comes to it... What Mr Foot has against Mr Tatchell is his attitude to Parliament. He has, so Mr Foot says, got the balance between parliamentary and extra-parliamentary activity wrong and, for this reason, must be refused endorsement. But how is this balance to be assessed? How are the scales to be weighted? To answer these questions, we have merely to imagine the scorn which the Michael Foot of the 1950s and 1960s would have visited upon such an exercise of weight-juggling if it had been proposed by, say, Herbert Morrison or Arthur Deakin... Perhaps the most shocking thing that was said to me last week about the case was: 'Well, you know someone has to get hurt and I'm afraid it has to be Tatchell.' It was said by an MP who makes a parade of her decent feelings and humanitarian instincts.

I quote at some length from this article to illustrate that not all the press coverage was hysterical and biased. Alan Watkins clearly did not endorse my left-wing views, but at least he was making a plea for some elementary justice and a rational discussion of the issues.

On the eve of the full NEC meeting, 19 Labour MPs and 28 GLC members signed a statement 'fully endorsing' my views in the *Briefing* article and calling for 'mass peaceful protests against Conservative government policies'. That same evening there was a crowded public meeting at the Rotherhithe Civic Centre. Despite heavy snow, over 600 people turned up, and there had to be an overflow meeting. The rally had been advertised in a leaflet with the slogan 'Don't let Bermondsey be trampled underfoot'. This plea found enthusiastic support in the audience and from the speakers, who included Tony Benn. He gave a brilliant speech, ridiculing the idea that extra-parliamentary action was in any way a new or dangerous concept in the politics of the Labour movement. He also argued that a vote for my reinstatement would be the best way to safeguard Foot's leadership and strengthen party unity. He claimed Foot was a prisoner of the right wing who were working to undermine his leadership. If Foot led a purge of left-wingers, this would isolate him from his natural supporters and cause such disunity and bitterness that the right would be able to use the chaos created as an excuse to force his resignation. As a riposte to our campaign, Solidarity, the centre-right grouping in the party led by Roy Hattersley and Peter Shore, called for more attacks on the left to stop what they alleged was the organised infiltration and manipulation of constituency parties.

Denial of Natural Justice and Defeat Again at the NEC

I had requested the chance to put my case personally to the full NEC at its meeting on 16 December. Telephone negotiations on this issue had already produced a blank refusal. But I was determined to highlight this amazing injustice by presenting myself at Transport House where the NEC was meeting in the hope of being granted an 'audience'. Accompanied by the acting chair and vice-chair of the Bermondsey party, I was kept waiting for nearly an hour while the NEC argued whether I should be permitted to enter the meeting and state my defence. In the end, I was refused a hearing on the grounds that it would set a 'precedent'. We had to leave and sit out the waiting time until the verdict came through. When it did come, we had lost by a single vote — 15 votes to 14. It was an astonishing decision.

Meeting in secret session, the NEC had turned aside the principles of natural justice. Despite my request for a hearing, I had been denied the right to face my accusers and speak in my own defence. Of course, that would have been quite difficult anyway because I had never been officially informed of the allegations against me. Nor, for that matter, did the NEC subsequently ever tell me its reasons for refusing my endorsement. Instead, like everyone else, I was left to conclude from the rumours of lobbyists and newspaper columnists that my candidature was voted down on the basis of alleged 'anti-parliamentary' views expressed in my *Briefing* article. When the members of the full NEC made their decision to deny endorsement they did not even have the article in question before them. Indeed, several members voted without ever having read it. They based their judgements instead on hearsay and the gross misrepresentation of its contents by my critics.

It is a perverse kind of justice where no evidence is presented and the defendant has no right to even know, let alone answer, the charges. What is more, the process of justice normally involves taking into account the character and previous record of the defendant before passing sentence. However, the NEC's judgement was apparently based solely on my authorship of a single article. It completely ignored my record of working with other local members to rebuild the Bermondsey Labour Party and campaign for the betterment of the local community. Given that my article was written as a contribution to the debate concerning Labour's strategy for fighting the Tories, was not this judgement by the NEC tantamount to denying freedom of speech and open debate within the party? Did it not signify an intolerance towards opinions different from those of the leadership?

What made the verdict so hypocritical is that it emanated from party leaders who only a year beforehand had shown such tolerance in their desperate attempts to persuade the 'gang of four' to stay within the party. Then, as now, they were prepared to accommodate within their ranks members who openly oppose our democratically agreed conference policies of withdrawal from the Common Market and unilateral nuclear disarmament.

It therefore still mystifies me what ideas in an altogether innocuous article were apparently so powerful and threatening to the party establishment that they required my disqualification as a Labour candidate. The proposition that I was somehow a mortal threat to parliamentary democracy that had to be exorcised from the body politic was a rather flattering but nevertheless absurd overestimation of my significance. It was an equal nonsense to suggest that my unexceptional writing had shown 'a contempt for parliamentary democracy' and 'brought Parliament into disrepute'. As if such a feat was in my power anyway! The truth is that the whole episode had little to do with my extra-parliamentary article. Myself and the Bermondsey party were scapegoats all along; we were cynically sacrificed to the threats of right-wing MPs in the erroneous hope of improving Labour's by-election propects. This sacrifice, in fact, achieved the exact opposite. It failed to stem the tide of defections to the SDP. Many months of hard work to build up the Bermondsey party membership and establish strong links in the local community were undermined — doing enormous electoral damage.

It was a real tragedy to see Michael Foot, who had himself been a victim and an opponent of witchhunts and inquisitions in the past, associated with the purge demanded by the right. Why couldn't he have admitted that he had made a mistake in his original Commons statement? Far from being a sign of weakness which would have forced his resignation, it would have been an act of political courage and principle. He would have brought a little honesty and integrity back into a political system which badly lacks it and therefore made himself all the more deserving of our continued support as Labour leader.

On 16 December it was defeat at the NEC again, albeit by only one vote. The soft left members, notably Neil Kinnock, had caved in and voted with Foot and the right out of loyalty to the leader and in a desperate desire for party unity, apparently at any price. Kinnock, especially, did lasting damage to his standing among the left of the party, not only by his vote on my endorsement, but also by his insensitive and reactionary remarks before and after the NEC meeting. Since he had become the shadow spokesperson on education Kinnock had noticeably lurched to the right, not an unfamiliar characteristic of many Labour MPs when the carrot of high office is dangled in front of their noses. Kinnock was quoted in the *Express* as saying: 'I'm not in favour of witchhunts but I do not mistake bloody witches for fairies.' It took no great insight to recognise the blatantly anti-gay tenor of those remarks. In a *Sunday Times* article the next Sunday Kinnock referred to himself as being on the 'balls wing' of the party. It was sad to see a 'socialist' pandering so crudely to anti-gay prejudice. Perhaps he felt he had to play to the macho, rugby-playing gallery, protesting his masculinity as he did in the same article where he told of 'beating the shit' out of someone who had kicked him in the elbow at annual conference.

The reason why the soft left on the NEC voted against my endorsement are more complex than personal loyalty to Foot. Labour MPs are repeatedly cajoled about the need to show loyalty to the leadership and to obey the principle of collective responsibility for decisions taken. However, when the leader has so clearly erred and acted against elementary justice, is it still the duty of MPs to back him up regardless? Clearly not; especially when the issue is such an important one as a constituency party's right to choose its own candidate and for that democratically selected candidate to be endorsed. What possible justification could so-called left MPs have for voting with Foot and the right? If Kinnock and people like him justify their action on the basis of personal friendship with Foot, what price are socialist principles when 'old pals' can supersede them? I was the victim, the sacrifice required, to ensure that Foot's face could be saved. Kinnock again implied as much when he said on television that as a good socialist I would understand why he had to vote in the way he did. I did not understand then and I still do not understand now.

One day after the NEC decision, Mellish announced that he would not be resigning as Bermondsey's MP after all. He said he had changed his mind after new talks with Michael Foot. He told a meeting of Labour MPs on the evening of the 17th that he would 'stay on for a bit'. It seemed conclusive proof that some kind of pact had been agreed between Foot and Mellish — Mellish had apparently threatened to resign unless Foot acted against me. Foot had panicked under the threat of a by-election which he had been induced to believe Labour would lose if I were the candidate; particularly if I had to stand against Roy Jenkins of the SDP and also face Mellish's public opposition. Foot won the vote for my non-endorsement; Mellish then kept his side of the bargain. The by-election was postponed. But it was only a postponement, because Mellish later broke his promise to Foot, as Foot himself admitted in a speech in Bermondsey during the by-election campaign.

Also on 17 December, the Bermondsey GC met again. We had received a letter from David Hughes, Labour's national agent, informing us that we had been instructed by the NEC to begin a new selection process to choose a new candidate. At the meeting, a regional officer of the party informed us that the assistant national agent had ruled that I would be ineligible to stand again for selection and that any nomination received in my name would be declared invalid. As we suspected and later discovered, the NEC had given no such instructions. Yet again, the party's full-time officials were overstepping their powers. The GC concluded by 'reaffirming its total support' and 'deploring' the NEC's refusal to endorse my candidacy. The overwhelming vote of 59 to 7 indicated that even members of the centre-right realised this was an issue which transcended the left-right divide. Party democracy and constituency rights were at stake. For the sake of all parties everywhere, we had to keep up the fight.

By the time that the Labour Party headquarters in Walworth Road closed for the Christmas period, more than 600 resolutions and letters of support for my endorsement had been received, according to the *Tribune* report on 1 January 1982. The same *Tribune* article went on to analyse the situation in this way: 'Bermondsey now has two choices. It can hold another selection and choose Tatchell again or it can refuse to select again on the grounds that the candidate of its choice has been wrongfully excluded. Sooner or later the NEC will be faced — just as in the bad old days — with having to dissolve the party. Since Bermondsey is now one of the healthiest and toughest Labour parties in London, the NEC can expect to meet stiff resistance, on top of which Peter Tatchell may wish to exercise his right to appeal to this year's annual conference. This one, as they say, will run and run.' Indeed it would.

Up until this point, the Bermondsey electorate only had the lurid and distorted picture of Peter Tatchell which they saw on television and read about in the newspapers. We had to counteract the media propaganda. Early in January 1982, therefore, the Bermondsey party finally produced the newsletter we had planned the previous November before national headquarters had intervened to block it. The newsletter, which was distributed to every household in the constituency, explained why I had been chosen as the candidate and the policies I was fighting for.

Around this time the idea was floated that I should stand for election to the constituency section of the NEC at annual conference in the autumn. We saw this as a means of pressurising the party leadership. Clearly we had immense support around the country and the prospect that this support might be enough to put me on the NEC created considerable discomfort among the leadership. Besides, it would be completely untenable for an elected member of the NEC to be ineligible to stand as a parliamentary candidate. This plan was later dropped in July when the NEC agreed to allow me to stand in a new selection and after it was decided that the left should all unite around an agreed slate of candidates to avoid splitting its vote in the face of a strong right-wing challenge for control of the constituency section. While the idea was current, however, it received wide support from Labour parties round the country. In any case, many members felt there should be more non-MPs on the NEC and more younger people, not just a token Young Socialist.

By the New Year, the backstage machinations that had led up to Foot's statement were fairly widely acknowledged. On 8 January, *Tribune* had this to say: 'They believe that their MP, Bob Mellish, did a deal with Foot: Tatchell's head in return for Mellish not standing down to create an embarrassing by-election. It is well-known that Foot and Mellish met to discuss the matter before Foot made his denunciation. Labour Party members are entitled to know what went on at that meeting.'

But it was another meeting that got most press and party attention that week. Labour Party leaders and trade-union bosses met at Bishop's Stortford, ostensibly to heal the left-right divisions and forge a new sense of unity. The *Guardian* reported: 'As they met their traditional enemy, the press, assembled outside, few of the participants could disguise their genuine pleasure at reporting the absence of blood from the floor or walls of the conference room. It was clear that they could scarcely believe it themselves that not only was there no disagreement to disguise, but for the first time in nearly three years, there was a positive move forward — what party chairman [sic] Dame Judith Hart described as "the will for unity". The meeting in fact managed to avoid trouble largely by not discussing matters that were controversial either between left and right, or between the party and the unions. They did not, for example, talk about the row over Peter Tatchell, Mr Tariq Ali as a prospective member of the party, or the role of the Militant Tendency. But these are issues that have created turmoil in the constituencies which will not easily subside.' There was much written about the new spirit born in the party after the Bishop's Stortford meeting. Party leaders were often to refer to the 'spirit of Bishop's Stortford' in the months to come. We saw little evidence of that benevolence spreading as far as Bermondsey.

The Bermondsey party sent a letter to the January NEC meeting asking them to reverse their earlier decision. When they met on 11 January, the NEC refused to do so, but confirmed they would dispatch the national agent, David Hughes, and Eric Heffer, chair of the organisation committee, to Bermondsey to discuss the situation re my candidature and our refusal to accept the nomination of long-standing councillors for the May 1982 borough council elections.

Foot's Parliamentary Route to Socialism and My Reply

The controversy over 'extra-parliamentarianism' led to Michael Foot setting out his faith in a parliamentary route to socialism in two articles published in the *Observer* on 10 and 17 January 1982. After referring to the 'terrible example' of Poland, he wrote:

> There is plentiful proof on our own doorsteps of the proposition that for Socialists — for those who accept that only by profound Socialist change can the deeper disease of society be cured — the dominant need is to turn the nation's mind to parliamentary action... Who, in the Labour movement, who on the left, even the so-called hard left, opposes parliamentary action? Of course it is needed. The real question concerns extra-parliamentary action which may be the handmaiden, the indispensable ally, of parliamentary action. Is not that a more profitable field of scrutiny? Should we not be seeking new and more effective methods of extra-parliamentary action, drawing some lessons from the past maybe, from Wat Tyler, the Levellers, the Chartists, the Suffragettes, all of whom did certainly engage in extra-parliamentary activity, and to some considerable effect? ...Extra-parliamentary action was imperative since they had no effective voice inside; actually to win the voice inside was the aim. Of course, to achieve such results, it was necessary to take action outside Parliament, and with every justice... And the Suffragettes, like the Chartists, resorted to legal or sometimes illegal action outside Parliament precisely because they too were denied the right to speak and act inside Parliament. It is an irony that they should now be paraded as the opponents of parliamentary democracy.

In the second of the articles Foot warned of the danger of a break-through of the 'so-called' Social-Democrats and their allies:

> Such could have been the calamitous result in the by-election at Bermondsey — and far beyond Bermondsey — if we had been compelled to fight on the declarations issued by the recently selected candidate there. And these declarations, let me underline, did not assert the equality and interdependence of parliamentary and extra-parliamentary activities as the Labour movement has practised them and the people of Britain understand and support them. Those declarations professed the superiority of extra-parliamentary activities as a means of securing change and progress in the Britain of the 1980s. They were anti-parliamentary and gave ruinous advantage and opportunities to our enemies — and to our

Social-Democrat enemies in particular. Sooner or later, if the Labour Party was to prove afresh its allegiance to parliamentary democracy — and I mean the widely held belief more than the actual institution — those declarations had to be repudiated. And, in my judgement as leader of the party, the sooner the better... For the men and women who made the Labour Party constitution, and who insisted on establishing a Labour Party inside Parliament as well as outside in the country, were not mistaken. They understood the place Parliament occupied in the history of the British people and the importance which our people attach to what Tawney called the 'elementary decencies' of parliamentary government.

Nowhere in these articles did Foot explain how 'the suffering millions', the victims of Thatcherism, could be rescued given a Parliament where the Labour opposition is in a clear minority. It faces a determined Conservative government which is impervious to the argument and oratory of Labour's front bench. Foot's treatise decried extra-parliamentary action but offered no alternative this side of a general election and the return of a Labour government. But the many victims of Tory policies — the homeless and the jobless — cannot wait that long. Indeed, in extreme cases, their lives depend on Labour taking action now — the thousands of elderly people who die from hypothermia during bad winters and the hundreds of kidney patients whose lives are lost every year for want of transplants and dialysis treatment.

Foot also seemed to be arguing that the winning of universal suffrage made extra-parliamentary protests unnecessary and perhaps even illegitimate. This was a surprising view from the parliamentary leader of the Labour movement. Surely he cannot deny that even since the granting of the vote, the recent history and finest moments of our movement have included struggles not only outside of Parliament, but sometimes even outside the law? To defend improverished tenants from onerous rates and rents, unjust legislation was defied by Labour councillors at Poplar in 1921 and Clay Cross in 1972. At the very time of Foot's *Observer* articles, twenty-four Scottish Labour MPs were backing the workers' occupation of the British Aluminium plant at Invergordon. Is Foot seriously suggesting that there are never any circumstances in which it is right to defy the law — that all laws enacted in parliamentary democracies must be obeyed, no matter how repressive? To my knowledge, Labour has never accepted that election by universal suffrage gives any government — least of all the Thatcher regime — a legislative carte blanche and automatic moral authority for its every action. That a government is elected by universal suffrage in a parliamentary democratic state does not make oppressive legislation any more defensible or any less worthy of opposition. Whenever governments such as the current Tory administration exceed their mandate, cease to be accountable to the electorate or pursue odious and draconian policies, they have always been challenged by the Labour movement through extra-parliamentary action. This was the case with the Jarrow marchers in the 1930s and fifty years later it is still the case today with the People's Marches for Jobs. The tradition of extra-parliamentary direct action and civil disobedience has an honourable lineage. It ws strongly epoused by the radical reformers of the 18th century such as Tom Paine who argued that citizens have a right to rebel against repressive laws and unjust governments. It has found modern champions in Mahatma Gandhi and Martin Luther King, and most recently in the 'Stop the Missiles' blockade of US nuclear airbases in Britain. Tory policies at the time of Foot's *Observer* articles were certainly denying millions of Britons the most elementary human rights of all — the right to employment, housing and medical care for all those who need it. More explicitly, the Home Secretary's bans on marches had denied Londoners the freedom of political demonstration for more than a quarter of 1981. Since then, the Tebbit Bill has curtailed the rights of workers to freely organise and take industrial action, while the Nationality Act has put legislation on the statute books which is blatantly discriminatory against black people. To challenge and defeat the government on such infringements of our civil and human rights is not only justifiable. It is the positive duty of every true democrat.

Extra-parliamentary action of this nature does not seek to usurp the rights of Parliament, but to restore the civil and human rights which Parliament has usurped from the citizens it governs. Far from leading to disillusionment with parliamentary democracy (millions are already disillusioned anyway given the failures of successive governments to bring about a real measure of justice and equality), this can only give hope that the House of Commons is accountable to the electorate and that it is the guardian of the rights and democratic freedoms of working-class people.

Foot's initial accusation against me, and he repeated it in his *Observer* articles, was that I was 'anti-parliamentary'. In the sense that I believe Parliament is neither sovereign nor fully democratic and requires reforming to make it so, Foot was right. The British Parliament is an assembly of three bodies — the Lords, the Crown which grants Royal Assent, and the House of Commons. Only the latter is elected, whereas the other two are hereditary or appointed through patronage. Though the House of Commons predominates in normal circumstances, the monarch enjoys very considerable reserve powers in exceptional situations such as a hung Parliament or civil emergency, when Parliament can no longer function in a 'normal' manner. The radicalism of Labour governments is undoubtedly inhibited by the very existence of these powers and by the fact that the army owes its allegiance exclusively to the monarch, and not to the elected Parliament and government. Unlike most electoral democracies, the British people do not enjoy the legal status of citizens. They remain subjects of the Crown, a vestige of a bygone feudal era in which absolute monarchy held sway. Parliament is not 'the people in power'. It is the Crown, rather than the electorate, which is sovereign over Parliament. Indeed, MPs swear allegiance not to the people or even to parliamentary democracy, but to Her Majesty the Queen. Nor is Parliament the sovereign institution which governs the whole of society. It is subject to influence and manipulation by extra-parliamentary formations of unelected and unaccountable capitalist power. They enjoy unequal and privileged access to Westminster and exercise their own power over vast areas of social life, particularly in the economic realm. These formations not only include major monopolies, the City and multinational corporations, but also the semi-independent branches of the parliamentary democratic state — the civil service, judiciary, media, armed forces, etc. It is inside these collective formations of capitalist power, and outside the forums of electoral democracy, that many of the *real* decisions affecting the lives of millions of people are made — often in secret.

Thus, the existence of representative democracy, and Parliament as the place where this unfettered representation takes place, is at best no more than a half truth. Parliament does not monopolise or exhaust the process of representing individuals and interest groups, nor does it represent them all equally or make its own sovereign decisions.

Perhaps the greatest single flaw in our 'actually existing' parliamentary democratic system is the virtual absence of any economic democracy to remotely parallel even the imperfect form of parliamentary democracy we have thus far achieved. Our present matrix of economic and political systems is no more than bourgeois democracy. In his essay 'Democracy and Parliament', Raymond Williams precisely defines this as 'the co-existence of political representation and participation with an economic system which admits no such rights, procedures or claims — the continuing bourgeois monopoly of predominant ecoomic power; the use of this power to influence and at times marginalise political democracy'.

It is thus the task of socialists to complete the unfinished democratic revolution — to win economic democracy, together with a reformed system of parliamentary democracy in which the people have supreme power over Parliament and Parliament has supreme power over the whole of society. This requires breaking up the rule of private capitalist monopolies and the centralised and secretive capitalist state. It necessitates greater common ownership and democratic public control of industry and wealth, together with the democratisation of the whole state apparatus, of which Parliament is only one aspect, to ensure greater public accountability, freedom of information and popular participation. This democratisation must also necessarily transfer military allegiance to the elected House of Commons and remove the monarch's sovereignty over the state, particularly her reserve powers over Parliament which would be more appropriately vested in the hands of the Speaker of the House of Commons who is accountable to the assembled MPs.

Contrary to the claims of the right, the real threat to democracy comes not from the relatively powerless minnows of the extra-parliamentary left. It comes from the capitalist classes who have most to gain from the present system and most to lose from any fundamental social change. Utilising *their* state apparatus, they have long been prepared for a 'slaveholders' rebellion' against the election of a radical socialist government. Having thwarted such an eventuality, the re-elected Thatcher government is more determined than ever to shore up class privilege and ready to ruthlessly put down the dissent and social disorder which its policies will undoubtedly provoke in the years to come. In response to unemployment, bad housing and police harassment, the Tory government offers riot squads, plastic bullets, CS gas and water cannons, plus new repressive legislation along the lines of the Police Bill. Some of its instruments of repression, such as the Prevention of Terrorism Act, are already on the statute book. Other emergency powers are ready, waiting in the wings, for activation to break strikes and crush the union movement. New technologies of surveillance, information control, psychological warfare and counter-insurgency against the 'enemies of the (capitalist) state' have been developed and put into operation in the north of Ireland and Falklands wars. The methods tested there are now being refined for use against civil unrest by our increasingly militarised police. Far from the left being a threat to parliamentary democracy, it is against the resistance of the 'slaveholders' that the left is seeking to actualise the democratic ideals which sprang from the English Revolution four hundred years ago.

Our socialist vision is indivisible from making parliamentary democracy a reality and establishing Parliament as the truly sovereign decision-making body in society, genuinely ruled by the people, rather than by the hidden hand of big business. Such views are, of course, against Parliament as it is presently constituted, though not anti-parliamentary in principle. It is this distinction that Foot seemed unable to appreciate or accept. But it is a distinction the Labour Party must recognise and act upon if we are to avoid the fatal delusion that a Labour government can simply take over Parliament and the rest of the state apparatus in its present form and wield it for socialist purposes on behalf of the working class.

The state is not neutral. It was not constructed by or for us. It has historically evolved over many centuries as the governing instrument of the business classes and it will have to be fundamentally transformed if it is ever to be the handmaiden of genuine socialist change.

A month after the Foot articles, in a clear challenge to the party leadership, 33 Labour prospective parliamentary candidates signed a statement supporting extra-parliamentary action. On 7 March, at the Greater London Labour Party annual conference, the chair of the party, Judith Hart, dismissed the Bermondsey affair as an 'organisational hiccup'. It was a 'hiccup' that had caused great discomfort to the party and would continue to do so. By a vote of 538,500 in favour and only 189,500 against, the conference called on the NEC to reinstate me as the Bermondsey candidate.

Clearly, Foot and the right wing were not winning the argument about extra-parliamentary action among the rank and file of party and union membership. Those arguments and the struggle for my endorsement by the NEC were to continue for the next year right up to the very eve of the Bermondsey by-election.

Chapter Four

The Fight to Become
the Official Candidate

During the initial furore over Foot's repudiation of my candidature in December 1981, the battle continued over our refusal to accept a few old guard councillors onto the approved list of candidates for the borough council elections in May 1982. The Southwark Labour parties — Bermondsey, Peckham and Dulwich — refused to accept a total of eight councillors out of over ninety nominees they approved. On 8 December, only five days after Foot's Commons statement, the Greater London Labour Party appeals committee turned down four of the councillors who had appealed against our decision to drop them, while reinstating four others. John O'Grady was one of the councillors whose appeal was turned down. By that stage he had been turned down by the Bermondsey constituency party, the Southwark local government committee, which represents all three Southwark Labour parties, and the Greater London Labour Party. John O'Grady was not, however, going to surrender the power he had become accustomed to over the previous fourteen years without inflicting further damage on the Labour Party.

The NEC's Imposition of Eight Councillors

On 16 December 1981 the NEC had 'frozen' our selection of council candidates and agreed to send David Hughes, the national agent, and Eric Heffer, chair of the organisation sub-committee, to meet us in a bid to resolve the councillors dispute. On 21 January 1982 that meeting duly took place with the officers of the Southwark local government committee and the three Southwark Labour parties at the House of Commons. Heffer opened by saying that we had to accept the eight councillors back on the panel of candidates in the 'spirit of Bishop's Stortford'. He kept repeating that a 'modus vivendi' had to be found. He admitted that no rules had been broken in the selection process. 'I don't give a damn about rules,' he said, 'Bishop's Stortford determines everything.' The party had to unite, because 'any Labour government is better than any Tory government'. He added that people who talked about betrayal by the Callaghan government were talking nonsense. I told him that if we reinstated the councillors as he requested, there was no way he could guarantee they would implement Labour's manifesto and not defect to the SDP. Uncharacteristically, Heffer got extremely angry and almost shouted at me: 'If you want my support in the future, don't come on with clever questions. I can't stand clever people. I am just a simple working-class chap.' We all took Heffer's 'threat' to mean he would withdraw his suport in my fight for endorsement if we did not toe the line on the councillors issue. He went on to say: 'This is not the 1950s and I'm not Ray Gunter.' Some of us felt, however, that he gave a very good imitation of Gunter at the meeting.

After hearing Heffer's demand that we accept the eight councillors, we left to go back and consult with our local parties. The next evening the Southwark local government committee met and overwhelmingly rejected the Heffer-Hughes demand that we accept the eight councillors.

Having failed the first time, on 29 January the NEC sent David Hughes and Judith Hart, then chair of the Labour Party, to meet the Southwark local government committee and persuade us to accept the eight back. Judith Hart was friendly and conciliatory in contrast to the bulldozing tactics of Heffer. She admitted that the Southwark parties had behaved perfectly constitutionally, but said that 'a dispute exists and I am here to settle it'. When she was challenged as to whom the dispute was between, it took half an hour for her to finally admit that the complaints were emanating from the hard right in the Dulwich Fabian Society (the branch that sent John O'Grady as a delegate to the Bermondsey GC) and several unspecified EETPU branches. Neither Hart nor Hughes would tell us the nature of their allegations despite numerous requests for them to do so. Contradicting Heffer, Hart said that 'modus vivendi' was irrelevant and the time for compromising was over. Prompted by Hart's declaration, a right-wing delegate moved to accept back the eight councillors, but his motion was lost by 28 votes to 3. In the 'spirit of Bishop's Stortford', we offered a compromise motion to accept back the four councillors whose appeal had been upheld by the Greater London Labour Party, but to reject the four whose appeal had been turned down. This was carried by 22 votes to 9. O'Grady was still excluded. That night I wrote in my diary: 'Bishop's Stortford is a farce. Unity at any price? They want total capitulation to the right. We are expected to give everything and get nothing in return.'

On 8 February the NEC organisation sub-committee unilaterally restored the eight councillors to the panel of candidates. Our compromise of four in and four out was flatly rejected. That evening the Southwark local government committee voted by 14 votes to 11 to reluctantly accept the decision of the NEC. This vote caused huge controversy within the

Southwark parties. I abstained on the vote, thinking that we should have taken the issue back to the three respective GCs for a fresh mandate before making any decision. This abstention on my part angered some of my supporters in the parliamentary selection process who accused me of betrayal because I had not voted against the reinstatement. The consistent bombardment from the media against me personally had already caused some to waver. This issue accelerated that process. In addition, the small group of Militant supporters exploited controversial issues such as the reinstatement of O'Grady to foment dissension among the left and gain more supporters for the Militant cause. From this point onwards, some Militant supporters ceased to be wholeheartedly behind me in my fight to be restored as the candidate. Publicly they spoke out for my endorsement and they always voted with the Bermondsey party to that end. But in private and behind the scenes they frequently sought to undermine my position. These 'workerist' comrades branded me a middle-class interloper and dismissed my socialism as mere 'community politics'. Some of them used my homosexuality and the fact that I had lived 19 years in Australia to prejudice other comrades against me. I have always defended, and continue to defend, Militant's right to exist and organise within the party. I have always opposed the witchhunt against them. It saddens me that some Militant supporters in Bermondsey did not back up their publicly stated views with actual firm support in the constituency.

Over the next few weeks, the personal animosity towards me by former close comrades was to hurt me very deeply. I remember at the time feeling very depressed following the local government committee vote and the anger it aroused among our own ranks. I felt very concerned that it could irrevocably split the left. Indeed, when the Southwark left caucus next met it was deeply divided over the reinstatement of the councillors. Many comrades said the Southwark parties should have continued to resist the NEC. It had to be faced, however, that such resistance would have been nominal. The NEC would undoubtedly have presented the wards with their own approved list of candidates, including the eight. It had also to be acknowledged that support among left members of the NEC was much less strong on this issue than on that of my endorsement.

There were only three months to go before the council elections, and the wards had yet to choose their candidates. Total resistance in these circumstances could well have been used as a pretext by the right-wing members of the NEC to push through the dissolution of the Bermondsey party, if not of all three Southwark parties. That could have resulted in O'Grady and his henchmen being automatically installed as official candidates while we would have been out in the cold.

Soon after the local government committee accepted the eight councillors, the NEC 'unfroze' the selection of candidates. The wards could proceed to select. In the event, only two of the eight former councillors were selected by their wards — John O'Grady and Harold Young. However, the selection of candidates in Riverside ward caused great controversy and shock waves that later significantly affected the result of the Bermondsey by-election.

Council Elections – Mellish Backs Independents

On 8 March the Riverside ward held its selection meeting to choose three candidates to fight the council elections. Coral Newell, a right-wing councillor for the previous four years and a supporter of John O'Grady, was not one of the three candidates who were selected at the meeting, despite the fact that she received 48 votes from the 86 members present. As was normal in Bermondsey selections, the choice was made by an eliminating ballot; every person eligible to vote at the meeting had to use three votes for three candidates otherwise their ballot slip was declared invalid. With this type of ballot, it is quite possible for a candidate to receive more than half the votes cast and still lose the selection. The reasons for this are various, but they include the possibility of one group at the meeting voting for the same slate of three on each ballot, while other people vote for the one candidate they really want but have to vote for two others they don't particularly want as well. This voting procedure is used in many constituency Labour parties and at Labour conferences. Indeed, Newell had been selected as a candidate four years previously, when she ousted long-standing councillors, by the very same method of ballot. However, this was conveniently forgotten by her supporters when they raised squawks of protest after she had not been re-selected. The meeting ended in uproar as the Newell-O'Grady faction vented their anger at being beaten.

The right wing complained that a few months prior to the Riverside selection, thirty new members had joined the ward branch. Many of these new members came from a particular nineteenth-century block of delapidated flats. Newell's supporters denigrated them as 'squatters' although these people had tenancy agreements with Southwark council. Unfortunately, 'squatter' is still a term of abuse with many Bermondsey people. The right wing knew that and used the term widely and inaccurately, but to great effect in stirring up hostile passions. The right also screamed wild allegations that one of the membership application forms had been forged by an unnamed person. Interestingly, they never made any formal charges about these alleged irregularities. However, to satisfy all concerned, the Bermondsey party set up an enquiry. Two outside observers from the Southwark local government committee had been present at the selection meeting. They testified that the selection process had been properly carried out. A later exhaustive investigation into the Riverside selection by London regional officials of the Labour Party brought forth no evidence of wrong-doing. The right's claims were seen to be baseless.

However, Newell and her supporters were not content with that verdict. The myths about a 'rigged' selection meeting began to spread round the district. It has to be said that Newell had considerable support in the neighbourhood. She was perceived as being a good, hard-working councillor. The myth that she had been 'cheated' and 'thrown aside' by a conspiracy of 'middle-class social workers', 'squatters' and 'hippies' who had been specially imported for the purpose gained wide credence in the area. Mellish weighed in with further support, saying he would back Newell if she ran as an independent. Encouraged by this, she decided to stand as an Independent Labour and Tenant candidate in the May council elections. She chose as her running mates two non-Labour Party members. Mellish made it clear he would canvass on her behalf. Subsequently, he sent out leaflets in his name to every household in the ward asking people to vote for the independent candidates against the official Labour candidates. Close to the poll, the local *South London Press* picked up on this and ran a huge front-page banner headline 'Mellish Says: Don't Vote Labour'.

Public support for, and canvassing on behalf of, candidates standing in elections against official Labour Party candidates is a cardinal sin which renders members liable to expulsion from the party. Any later bleating from Mellish about being forced to leave the Labour Party because of a witchhunt against him and his supporters was nonsense. An old party member such as Mellish knew exactly what he was doing, and the inevitable consequences, when he came out in support of Newell and her two non-Labour Party running mates. By the time of his public support of Newell, he must have made up his mind to leave the party. It seemed he was hell-bent on causing as much damage as he could before leaving.

Whether or not Coral Newell had been a good councillor during the previous four years or not, the ward did not choose her as a candidate. That was their straight democratic choice. Most of the time she had supported the O'Grady line on Southwark council and this weighed against her when the ward members made their decision.

Rather belatedly, just before the poll the NEC issued a statement calling on people in Riverside ward to vote for the official Labour Party candidates — three long-standing, older working-class members from the area. But Riverside members were very dissatisfied with the support they received from the party's national headquarters and felt particularly aggrieved at the high-handed attitude of David Hughes, the national agent. Given the already fraught situation in Southwark and the prospect of a parliamentary by-election looming, it might have been a good idea for the party leadership to come out heavily against unofficial Labour candidates backed by a Labour MP who had already indicated he would support an opposition candidate in a by-election. To many of us it seemed clear that some of the party's top brass were pleased when we lost Riverside ward in the borough elections of 6 May.

Newell and her two running mates were returned with large majorities in Riverside. But elsewhere in Southwark the Labour Party's mainly new left candidates swept the board. All fourteen SDP defectors were defeated, and Labour gained back a seat from the SDP that we had lost shortly before in a by-election. Labour won 52 seats to the opposition's 8. The Alliance was decimated. By any standards it was a good victory. O'Grady and the handful of right-wingers returned to the council were in a clear minority and were quickly displaced from their old power base by the new Labour Group, ending up with no chairs or vice-chairs of committees.

However, it was a sad blow losing Riverside to the independents. It was made all the worse because our MP's endorsement of the unofficial candidates had clearly made a considerable difference to the way people voted. It was quite evident that Mellish still had the confidence of many Bermondsey electors. The other worrying sign from the Riverside result was that the Alliance candidates in the ward, which was their one base in the constituency, polled more aggregate votes than the official Labour candidates.

Bermondsey people have a natural pride in being Bermondsey 'born and bred'. When that sense of local rootedness is unscrupulously manipulated, it can generate prejudice against 'outsiders', whether they be 'squatters', 'niggers', 'queers' or just people with a different lifestyle. Those prejudices were manipulated with success during the Riverside election, and were to surface again during the parliamentary by-election. On the credit side, the Bermondsey people, and the Southwark people as a whole, had chosen to vote for a body of Labour Party candidates fighting on a socialist manifesto — a genuinely socialist programme. This was the first time that had happened in Southwark for over thirty years.

One lesson we had to learn from the Riverside defeat was the importance of having influence in the local tenants' associations. In Riverside ward, the tenants' associations were mainly under the control of people favourable to the O'Grady camp or with even more reactionary political views than that. Our canvassing and campaign literature were not sufficient to counter-balance the unceasing tide of 'bush telegraph' misrepresentation. As ever, the local press were not neutral and the official candidates had no weighty local figures such as Mellish to endorse them. That absence might have been counteracted if we had more backing from the national Labour Party leadership, but that was never forthcoming.

After the taste of success in Riverside, it seemed almost certain that Mellish would support an independent candidate against me when he eventually resigned to cause a by-election. Speculation centred round the question whether it would be O'Grady or Newell in the wake of her Riverside success.

Naturally, the level of bitterness in Bermondsey political circles was even higher after the Riverside debacle. Mellish had clearly burnt his boats, and even before the election took place discussions of how he could be expelled from the party had begun. Despite his boast of being a 'Bermondsey boy' and loving the place, he did not actually live in the constituency. His home was in the nicer end of Catford; so he belonged to the West Lewisham party and it was up to them to start expulsion proceedings. They were as shocked as we were by his disloyalty to the party and at our request quickly began moves to consider his expulsion.

Back in Bermondsey, more or less immediately after the council elections, we put into operation moves to expel Newell and those party members who had nominated or supported her. Unfortunately, once again the Bermondsey party was to suffer the throes of internal strife instead of campaigning in the community and rebuilding its lost support. No one in the Bermondsey party seriously objected to Newell being expelled, because she had clearly offended against the party constitution and caused great damage to Labour's standing in the local area. There was more controversy, however, about the expulsion or suspension of those party members who had signed Newell's nomination papers and had actively campaigned for her. Unfortunately, the desire for revenge became dominant in some comrades. Those who had broken the rules of the party, including Newell, were given a fair hearing in front of the executive and the GC of the Bermondsey party. Newell was expelled indefinitely and three supporters who had signed her nomination papers were expelled for a year. Four others were suspended from the party for various periods of six to twelve months.

Grassroots Community Socialism Versus the Liberals

To help counter the bad publicity the party had received over the council elections and subsequent expulsions, some of us made strenuous efforts to campaign out in the community during the summer months. The new district health authority was planning to reconsider the future of St Olave's Hospital later in the year. To put pressure on them, the party decided to draw up a petition demanding the restoration of in-patient services. From June to September I went door to door with the petition and personally collected 3,000 signatures. I managed to meet and chat with a great many local electors through this doorstep work. Often people would mention particular problems they had with repairs, or transfers that had not come through. This led to me having a very large constituents' caseload which I handled with assistance from councillors. From the summer onwards, the party also held a regular Saturday morning pitch in The Blue, a small marketplace in the middle of Bermondsey, where people could get consumer and citizen's advice and leave details of housing problems which would then be passed on to the relevant councillors. We also held a street corner meeting nearby on a different theme each week — 'Homes before Offices', 'Jobs not Bombs', 'Save St Olave's', 'Quit the EEC', etc.

I was receiving an increasingly favourable response in my canvassing. During the months of June through September 1982, I canvassed 4,500 people and encountered only 40 overtly hostile responses. Things were beginning to look more promising and I was feeling very optimistic. My efforts were not without detractors in the Bermondsey party who derided my community-based socialist approach. They compared me disdainfully with the Liberals and claimed they could not see much difference between my 'grassroots community socialism' and the brand of 'community politics' peddled by the Liberals. But there is all the difference in the world. Liberal community politics is the politics of drains and dustbins. It is not really politics at all. Instead of focusing on the issues, the Liberals indulge in a glorified form of social work which deals more or less exclusively with people's individual problems. With an insatiable appetite for 'parish pump' and negative 'knocking' propaganda, usually against Labour councils, the Liberals take up a few individual cases of broken windows and cracked paving-stones and then make a huge blaze of publicity about them through their *Focus* newsletter. By this means, they project the appearance of being much more concerned and successful than they really are, while dodging the far trickier questions about what they actually stand for. Liberal 'community politics' never explain or agitate against more fundamental causes of people's everyday problems, such as cuts in central government finance to local councils which means less money and longer delays for council house repairs. In concentrating on the effect rather than the cause, the real roots of people's problems remain unquestioned and untouched. Nor do the Liberals state or campaign for the alternative policies required to put these problems right so that people don't have to go begging for help.

Liberal 'community politics' is a fundamentally dishonest evasion of the issues and a cynical vote-catching exploitation of people's grievances and frustrations. Behind the facade of 'community politics' lies a basic elitism that imitates the Labour right in that it never actively encourages people to take part in local decision-making and politics themelves. The Liberals are not interested in people taking action into their own hands. In response to individual complaints, their approach is to say: 'Leave it to us. We'll sort it out for you.' In fact they actually want to take decisions away from ordinary people and vest them solely in the hands of professional politicians and officials — preferably themselves. This Liberal style of 'community politics' is ultimately the politics of paternalism and dependence. It sees people and their problems in an individualised client-type relationship which shuns collective political action.

The concept of 'grassroots community socialism' is very different. It envisages the Labour Party as being firmly rooted in the local community, participating in its struggles against the root causes rather than the superficial manifestations of people's problems, and through a more decentralised and self-help approach to politics encouraging them to organise together to defend their interests and take a little power for themselves, rather than leaving everything to full-time politicians. Of course, Labour councillors and party members should, and do, help constituents with their day-to-day problems. But more importantly, we have to fight the structural causes of those problems — to confront the disease rather than the symptoms, and in the process, come to an understanding of how society works and how it can be changed. A good example of this was our battle over the riverside. Many Bermondsey people live in sub-standard housing built before the war which is now in urgent need of replacement. All along the river, the derelict wharves and warehouses presented ideal sites for new council housing. But that land was privately owned, and on the property market it was subject to speculative bidding which pushed up its price. The developers were not interested in non-profit-making housing for local Bermondsey folk, and Southwark council could not afford the inflated land prices. So the riverside sites were sold for speculative offices, hotels, luxury flats and yacht marinas. Private greed triumphed over public need.

In the process of local struggles against these developments, we argued — and many people soon realised — that the private ownership of land and the capitalist property market were impediments to the solution of our local housing needs. Thus a purely parochial perception of these problems expanded to become a much wider consciousness that the very nature of our present economic system works against people's most basic needs and that to resolve the root cause of the housing crisis land must be brought into public ownership.

Unlike the patronising Liberal approach, 'grassroots community socialism' is about the Labour Party being actively involved in local struggles, and promoting and enabling other people to organise themselves to defend their own interests and take some power into their own hands, through representative community organisations such as tenants' associations, pensioners' groups, women's committees, workers' and consumers' coops, etc. By joining with others in this way, they have the power to shape and influence the decisions that affect their lives. Just as national affairs cannot be left entirely up to Parliament and MPs, so local affairs are not the exclusive preserve of the council chamber and its councillors. It is not only important that these MPs and councillors are accountable to the wider electorate, it is also important that they share their decision-making with the people and their representative organisations. Whereas the Liberals believe *they* should run the community, as far as possible the people should run their own community themselves and not leave everything up to politicians, experts and officials.

This decentralist and self-help dimension of 'grassroots community socialism' is best exemplified by the grants policy of the Labour-controlled Greater London Council, which has made available funds for community groups who want to do things for themselves rather than wait for professionals to do everything for them. It is no coincidence that the Liberals have been such vocal critics of this policy. They fear it like the plague because they see the power they aspire to exercise being dispensed to groups of people whom they may not be able to control.

The NEC Agrees to a New Selection and Mellish Resigns

At the Bermondsey GC meeting in June, which was poorly attended because we had had so many extra meetings to discuss the expulsions and suspensions, Militant supporters were able to organise and defeat my nomination to be the delegate to the Labour Party annual conference in September. The vote went against me by 17 to 16. Naturally, I had no automatic right to be the delegate to the annual conference, and Militant had every right to put forward their own nominee. Indeed, in normal circumstances I would have argued that someone else should represent the Bermondsey party at Blackpool. But to many of us there seemed to be a strong argument for my being there in September to put the case for the party's right to choose its own candidate, since I happened to be the candidate in question and in the forefront of the campaign against the witchhunt. However, the pro-Militants were more interested in winning the vote for their own candidate than in the wider issues involved. For several months some Militant supporters had been waging a very divisive word-of-mouth campaign against me and the Chaucer ward branch of which I was a member. Appealing to some very chauvinistic ideas, they branded us lock-stock-and-barrel as 'middle-class outsiders' and succeeded in splitting the left — something that not even the right had managed to do! The Militant faction also began to argue that if the Bermondsey party got the go-ahead for a new selection procedure, there could be no question of automatically selecting me again. They argued there would have to be a full and open selection procedure and the party would have to choose the best candidate, whether it was me or someone else. To many members, this seemed to be reneging on an important issue of principle and going against the Bermondsey party's policy of standing by our original democratic choice of candidate. Certainly the Militant supporters had voted publicly to defy the party leadership on that vital issue. But with this kind of talk in the Bermondsey party there seemed a distinct possibility that Militant might back their own candidate against me in any new selection process.

On 7 July there was a special meeting of the Bermondsey executive with Hughes and Heffer at the House of Commons. Eric Heffer is a good socialist with many sterling qualities, but he can be very paternalistic. That evening he was in one of his most amiable but paternalistic moods. The Bermondsey party had not long beforehand sent another motion to the NEC requesting my endorsement. Heffer asked us to withdraw that motion and not to attempt to bring the issue up before annual conference. He implied that all would be well if only we left it up to 'Uncle Eric' and his friends in high places. He made many a reference to the 'leader', but stopped short of telling us what Foot's actual thoughts were. Heffer was in his best 'king-maker' form. With many a nod and a wink, but without actually saying that Michael Foot had withdrawn his opposition, he suggested that the way was now clear for us to move to a new selection and, hopefully, my eventual endorsement.

The Bermondsey executive asked for time to consider what Heffer and Hughes had said. So they withdrew from the room while we discussed their proposition. The executive decided not to play ball with their machinations. Heffer was actually offering us only vague may-be's, without guarantees, in return for our cooperation in withdrawing our motion to the NEC and not raising the matter at conference. Besides, if what he was implying was true, how could we be sure that a shift to the right on the NEC at annual conference would not scupper his offer? When Hughes and Heffer came back into the room, we told them we wanted our motion to stand. We voiced our fear that the NEC would shift to the right at annual conference. Heffer's nods and winks about Foot's change of heart would be worthless with an NEC packed full of members hostile to Bermondsey and the left. We had every right to be suspicious and sceptical. But Heffer was clearly displeased. Though he initially reacted with some exasperation, like a schoolmaster dealing with naughty children, we ended up parting ways on friendly terms that evening.

The *Guardian* of 12 July summed up the situation thus:

> At today's meeting of the NEC organisation sub-committee, Mr Tony Benn is expected to try to overturn the blocking of Mr Tatchell's candidacy which occurred after the row over his call for extra-parliamentary action last autumn. But last night the signs

were that the majority on the sub-committee would prefer a solution being mooted by its chairman, Mr Eric Heffer... He apparently favours another selection conference at which anyone, including Mr Tatchell, could contest the nomination for what has long been a safe Labour seat... A timetable would have to be agreed with Labour's national agent. But some of the NEC left-wingers have taken comfort from the conviction that Mr Tatchell himself — if not all his supporters in what has become a cause célèbre — appreciates the need for some face-saving, particularly for the Labour leader, who denounced Mr Tatchell's candidacy in the Commons. They believe that Mr Benn's initiative, which may be ruled out of order, is unhelpful, to say the least.

The committee duly voted for a re-run of the selection procedure and confirmed my eligibility to stand for selection. The *Guardian* reported the next day:

It is now certain that such a conference would again pick Mr Tatchell and that his candidacy would then be endorsed by the national executive committee... A move by Mr Tony Benn to endorse Mr Tatchell immediately — which he tabled, he said, to 'test the waters' — was defeated by 13 votes to 4. The committee then unanimously endorsed the compromise worked out by the chairman, Mr Eric Heffer. It was backed by Michael Foot, who raised the original objection in the House of Commons last December... Mr Foot reminded members of the organisation committee yesterday that at the time of the original objection he made to Mr Tatchell circumstances were rather different. There was a strong possibility of a by-election and he said that his opposition had been based on the consequences of adopting Mr Tatchell at that time. He regarded the offending article as anti-parliamentary, Mr Foot also explained. He went on to criticise Mr Mellish's subsequent action in backing anti-Labour candidates in the local elections this May. Although Mr Foot made it plain that he feels the new plan is the best way to proceed, it is obvious he thinks further problems remain.

Clearly, this vote was a decisive step on the path to my eventual endorsement. But the climb-down by the party leadership was not a magnanimous gesture on their part. They were forced to relent by the massive pressure of constituency parties up and down the country who had rallied to Bermondsey's aid. Faced with our collective determination not to submit to its arbitrary and autocratic will, the NEC had no choice but to allow the democratic process to run its course.

The NEC's decision was probably also partly influenced by Mellish's actions. He had put himelf beyond the pale by committing the unpardonable sin of supporting non-Labour Party candidates. It is likely that this, more than anything else, brought home to Foot that Mellish's loyalty to the party was paper thin. Realising that Mellish could not be trusted, Foot no doubt also began questioning the information he had been fed in late 1981 which led him to denounce me in the Commons.

By agreeing to the face-saving solution of a new selection conference, Foot had publicly backed down on his statement that I would 'never' be an endorsed candidate while he was leader of the Labour Party. The press were not slow to seize on this. The *Mirror* the next day rubbed it in: 'Labour leader Michael Foot made an amazing about turn last night over militant left-winger Peter Tatchell.' (Even the *Mirror*, which claims to be a Labour paper, was not above tarring me with the 'Militant' brush by referring to me as 'militant' with a small 'm'.) The *Guardian* said of Foot's change of heart: 'Mr Foot will have alienated those who thought that the attack should never have been made and those who expected him to deliver, while leaving the world at large in a state of total confusion.' The *South London Press*, a local paper read by many Bermondsey people, stated in its editorial: 'In less than a year, young Peter Tatchell has achieved more fame and notoriety as a non-MP buzzing round the Bermondsey constituency than many sitting MPs have achieved in a lifetime of parliamentary service. The Australian who fled to England to escape conscription a decade ago has, within three years, been chosen to replace veteran MP Bob Mellish in Bermondsey and vociferously rejected by his party leaders after writing an article full of jargon about extra-parliamentary activity in a left-wing journal. He was back in the news again this week after successfully forcing poor old Michael Foot to shoot off another of his toes, thereby making it more painful for him to lead his party on.'

Following our requests, during June and July the West Lewisham Labour Party began moves to expel Mellish for supporting the Riverside independents in the council elections. Mellish, in his statements to the press, indicated that he was determined to stay in the party and would fight all the way against any moves to expel him.

Then, on 2 August, Mellish suddenly resigned from the Labour Party. The timing may have been chosen because of the imminent expulsion moves and the knowledge that the *New Statesman* was about to publish a long and damning indictment of Mellish's business and political associations. Mellish predictably tried to extract maximum emotional and political mileage from his resignation. He even managed to cry for the television cameras, explaining that he couldn't leave the party he'd belonged to for fifty-five years without shedding a few tears. That evening, the *Standard* plastered the story of his resignation over its front page with the sub-heading 'Veteran MP turns his back on the party of "hit lists" and its Bermondsey "mafia".' He was quoted in the article as saying: 'It is not the Labour Party I joined and worked for. Today it has hit lists of decent men and women.' He described the Bermondsey party as a 'mafia' and the Labour movement in London generally as being in a 'terrible mess' with 'all tolerance gone after a left-wing takeover'. The next morning's papers backed up this image of the old stalwart tearfully retiring because of the viciousness of the extreme left. The *Express* headlined its story 'Why I Quit: Bob the Mod' and followed with: 'Defiant Mr Bob Mellish quit the Labour Party yesterday declaring "I am my own man. Nobody shoves me around".' Protesting its deep concern for the future of the Labour Party, the *Sun* asked: 'What hope is there for any political body which spurns an old warrior like Bob Mellish and instead embraces an immigrant upstart who is most usually described as a "former activist for gay rights"?'

However glowingly the press epilogued his parliamentary career, Mellish represented that machine-type of Labour politician who through long tenure of elected office eventually considers he *is* the party and that any challenge to his views and decisions is therefore tantamount to disloyalty and treason to the Labour cause. Duncan Campbell, in an article for the *New Statesman* the following Friday, brought out the full disreputability of Mellish's political career and the unsavoury friends he had acquired. A few days later, Mellish made a startling admission about his years of complacency to the *Sunday Times*: 'All of us here were at fault. I'm as much to blame as anyone. We took everyone for granted and never supported our rear.' Certainly for years Mellish had been taking many things and people for granted. The manner in which he finally left the party showed that he had no concept of loyalty to the unsung party workers and ordinary people of Bermondsey whose backing made him the public figure he became.

On 11 August, at my request, I met with Michael Foot in the Commons to discuss the future of my candidature. I was immediately struck by the immense warmth and friendliness of his welcome. It was such a contrast to the coldness of our meeting the previous December. Foot stopped short of confirming he would support my future endorsement, saying he couldn't guarantee it. He said his attitude would 'depend on the circumstances at the time'. But it was clear that his view of my 'extremism' had been tempered by events and a more informed understanding of what had happened in Bermondsey.

Foot's acquaintance with Mellish over many years in Parliament had no doubt led him to trust too much Mellish's account of what had gone on in Bermondsey. It had encouraged him to err on the side of the devil he knew and strike a bargain with Mellish, a bargain which was soon to be welched on. Certainly, although I had no firm assurances from Foot, I left the meeting feeling he would no longer oppose my candidature.

Reforming the House of Commons

Also in August, I was once again in trouble, inadvertently ruffling the feathers of the Labour establishment. In a number of speeches and articles, I expressed the view that Labour's commitment to abolish the House of Lords was overshadowing the equally important task of reforming the House of Commons. Surely it is about time Labour had a firm commitment to modernise the Commons and rid it of petty and antiquated traditions which serve no useful purpose, and indeed impede it as an efficient and effective legislative body?

To begin with, we could consider what justification there is for the present inordinate length of parliamentary recesses, which amount to nearly four months of the year. It is difficult to discover any compelling rationality for the twelve-week summer recess from the end of July to mid-October. On the contrary, it is deplorable that in the midst of major political events, such as the 1981 inner-city riots, Parliament was not sitting. It seems absurd that for a huge segment of the year the House of Commons is not in session, and that events occurring then are not subject to parliamentary questions and debate. It would seem quite reasonable for the Labour Party to have a clear commitment to drastically cut the summer and Christmas recesses and to abolish the Whitsun recess altogether. This would ensure that the House of Commons sits more or less continuously throughout the year to scrutinise all political events and the government's response. By reducing the length of recesses in this way, perhaps Parliament could adjourn for the week on Thursday evening instead of Friday. This could be an important reform for those of us who want to encourage a new style of grassroots MP, strongly linked to their constituency parties and with deep roots in their local communities. An adjournment a day earlier would have the advantage of giving MPs all day Friday, plus the weekend, to campaign, attend meetings and deal with constituents' problems locally. It would enable MPs to have more regular and continuous contact with their constituents, thereby helping diminish the separation between MPs and their electorate and the sense of remoteness and inaccessibility that many people feel towards Parliament and their elected representatives.

Related to the question of cutting the parliamentary recesses is the issue of establishing more sensible hours for the conduct of parliamentary business. What other group of employees start work at 2.30 p.m. and finish work at 10.30 p.m. or later? Is it wise that the future of the nation is frequently decided in the middle of the night, often by a small number of tired MPs? It is all very well for MPs to complain about long hours and the stress this places upon their marriages. However it is difficult to sympathise when they show not the slightest inclination to reform the ridiculous hours of Parliament.

It is perhaps time that the Labour Party and its MPs officially campaigned for the House of Commons to begin sitting at 10 a.m. and conclude by 8.30 p.m. This would reduce the need for late night and all night sittings. It would enable MPs to have a less strained and more normal family life and put an end to the 'moonlighters' doing other jobs in the morning. Hard luck for the Tory barristers and company directors! Indeed, perhaps we should go one step further and actually campaign for a ban on MPs holding outside paid jobs.

I thought these ideas were fairly harmless and innocuous. They weren't even particularly new. Quite a few left Labour MPs had expressed similar views. To me, they seemed plain common sense. But they weren't to many Labour MPs who were soon on my back again.

Press Harassment, New Smears and Hate Mail

In the latter half of 1982, there was to be a new upsurge of press hysteria against myself and the Bermondsey party. Right from the day of my original selection, and particularly after Foot denounced me in the Commons, I was subjected to peaks and troughs of press harassment plus a hate campaign of smears and lies by much of the popular press. Fifteen months of misrepresentation and vilification in turn produced a ripple effect of death threats, assaults and obscene letters which continued months after the by-election was over. When the media first descended on Bermondsey, most of them did not come with open minds willing to search out the truth. They arrived with preconceived ideas of what they would find. They were actually looking and hoping for confirmation of their stereotype of what the *Sun* would describe as Labour's 'loony left'.

When our local campaigning record didn't fit the image Fleet Street wanted, they just remained silent. Most of the press refused to print a word about our success in re-opening the local swimming baths which O'Grady had shut down, or the help given to hundreds of Bermondsey constituents through my advice surgeries. In a desperate bid to dig up some dirt, sections of the media went to extraordinary lengths of harassment and intimidation. There were constant phone calls and visits to my flat from journalists who would not take no for an answer. These would sometimes begin as early as 6.30 a.m. and not end until after midnight. Even if I refused to answer the door, they would just keep on knocking for hours. In a few extreme cases, journalists' questions and comments bordered on the threatening: 'We will get you' and 'We are going to turn your life inside out', they said. Whenever Bermondsey was a hot news issue, reporters would 'doorstep' my flat and sit in cars outside to photograph everyone going in and out with telefoto lens — often without their knowledge, let alone their consent!

Occasionally, I was surreptitiously trailed on foot, by car and even on the underground. Periodically, the rubbish chute outside my flat was blocked by journalists so they could sift through the contents of my garbage in the hope of finding some incriminating letters, thereby adding a new dimension to the term 'gutter press'. Equally, my neighbours on the Rockingham Estate were subject to the same barrage of late night visits and phone calls for days at a time, with the evident intention of wearing down their resistance and forcing them to 'tell all' for the sake of getting some peace and quiet. Those neighbours who consistently refused to speak to the press were subject to obscene and racist abuse by certain journalists. When these journalists were not able to get the damning quotes they wanted, they resorted to more devious methods. They scoured neighbourhood pubs posing as local tenants and Labour Party colleagues of mine to scavenge for gossip.

On one occasion, reporters turned up on my neighbours' doorstep claiming to be Southwark council officials who were investigating complaints that I had been holding rowdy, all-night, all-male parties. They wanted to know if my neighbours could give them any details for their report. On other occasion, an enterprising journalist went knocking on nearby doors, complete with suitcase and suntan, claiming to be a long lost cousin of mine from Australia.

Some of the lower creatures of Fleet Street went so far as to quiz local kids as young as ten years old about intimate details of my personal life. But the papers did not stop there. Two of them are said to have put a £3,000 'bounty' on my head for a good scandal story, 'preferably with photographs'. They set a dragnet through the gay bars of London to find someone who would 'reveal all'. The *Daily Mail*, in particular, compiled a list of twenty alleged former lovers which they touted around seeking confirmation from gay Liberals and Social-Democrats.

At the North Lambeth Day Centre where I was employed, my co-workers and the single homeless we assisted were put under enormous strain. For weeks on end reporters telephoned and walked into the Day Centre uninvited, interrupting our work and demanding to speak to me. It seemed that my home and work addresses had passed into some kind of international journalists' directory. During Thatcher's visit to Japan in 1982, hordes of Japanese reporters descended on the Day Centre to interview me. At times the phone lines were so jammed with journalists that we were prevented from carrying on our jobs. When other staff members quite rightly refused to take this endless stream of press calls for me, they too were sometimes savagely abused and threatened by journalists. In one instance, a newspaper threatened to print a scandal story about the Day Centre and ensure that its funding was cut off if the staff did not let them speak to me. In the end, this harassment so seriously interfered with the operation of the Day Centre that I was pressured to resign my job.

Press harassment was not confined to these shores either. At a cost of tens of thousands of pounds, reporters were dispatched to Australia. Local journalists at that end were also hired as full-time 'Tatchell-hunters' to 'dig up everything you have ever said or done from the day you were born', to quote one journalist. In Australia, within twenty-hours of Foot's statement in the Commons, they put my family through the same nightmare of round-the-clock phone calls and doorstepping.

On one occasion, reporters waited till all my family, bar my step-father, had gone away for the weekend to stay with relatives and escape the press. Then, with the incentive of some bottles of wine, an 'especially attractive' woman reporter pressured my elderly and invalid stepfather to respond to malicious and leading questions about my political and personal life. Another time, journalists led my family to believe I'd had a serious accident as a means of gaining entry to their house. Being in a state of shock at such news, with their guard lowered, these journalists then persuaded my family to talk.

For fifteen months, myself, my family, neighbours and co-workers were also subject to a never ending stream of false, but very intimidating, allegations by the press. My support for troops out of Ireland resulted in accusations of membership of the IRA. I was asked why I had taken 'monthly trips to Belfast for the past three years'. In fact I have never been to Ireland in my life. Reporters suggested that the rumpus at the World Youth Festival in East Berlin in 1973 had been a carefully planned stunt to establish 'anti-Soviet' credentials in order to disguise my work as a KGB agent. Over the months I was variously accused by reporters of frequenting gay brothels, underworld associations, involvement in terrorist activities, and sexual assaults on young kids. These same false allegations were put to my family and friends in order to undermine their support and provoke them to make critical and damaging statements which could then be quoted against me. At one point journalists claimed that my mother had disowned me as a 'bastard child' and a 'queer communist'. Though I knew it could not be true, it is not hard to comprehend the anxiety provoked by such fictitious allegations and the possibility they could be published and perhaps accepted as true by millions of newspaper readers.

When, despite all these extraordinary methods, the press failed to find the filth they wanted, they simply resorted to outright fantasy. The following three examples are typical of many stories lacking any factual basis. On 3 August 1982 the *Daily Star* editorial described me as 'Mr Peter Tatchell of the Militant Tendency'. It went on to associate me with activities in the Labour Party which were 'secretive, behind closed doors and using every trick not in any rule book'. Of course I have never been a Militant sympathiser and my selection was fully in accord with Labour's constitution. *Private Eye* exemplified the innuendo and ridicule with which my sexuality was treated. Its 3 December 1982 issue ran this fictitious item in the news section: 'One of 30-year-old Tatchell's haunts is Bangs, the disco-gathering of London gays in Charing Cross Road. Sadly, the parliamentary candidate for Bermondsey is given a cool reception by gays there, because of his mannerisms. "My dear she's always so outrageous!" confides Vince, a teenage rent-boy regular. "The other night she was wearing pink trousers and a pink shirt covered in frills! Quite fashionable, I suppose, but just too much! No one would talk to her and she had to dance by herself."'

Just how far the web of poison spread is indicated by an article which appeared in the Trinidad newspaper *The Bomb* on 24 September 1982. The article claimed, quite falsely, that I was planning a holiday in Trinidad, and its author, Harold Poliah, urged the Minister of National Security to ban my entry on the grounds that: 'Tatchell is a communist. His party group, which belongs to Britain's opposition Labour Party, has mafia connections. And Tatchell is a man who preys on young, gullible Negroes and East Indians. They do what he wants them to do... and brother, it isn't nice!'

But media reportage of Bermondsey was not just inventions and smears. It involved suppression of the news as well. A while before the by-election, the Thames Television programme *Reporting London* approached the Bermondsey party saying they thought we had been really unfairly treated by the media. They offered to correct the bias with a more balanced report about the 'real Peter Tatchell' and my record of local community action. We readily cooperated. At last, we thought, the truth would out. Alas, two hours before transmission, senior officials in Thames Television pulled the plug on it. Publicly the pretext was that two of my critics had withdrawn their permission for their interviews to be shown. But privately, the real reason was that the programme presented me in too favourable a light. What had happened was that over many months the lies and scares about Peter Tatchell had become the consensus; so anything that tried to present me as I really was appeared to be biased.

Naturally, Fleet Street's falsehood and muck-racking was not without its consequences. I hold the popular press, with its appeals to people's basest emotions and most irrational fears, responsible for much of the hate mail and death threats which I received in the fifteen months leading up to the by-election. Throughout that period, abuse and violence became an almost everyday part of my life. The catalogue of incidents between December 1981 and February 1983 runs into the hundreds. Least of my worries was the verbal abuse. It was of a very limited vocabulary, almost invariably along the lines of 'Fuck off back to Australia, you communist poofta' and 'Why don't you go and fight in Vietnam, you bloody coward?' Similar sentiments were plastered in graffiti all over

Bermondsey. In the end, even kids as young as eight or nine were shouting at me the obscenities they had learnt off the hoardings.

While leafleting in local shopping centres, on several Saturday mornings, I was manhandled and warned with threats such as 'Fuck off out of Bermondsey before we send you out in a coffin' or 'Get off the streets or you'll be dead by midnight'. Chillingly, on one occasion, I was then given a detailed and graphic description of my flat and the stairway leading up to it. Even just doing my shopping or going to work became an ordeal of running the gauntlets of abuse and threats. One time, a middle-aged man boasted to me that he had a little silver bullet which he was saving to 'plant between your fucking eyes', and yet another claimed he had contacts with Bermondsey's gangland and was going to have me knee-capped.

Perhaps the most dramatic threat of all occurred when it was announced over Capital Radio that I would be visiting the Dun Cow disco in the Old Kent Road. Shortly afterwards, the manager was swamped with threats to fire-bomb the pub and kill me if I appeared there. Nevertheless I did appear, though the pub had to be placed under police surveillance and I remained sandwiched between two hefty bodyguards all night. Apart from these threats, there were several actual attempts to injure or maim me, including three attempts to run me down in a car. One of these attempts was directly related to a fabricated *Sun* story, as my assailants drove at me shouting 'Fuck off back to the Gay Olympics, you communist cunt'.

When out canvassing on several occasions, bottles and bricks were hurled at me from flat balconies and passing cars, and I was once chased and menaced by two youths with an iron bar. Less serious, but no less unpleasant, my flat was daubed with swastikas and Column 88 slogans, and at the time of the Falklands war I was sent white feathers and abused as a 'traitor'.

Throughout this period, coinciding with the more sensational press smears, the steady stream of hate mail continued unabated. Letters dropped on my doorstep, some simply addressed to 'Peter Tatchell, Communist Traitor, Bermondsey'. One, postmarked SE16, described me as a 'low down scum of a whore — get back to that goddam country you came from. We don't want sodomites you sewer rat. Or better still, go to Russia. They like filth like you...drop dead with the filthy disease you are carrying. You are not wanted here.' Another advised me to 'go hide yourself in Soho instead of flaunting youself in public... What a load of poofs the Bermondsey Labour Party must be to pick you.' Others were in a similar vein:

> Tatchell, I don't know whether to address you as Miss or Mr, but when I lived in Bermondsey until my family were bombed out in

1940 while I was in the army fighting for scum like you, we had a saying that 'a man should never push shit uphill without a wheelbarrow'. So why don't you go back to the gay tribe and leave Bermondsey to real men.

Dear Sir,

I always understood that East Londoners loved city and country. For God's sake, why are they choosing that loud-mouthed little commissar, Tatchell? I pray he will not get to be an MP. He and Benn should be put in their soap boxes and sent to Russia with love — or shot.

Signed D. Thomas, Tenerife.

But in the midst of all the hate and obscenity, there were still plenty of messages of support as well. Some of them came from the most unlikely quarters. A retired naval commander wrote:

Little did I think that as a die-hard Tory I would write a letter of congratulations to a left-wing socialist to compliment him on his honesty. I refer to your article in the *Telegraph* in which you emphasise the humbug of MPs styling themselves as 'Labour' and then having a lifestyle worth at least £20,000 a year which they would not give up at any price. There is not one that does not relish the perks and prestige of being an MP and you have had the courage to point that out. If I lived in Bermondsey I would be inclined to vote for you.

I was most touched, however, by two letters I received from former members of the Bermondsey party:

As an old member of the Bermondsey Labour Party I wish you every success in getting to Westminster. The media, assisted by Mellish, are doing a great job of character assassination. But bear in mind, you are in good company. Dr Salter suffered for speaking the truth... I've waited all these years since Mellish came from Deakin's TGWU to oust all the old Independent Labour Party members from Bermondsey. Now the pendulum has swung full circle and its our turn.

Another ex-Bermondsey member who is now almost eighty wrote:

Mellish brags in the media about his 54 years in the Labour Party. I can never remember seeing him before he was selected as our future MP. I was there at his selection... I can see him now in his army captain's uniform being questioned and after he left I was asked what I thought of him — not much. The other selectors shrugged their shoulders and said we had to have a young man, not one who is getting on in years. He was chosen because he was a young man. So what is he crying on the media about? After all, the wheel has come full circle. I don't remember seeing him cry over the previous member being dropped because of his age.

By the time the by-election was over, I had received several hundred hate letters, two bullets, and thirty threats to kill me and petrol-bomb my flat. For fifteen months the threat of violence cast a shadow over my life. Whenever I answered the door, I kept a weapon handy. As I left my flat each morning, I was forever looking over my shoulder and often wondered if I would return home in one piece. Out riding my bicycle, I was always conscious of how vulnerable I was to a hit-and-run attack. When I went to bed at night I pondered whether that would be the night a fire bomb would come crashing through my window. All of this was at least partly due to the bigotry stirred up in the pages of the tabloid press. So often I wished the journalists who wrote those smears could have been forced to experience the consequences of their actions. But despite all our pleas for fair play and objectivity, Fleet Street just went on sharpening its knives.

The Media's Anti-Gay Campaign at Annual Conference

The next great media onslaught began soon after the NEC's green light for a new selection and Mellish's resignation. The press knew that a re-run selection procedure would take place in the near future. They clearly wanted to defeat my chances of being selected, or failing that, scupper my hopes of being elected MP. So they again began hammering away at issues that they believed would undermine my support, both in the party and among the Bermondsey electorate.

Just before the opening of the 1982 Labour Party annual conference in September, Fleet Street stepped up its attacks with a vengeance. It was not coincidental that a barrage of outrageous smears took place at this time. These were designed to cause me and the party maximum embarrassment and sow discord in the ranks of my supporters. The first taste of what was to come took place in early September. The *Daily Express* ran an unpleasant and ridiculing story about me 'slipping around the seafront hotels' at the TUC conference in Brighton. In fact I was away on holiday and not even in the country at the time!

At the beginning of September I flew to San Francisco for a much needed three-week break with some close friends. I had thought I could escape the attentions of the media all those thousands of miles away. In a sense I did. But on returning home, I was doorstepped by *Sun* reporters. At one point, three of them waited outside my workplace for five hours in unseasonal cold and pouring rain to question me about an alleged visit to the Gay Olympics in San Francisco. I told them I had known nothing about the event before I went on holiday and did not attend it. Despite my denials, they kept up non-stop pressure on me for the next three days and nights to force me to 'confess'. In the end I am sure they knew the story was a fiction. But they were determined to use the coincidence of my San Francisco holiday for a sensationalist story anyway. They admitted as much when, in reply to my denial and warning about possible legal action, one of the *Sun* reporters actually said to me: 'Sue us. So what? What do we care? What's a few thousand pounds to us? This is a good story and we are going to use it.' And use it they did.

On 25 September, the Saturday before annual conference, the *Sun* had the front page headline 'Red Pete Went to the Gay Olympics'. Below this it revealed:

> Left-wing Labour candidate Peter Tatchell has upset his tough dockland supporters, who say he has been to the Gay Olympics. They claim the 30-year-old bachelor spent two weeks in the company of homosexuals at the bizarre sports event in San Francisco... Last night Philip Corr, the chairman of the local Young Socialists, said: 'Going to these Olympics is the last straw — he is not doing the image of the party any good at all. He should be spending his time in Bermondsey looking after the problems here — not swanning about at the Gay Olympics in California. What's more, as a socialist, I just don't know how he can afford it.' Mr Corr added: 'He only left Australia because he was called up into the army in the early seventies and didn't want to fight in Vietnam. Before that he was apparently a marathon runner in, would you believe it, Queensland.'

At the very end of the article, on the inside pages, I was quoted as denying I had been to the Gay Olympics, which was, of course, absolutely true.

We eventually discovered that Phil Dampier, the *Sun* reporter who wrote the story, was known to us as 'Phil Wilson'. Under this guise he had befriended Bermondsey party members on the TUC day of action to support the health workers' strike. Claiming to live in Bermondsey and support Labour, he expressed an interest in joining the party. His masquerade even went so far as leafleting local estates with members of the Young Socialists. At no time did he ever reveal that he was a journalist. According to Phil Corr and other local party members 'Wilson' had befriended, they never made any such remarks. The *Sun's* quotes were pure fiction.

As a companion piece to its Gay Olympics story, on another page on the same day the *Sun* exposed in bold headlines the 'Middle-Class Past of Working-Class Hero'. It began: 'Labour Leftie Peter Tatchell's proud boast to be a son of the working class is BUNKUM, the *Sun* can reveal today.' In this article, the main evidence for my alleged middle-class background was the fact that my parents lived in a 'tree-lined' street. This 'special report' claimed that my stepfather 'owned a taxi' and my mother worked as a 'bank clerk'. In actual fact, my stepfather didn't own his taxi; he was employed by a company and his take-home pay was well below the average industrial wage. My mother did work briefly as a bank clerk thirty years ago, but more recently she had been working in local biscuit and engineering factories. The article also impressed on *Sun* readers that my 'extremism' was not the recent waywardness of a good boy gone wrong. I had a long and premeditated history of it. At school my 'militant tendencies were obvious then...schoolpals and teachers used to call him Chairman Mao because of his left-wing views'.

Next day, on the eve of the annual conference, the *News of the World's* headline was 'Gay Row Rocks Labour — Freedom Plan Was Butchered, Say the Lefties': 'The Labour Party was plagued with fresh turmoil yesterday in a row over demands for freedom for homosexuals. The far left accused party leader Michael Foot of butchering a plan to sweep away restrictions on the activities of "gays". Mr Tatchell is a key figure in a massive campaign to make homosexual rights a dominant issue at this week's Labour conference in Blackpool. He and Greater London Council leader Ken Livingstone will be among speakers at a rally on Tuesday to demand a special debate.' The *News of the World* went on to slam *London Labour Briefing* for being 'devoted to a crusade for gay rights'. It denounced perfectly reasonable articles which dealt with gay rights issues as 'outrageous and sometimes obscene articles by homosexuals, lesbians and a transvestite'. The story was accompanied by an obviously retouched photograph which made me appear to wear eye-liner and lipstick. The *Mail* followed the day after with similar fantasies under the title 'MPs Shocked By Explicit Sex Pamphlet'. Inside, the *Mail* had a full-page feature article headed 'What Makes Tatchell Tick?' which explained my commitment to socialism as resulting from the trauma of my parents' divorce. It revealed how my opposition to the Vietnam war turned me into a 'social leper' in Australia. Naturally enough, no *Mail* article about me could appear without reminding readers: 'He is an active and open campaigner for gay rights. But he wards off questions about his own sex life with routine protests against personalising politics.' The article in question quoted schoolmates and friends going back eighteen years who had been tracked down by *Mail* reporters in the remotest corners of Australia. In particular, it referred to my friendship with 'a young window-dresser called Robert Kroening' and described how we had shared a flat together. Pandering to the *Mail*'s own pathetic stereotype of a homosexual relationship, the article fictitiously quoted Kroening as saying: 'Peter did most of the cooking and cleaning and I was the major breadwinner.' The *Mail* reporter concluded with a rhetorical question which he clearly considered his article had answered in the negative: 'But are the working class — whom he so avidly defends — convinced enough to vote him in?'

At annual conference, the right-wing caucus was very well-organised. Its slate of candidates managed to knock several prominent left-wingers off the NEC. The right also won the vote to set up a register of 'approved groups' within the party. This register was merely a respectable camouflage for plans to expel Militant supporters and, perhaps later, others on the left as well. During the debate on the register, Jim Mortimer, the general secretary, let the cat out of the bag. He began his speech with the claim that the register was merely a means of upholding the party constitution and there was no question of it being used as a weapon to witchhunt party members on account of their political beliefs. Astonishingly, he then proceeded to launch a direct political attack on Militant's policies. The register was a backdoor reintroduction of political bans and proscriptions from the 1950s and we all knew it.

That week in Blackpool there was a fringe meeting called by the Labour Campaign for Gay Rights at which I spoke together with Ken Livingstone, Jo Richardson and Joan Lestor. At the start of the meeting there was an overwhelming vote to eject reporters from the *Sun*, *Mail* and *News of the World* in view of the scurrilous anti-gay stories they had published earlier in the week. Tony Benn made a surprise appearance and an impromptu speech as a 'gesture of solidarity' in view of the savage press smears over the previous days.

Discord and Doubts in Our Own Ranks

In the period immediately after the conference, I seriously considered standing down as Bermondsey's candidate. I was very concerned by the deep split in the left within the local party and the atmosphere of distrust and animosity generated. Particularly distressing was my opponents' resort to spreading details of a relationship I had with a well-known public figure; this relationship had collapsed some months earlier under the strain of constant press surveillance and his fear of consequent exposure to the detriment of his career. I felt shocked and disgusted that, in order to destroy me, some people were prepared to destroy another innocent person as well. I began to seriously ask myself whether I wanted to represent such a divided party. Even if I became the candidate, would all of the left in Bermondsey work for my election? It was that sense of lost comradeship and what appeared to be the crumbling away of three years of effort to build up a united broad left which was uppermost in my thoughts at this time.

Though the new wave of press attacks was a comparatively minor consideration for me, these were having a significant effect on my support within the Bermondsey party itself. Good comrades who had supported me from the start, and others who had stuck by me out of support for the principle of the party's right to choose, were now beginning to waver. A few men expressed their embarrassment at being ridiculed and tainted by workmates and neighbours as one of 'poofta Pete's' friends. They resented the attendant jibes and innuendos about their own sexuality as a slur on their personal reputations. Others became extremely worried that the constant press vilification would prejudice Bermondsey people against me, making it very difficult for Labour to hold the seat. My closest friends also expressed concern that such incessant exposure to smears and threats might begin to affect me personally and adversely. Some party members began to believe we were headed for defeat, and feared that the loss of the Labour stronghold of Bermondsey, possibly a few months before a general election, would be disastrous for the party in the country. The stakes were very high. It is hardly surprising, then, that good socialists at this juncture suggested to me the possibility of my standing down as the candidate. In weighing up the arguments, most of our discussions revolved round the principles at stake versus the importance of winning the by-election.

After several days of crisis talks, a group of my closest supporters insisted that I continue the fight for endorsement. It was a view I shared. What was at stake was the fundamental democratic principle of a constituency party's right to choose its own candidate. Many other constituency parties around the country were looking to us to uphold this principle and resist the witchhunt. We could not let them down. At the October GC meeting the Bermondsey party put on a public show of unity by passing a unanimous motion reiterating its support for my candidature.

At the end of the month the by-election in Peckham took place. Labour's Harriet Harman was elected with a majority that had been reduced by 7,000 votes. Only 38 per cent of the electorate bothered to vote. It was a victory for Labour but hardly a convincing one. If a non-controversial candidate such as Harman could suffer such a humiliation, what would be in store for us?

The Monday after the Peckham by-election, 1 November, Bob Mellish at last resigned as MP. That meant a by-election would follow within a few months. Mellish had always said he would resign as MP when I was endorsed as the candidate. But he did not even keep to that promise, stating that Foot and the leadership were clearly preparing the way for my candidature. Why Mellish chose early November for the timing of his resignation was obviously the subject of speculation. The general opinion among us was that he wanted to inflict the maximum damage possible on the party he claimed to love so much. The prospect of Thatcher calling a general election some time in the first half of 1983 was clearly on the cards. If he delayed his resignation much longer, there might not be a by-election at all and he might lose his chance to rub dirt in the face of the left. If he missed the opportunity and let a general election preempt him, myself and the Bermondsey party would be far less vulnerable to sustained press publicity and vilification. Mellish wanted the full glare of a by-election to work against us and for the benefit of O'Grady, who by this time had emerged as his chosen successor.

On Mellish's resignation, I immediately started taking over his official constituency advice surgeries. Already, ever since my original selection, many Bermondsey people had taken up problems with me. But throughout 1982, as Mellish's interest in the area waned and local people found him hard to contact, more and more of them turned to me for assistance.

More Right-Wing Plots and Unexplained Burglaries

At around this time, from early November, we became increasingly uneasy after the NEC shifted further to the right at annual conference. There followed a flurry of reports that the hard right wanted to impose a candidate outright or, alternatively, a short-list of three candidates excluding myself, from which the Bermondsey party would be asked to choose.

Our fears of this possibility were increased when a full-time regional officer of the party attended the November meeting of the Bermondsey executive. She said that on instructions from David Hughes, the national agent, I had to stand down as constituency party secretary and cease campaigning publicly on behalf of the Labour Party. Hughes later denied having issued that instruction. But in view of the tip-offs received, we interpreted the directive as evidence that the party leadership wanted to withdraw me completely from the public eye as the Bermondsey candidate, as a prelude to the installation of someone else. This new external threat encouraged a closing of ranks and helped heal some of the wounds of internal division. At the November GC meeting a motion was again overwhelmingly passed reiterating support for me and stating that we would not accept an imposed candidate.

Despite the seemingly endless round of internal battles with the party hierarchy and the Mellish-O'Grady faction, we did not allow ourselves to be diverted from the task of outward public campaigning. Indeed, with the prospect of a by-election this was still more important than ever before. I continued to spend every spare moment out 'on the knocker', meeting the voters and counteracting the distorted image they had been fed by Fleet Street.

On Wednesday 17 November a group of us from the Bermondsey party joined with the Southwark Docklands Campaign to occupy Corbett's Wharf on the south bank of the Thames in protest against the former riverside warehouse being turned into luxury flats for the rich at prices ranging from £117,000 to £170,000 each. To add insult to injury, these deluxe apartments were right next door to decaying pre-war council estates where local tenants were trapped with little hope of ever moving out to something better. Yet again, the developers were grabbing land the council urgently needed for new housing. At ten in the morning, half a dozen of us climbed up the exterior scaffolding to unfurl banners: 'Council Houses with Gardens' and 'Homes not Offices, People not Profits'. The occupation lasted two hours. Though the police took our names, no arrests were made and we left peacefully.

In mid-November I was finally hounded out of my job at the North Lambeth Day Centre. The media harassment relentlessly interfered with the operation of the Centre. There was no end to it in sight. For the sake of my co-workers, I felt I had no option but to reluctantly resign. To make things even worse, my unemployment benefit was initially suspended for six weeks on the grounds that I had left work 'voluntarily'.

Later the same month, the Bermondsey party executive was asked to discuss a new selection procedure with senior party officials in the persons of Jim Mortimer, general secretary, Russell Tuck, the new right-wing chairperson of the NEC organisation sub-committee, David Hughes, the national agent and two London regional officers. With the by-election in the offing, the media were hoping for something sensational. Reporters and live outside broadcast units were at the Rotherhithe Civic Centre in strength when we arrived for the meeting. Given that this meeting was of vital importance to the future of the Bermondsey party, we had decided that non-executive members should be allowed to attend as non-participating observers. Six members of the party duly turned up. But this was too much for the head office delegation. Hughes, especially, was most insistent that the observers must leave. Several of us argued that we could see no reason why six rank-and-file party members should not be allowed to stay. The party bureaucrats insisted that unless the observers went, they would go. They decided to withdraw to deliberate about what attitude they should take to our insistence that the observers be allowed to stay. They could not leave the annexe as the waiting vultures from the media would seize on this as a sign that something was wrong. So all five of them had to crowd into the tiny gents' toilet that adjoined the room, including Kath Butler, the only woman in their delegation. They emerged a few minutes later; Mortimer explained they were insisting that the six observers leave. It was quite obvious that if we refused to accede to this, they would walk out without our having discussed anything. And presumably they would announce to the assembled media that no discussion was possible with the rebellious Bermondsey party. There would be damaging headlines the next day and the leadership could well have used the pretext that we had been uncooperative to justify imposing a candidate.

It seemed incredible that Mortimer and Hughes were willing to jeopardise the fragile peace that had broken out between the Bermondsey party and the Labour leadership over such a trifling issue. We had no option but to give in. The six observers had to leave. The incident, petty as it seemed, worried us. It showed to what extraordinary lengths they were prepared to go to assert their authority over the Bermondsey party, and how little they cared about losing further ground to our opponents in the run-up to the by-election.

After wasting nearly an hour on this petty issue of observers, Mortimer and Hughes said we should proceed to a new selection. Hughes, especially, emphasised that we should take the selection very seriously, as if we didn't! We should have a full selection procedure and invite a wide range of applications. He urged us to consider the merits of each nominee very carefully and to bear in mind the implications of our choice for the party nationally. The gist of their advice was that we should be open-minded and look on the new selection process as starting all over again without any pre-determining restraints on the outcome. To most of us the clear message was that they still hoped we would come to our senses and select someone other than myself. The next day the NEC formally agreed that a new selection should take place.

No sooner had the new selection been agreed than we were tipped off about plans by some right-wing unions to block my re-adoption by claiming there had been irregularities in the selection procedure. This was not paranoia on our part. One right-wing union, the EETPU, had already tried to flood our GC with delegates.

We were also concerned about certain unexplained burglaries which took place around this time. In late October, the Greater London Labour Party headquarters in Walworth Road was broken into. Valuables and cash were left untouched. The only things stolen were files on Bermondsey Labour Party — in particular, records of the inquiry into the Riverside ward selection meeting. About two weeks earlier, GC minutes, as well as files on our membership, delegates and affiliated organisations, also went missing from the Bermondsey party's Lower Road headquarters.

We never discovered who was responsible for these Watergate-style break-ins. But they did occur in the run-up to a new selection, and the material taken was relevant to the conduct of the selection procedure. The right's plans were to allege that certain union branches had not received nomination papers and their delegates had not been given proper notice of the selection meeting. We immediately preempted this plot to disrupt the selection procedure by publicising details of the planned manoeuvres and insisting that full-time regional officials handle the entire selection procedure.

Despite this our worst fears were confirmed soon after the selection when a branch of the EETPU did allege procedural malpractices. But given the imminence of the by-election and the overwhelming backing I had received in the selection meeting, national party officials were forced to treat the fabrication with the contempt it deserved. They ignored it.

On 23 December, the day after a small incendiary device had exploded at Hornsey Labour Party offices, the national Labour headquarters received a telephone threat to kill me — a pleasant little Christmas present. The police were immediately informed. They visited my flat and advised me to be cautious about handling mail and answering my door. They also promised some sort of surveillance — as if I had not been under surveillance by them for some time!

Re-Selection and a New Row Over 'Anti-Parliamentary' Views

On 5 January 1983 the Bermondsey executive drew up its parliamentary selection short-list. It included myself, with fifteen nominations including those of all eight ward branches, Eric Moonman, who had been nominated by the National Graphical Association, and Jim Little, an ex-Bermondsey colleague of Mellish and O'Grady who had years ago moved down to Kent. Moonman was a former MP. It puzzled us why he was so keen to get himself nominated. He must have known that constituency parties throughout the country would not look favourably on anyone who challenged Bermondsey's right to re-select their original candidate. It worried us. We felt there must be some ulterior strategy behind the move. It was not until much later that we caught a glimpse of what that strategy might have been.

The morning of the selection, 9 January 1983, the *Mail on Sunday* ran a story on its front page: 'Unpopular Tatchell Set to Become MP'. It published only part of an NOP poll result in Bermondsey, reporting that 62 per cent of those who had voted Labour in the 1979 general election intended to vote Labour in the by-election as well, 'despite the fact that most Labour supporters in the area where he [Peter Tatchell] will be a candidate say they cannot stand him'. In this poll, Labour voters in 1979 were asked: 'Do you approve of Peter Tatchell as a candidate?' According to the findings, 30 per cent said yes, while 37 per cent said no and 23 per cent did not mind either way. It might well be asked why such unusual questions were being put at all, particularly for publication on the morning of a selection conference. They are certainly not the normal questions asked in an election opinion poll. The *Mail on Sunday* was obviously quite disappointed with the findings. It suppressed the poll result for the electorate as a whole which showed me with 47 per cent support, while the Liberals, Independent Labour and Conservatives had less than 20 per cent each. It was a classic example of how the findings of opinion polls can be manipulated for political motives.

When the results of the selection meeting were announced that afternoon, I had received 52 votes, while Moonman got eight and Little only two. Under pressure from the left nationally and faced with such a limited choice, even those on the left in Bermondsey who had earlier stirred up opposition to my re-selection agreed to sink their differences and cast their votes in my favour. Ironically O'Grady was still a delegate to the Bermondsey GC at that stage. He had a vote at the selection even though by this time he had strongly intimated that he would run against me if I was chosen as the candidate. O'Grady stormed out after the announcement of the result, pursued by reporters trying to get him to officially announce there and then he would stand against me.

The next day, the NEC organisation sub-committee recommended that the full NEC later in January should endorse my candidature. Michael Foot wrote me a letter that night. In it he said:

> When you were originally selected, I strongly opposed your candidature for two reasons. You wrote an article appearing to favour not merely extra-parliamentary activity which has been a traditional part of Labour campaigning but anti-parliamentary action which is something quite different. If an election had been held at that time, I was sure that such an article could have been used to damage the party as a whole throughout the country. Moreover, there were at that time some difficulties arising from the infringement by the Bermondsey party of the right of wards to select their own candidates. These difficulties have now been overcome following discussions with representatives of the NEC, and I was glad to see the statements which you made, both before and after your selection, about your allegiance to the Labour Party's views on parliamentary democracy... When the NEC confirms today's decision, you will be the official Labour Party candidate and you will have my full backing in the election.

The press were not slow in focusing on Foot's turnabout. The *Daily Mirror* devoted an editorial to the subject. Referring to Foot's letter, it said: 'Mr Foot, an honest man trying not to look dishonest, wrote to Mr Tatchell last night explaining his change of mind. Houdini did easier tricks. Given Labour's overwhelming past support in Bermondsey, the Tatchell constituency, it will take all the party's talent for self-destruction to lose the seat in the coming by-election. Even then, it might be impossible. Mr Foot's letter to Mr Tatchell lacked the normal warmth expected of a party leader to a candidate. At least that made it more convincing... When he said "Never" he made the oldest mistake in the politician's handbook. That word will haunt him throughout the campaign. He should never have said it.'

Other sections of Fleet Street, however, had not given up the extra-parliamentary issue. I still had to be endorsed by the full NEC. The *Standard* on 13 January tried its best to stir things up by running a sensationalist story about an introduction I had written to a Socialist Society pamphlet by Raymond Williams entitled *Democracy and Parliament*. It had been written in September of the previous year, and published in November, without causing even a ripple of controversy anywhere. Then, suddenly, just three days after the organisation sub-committee's decision, the *Standard* hit the streets with a front-page headline 'Tatchell Says It Again': '"Power to the People. Parliament Is a Charade" says Foot's unrepentant candidate.'

Nowhere in my introduction did such words appear. They were fabricated by the *Standard*. The whole story implied that I had just written the introduction, even though it was clearly dated September 1982, and portrayed what I had written as a new and direct challenge to the authority of Foot and the NEC in the wake of my recommended endorsement. The *Standard* could hardly claim to be impartial. That paper is part of Trafalgar House, headed by Nigel Broackes. He is also chair of the London Docklands Development Corporation which myself and the Bermondsey Labour Party have always opposed. The LDDC's vice-chair is Bob Mellish and one of its board members is John O'Grady.

The *Standard* never bothered to check the introduction with me before going to press. After the early editions, I informed their newsdesk that my original text for the introduction had been altered without my knowledge or consent. After I had submitted it to the Socialist Society for publication, the editors had changed it on 'stylistic grounds', and in so doing, had inadvertantly altered the meaning of a few key sentences. For example, the sentence 'Nowhere in the world has radical social change ever been accomplished by Parliament alone' had the word 'alone' excised, altering the meaning completely.

None of my corrections to this effect appeared in the late editions of the *Standard* as I was told they would — though a correction did appear the next day. The whole tenor of the *Standard* article misrepresented my introduction as a 'repeat of the original attack on Parliament' in *London Labour Briefing* in November 1981. It was clearly another attempt to put Foot and the NEC on the spot when I came up for endorsement at the full NEC later that month.

Predictably, the rest of the tabloid press went to town on the story the next day. The *Guardian*, however, in its editorial of 15 January, was moved to admit that what I wrote was 'less exotic' than my critics alleged and 'should not trouble democrats'. It went on: 'He thinks Parliament works better under outside pressure than in a vacuum; but he does not say protest should supplant Parliament. He thinks our parliamentary democracy imperfect, but he would improve, rather than remove it.'

The way in which much of the press treated this issue illustrates the extent to which Parliament has become a 'sacred cow', and how it is virtually impossible to have a reasoned debate on the question of parliamentary reform. But if Parliament is so perfect and beyond criticism as some people would have us believe, why are four million workers on the dole? Why are a million people living in houses unfit for human habitation? And why are eight million Britons living near the poverty line in the 1980s? It is Parliament, and the government formed out of Parliament, which is responsible for all this hardship and suffering. It is Parliament which passed the Employment Act of 1982 to weaken the collective ability of workers to defend their interests through trade-union organisation. It is Parliament which passed the British Nationality Act of 1981 to undermine racial equality and curtail the rights of black Britons and their families. It is Parliament which passed the Local Government and Land Act of 1980 to usurp local democracy and weaken the powers of elected local councils.

No, Parliament is far from perfect.

Despite this latest press furore, on 26 January the full NEC met and officially endorsed me as the Labour candidate, though not without a sour note. John Golding, as ever, held out to the bitter end aginst my endorsement.

It had been a very long, and sometimes painful, haul from the original selection meeting on 7 November 1981. The Bermondsey party and myself had to struggle against many immensely powerful forces, especially the press and our own party leadership. We had to endure vilification, threats and assaults on a scale we had never imagined possible. We saw good comrades buckle under the pressure and others turn against us. But the long battle for endorsement had to be won because of the fundamental principle at stake.

For many of us, the strength of our socialist conviction was put to the ultimate test. Time and time again we had to decide whether our beliefs were strong enough to justify carrying on the fight against such enormous odds. In the process, most of us emerged with a commitment that was stronger and more determined than ever. It drew many of us closer together with a real bond of comradeship and loyalty, not merely to one another, but also to socialists much further afield who had rallied in solidarity to our defence.

By the time the by-election had been fixed for 24 February, I had done a vast amount of preparatory constituency work. Since November 1981, going around door to door three nights a week and often Saturday and Sunday as well, I had personally met 23,000 Bermondsey people, nearly half the entire electorate. During the same period, I had dealt with over a thousand constituents' advice cases and attended 140 local meetings ranging from tenants' associations to schools, unions, youth clubs and pensioners' groups.

We entered the by-election campaign with a fierce determination to win, despite everything that had gone before. But we knew there were many people, even in the highest reaches of the Labour Party, who did not want me to win. This was to become apparent from day one of the campaign.

Chapter Five

The Dirtiest and Most Notorious By-Election

Labour's by-election campaign started disastrously and generally continued on the same path till polling day on 24 February. Nevertheless, until the end of the second week of the campaign, ourselves and most observers felt sure that, despite all the disasters, we were going to win. Why it eventually turned into such a debacle raises enormously important questions, not only for the Labour Party, but also for the whole conduct of elections in this country.

For the first disaster of the campaign, the party leadership were entirely responsible. If they had wanted us to lose the by-election, and it seemed they did, there could have been no better way of achieving this than their antics over the period from 4 to 7 February.

Our Leaflets Confiscated and Press Conference Cancelled

In mid-January the Bermondsey party had ordered the printing of 25,000 introductory leaflets ready for distribution on 6 Februry to every household in the constituency. We had chosen Cambridge Heath Press, which is linked to the *Militant* newspaper, to do the printing. This decision was taken by the campaign committee of the Bermondsey party. It was not a sudden switch for us. Like many other constituency parties and the national Labour headquarters, we had used the Cambridge Heath printers for three years previously. We did this not out of political sympathy with Militant, but because they were fast, cheap and knew what we wanted. More importantly, they were a trade-union shop and all the workers were Labour Party members.

Suddenly, at a meeting of the campaign committee on 27 January, David Hughes, the party's national agent, expressed the wish that we not use Cambridge Heath Press for printing our election literature, in view of the NEC's plans to expel five members of *Militant*'s editorial board on the day before the by-election. If we went ahead, Hughes said, it would be embarrassing to the NEC and they would have to disassociate themselves from our action. What Hughes said to us was never expressed as an instruction and it certainly was not a directive from the NEC which had never discussed the matter. It seemed more a personal wish on the part of Hughes and the party leadership. After Hughes left the meeting, the campaign committee decided we had little option but to go ahead and use Cambridge Heath Press as planned, on both practical and political grounds. They had already typeset the leaflet. With the start of the by-election campaign only just over a week away, we thought it too late to get a new printer who would do the job in time and at a competitive rate. Besides, if we suddenly switched from Cambridge Heath after three years, it would be tantamount to collusion with the NEC's witchhunt against Militant. That in itself would be a big story for the press. This was the view of the campaign committee and it was my own personal view as well.

Hearing of our decision, David Hughes summoned the Bermondsey party officers on Thursday 3 February, and instructed us in the name of the NEC, though they still had not discussed the issue, that we were 'forbidden' to use Cambridge Heath Press. His instruction was relayed to the campaign meeting that night. With only four days to go before the scheduled distribution of the leaflets, and printing already begun, we felt compelled to reject Hughes' demand.

The next day, myself, the Bermondsey party chair, Ann Coltart, and our election agent, David Fryer, were called to appear before Hughes. He ordered us to have the leaflets impounded and reprinted. He strongly implied that if we didn't do this, the Labour Party regional and national headquarters would withdraw all their support from the by-election campaign, including all their full-time organisers and the use of their offices. Judith Hart, the chair of the party, would not appear at the opening press conference of the campaign the following Monday. Michael Foot would not be available for the eve-of-poll rally and no front bench spokespersons would attend the daily press conferences. We would be left to fend for ourselves, more or less disowned by the national party. Hughes then instructed Fryer to accompany full-time officials in a van to collect the leaflets from Cambridge Heath Press. Faced with this monstrous ultimatum, Fryer felt compelled to oblige. The 25,000 leaflets were duly collected and taken under official escort to the London Labour Party headquarters, where they were impounded in the locked basement pending pulping.

The 'coming attraction' of Militant expulsions was very much on the collective minds of Hughes and the party hierarchy when they confiscated our introductory leaflets. Certainly their fury was quite out of proportion to the supposed crime. It was made absolutely clear that there was nothing in the content of the election leaflet that offended. The 'offence' lay merely in our choice of printers. While authoritarian political regimes ban literature on account of its content, the Labour hierarchy had taken to destroying election leaflets because of where they were printed.

Naturally such a dispute on the opening day of the campaign was a godsend to the press and our political opponents. The *Sunday Express* of 6 February had got hold of the story. Its source can be reasonably guessed at, especially as it was quickly followed by another leak that the first press conference of the campaign, due the next day, had been cancelled, which even we were not aware of at the time. The *Sunday Express* article began: 'A bizarre new row between Mr Michael Foot and the controversial Mr Peter Tatchell has come close to wrecking Labour's campaign in the crucial Bermondsey by-election'. How close perhaps no one will ever know for certain. It seems extraordinary, even with hindsight, to believe that for such a paltry reason the party leadership and bureaucracy were apparently willing to withdraw all their support at the very beginning of a crucial by-election campaign. But we were convinced this was what they intended. It may be that they were thinking of going even further, such was their overriding desire to impose their authority on what they considered to be a rebellious left-wing party. In the same *Express* article Michael Toner wrote, referring to our decision to go ahead and use Cambridge Heath Press: 'The fury of Labour's official hierarchy at learning of this "treachery" was described by one source as "amazing".' Indeed it was, and most observers were astounded by the destructive moves of the leadership over such a very minor issue. It was hardly surprising, therefore, that more and more stories began circulating in the press that the Labour leadership, or at least a section of it, actually wanted us to lose Bermondsey. Their first priority seemed to be to re-assert the authority of the right by rolling back the left tide and expelling Militant. They did not appear to care if they lost Labour the by-election in the process. To them it was perhaps a price that had to be paid to get the party back on the right track. In any case, they could use the defeat of a left candidate in Bermondsey as justification for further purges of 'extremists' on the grounds that they were an electoral liability for the party. These certainly were the arguments of the hard right.

On Monday the 7th all the papers led with headlines such as the *Telegraph's* 'Tatchell Leaflets Seized'. On what was supposed to be the opening day of our campaign I arrived at the London Labour Party headquarters to find that not only had none of the Labour leaders turned up, but the planned press conference was cancelled and I was forbidden to speak to the press. Instead I was sent off canvassing.

Later that afternoon, at the NEC organisation sub-committee, the right easily won the vote to outlaw our use of Cambridge Heath Press. After the meeting, Jim Mortimer, the party's general secretary, went on television to explain that he was summoning myelf and the Bermondsey

Labour agent, David Fryer, to the House of Commons to enforce the NEC's decision. But we had a very important campaign committee meeting arranged for that evening at the local party offices in Bermondsey, followed by a public meeting in the Rotherhithe Civic Centre. It was a tight schedule and impossible to change. We insisted they would have to come to us. Thus, amid much publicity, Mortimer, Hughes and Russell Tuck, chairperson of the NEC organisation sub-committee, came down to Bermondsey to read us the riot act. There was no doubt about their intentions. They told us we had to 'fall into line' over this issue. They very firmly asserted their authority, falsely claiming they had a mandate from annual conference to ban us from using Cambridge Heath Press. I told them that as far as Bermondsey was concerned they had no constitutional or conference mandate for their ban. Without any authority from the party membership, they were widening the witchhunt to include certain printers which they had personally decided should be blacklisted. It was absurd for the NEC to forbid us to use a Labour and trade-union printer and instruct us to get our leaflets printed on capitalist presses instead. This would mean that we would have no leaflets for the first week of the campaign and the £400 cost of the Cambridge Heath leaflets would have to be put down to our election expenses, leaving us short of money in the last few days before the poll.

The party leaders were adamant and unmoved. In a most charming manner, Mortimer went on to repeat more or less the same threats Hughes had made the Friday before. He said we had to give an undertaking to submit ourselves to the authority of the NEC, with the clear implication that if we didn't, the national party would 'take over' the election. What exactly was meant by 'take over' remained in some doubt. There was speculation that it could have meant the NEC appointing their own agent and running the campaign from Labour Party headquarters without reference to the local party. That would have amounted to disowning the Bermondsey party and risking handing the seat to the Liberal or O'Grady, who by this time had emerged as the Real Bermondsey Labour candidate anointed with the blessing of his political mentor, Bob Mellish. Other comrades speculated that there might be a more extreme threat behind Mortimer's statement. Their speculation was further fed by the curious instance of my nomination papers. Each candidate in a parliamentary election has to be nominated by ten people eligible to vote in the election. Those signatures for my nomination had been gathered from Bermondsey party members over the weekend by Janice Muir, a full-time party official. She had approached ten party members who had given their names willingly. However, at the time of their signing, my name as the Labour candidate had not been filled in at the top of the nomination form. Cynics in the Bermondsey party wondered if the nomination paper had been deliberately left blank to

allow for a last-minute switch of candidate if we proved intractable on
the leaflets issue: possibly Eric Moonman, who had been runner-up in the
selection contest with 8 votes to my 52. Perhaps such a theory is too
Machiavellian, even for the Labour Party bureaucracy. But there
remains a suspicion in some of our minds, even to this day, that such a
manoeuvre was possibly on the cards at the beginning of the campaign.

The Bermondsey party had no real choice. On hearing the Hughes and
Mortimer ultimatum, the campaign committee reluctantly accepted
their conditions. We wanted to win the by-election for Labour, despite
the fact that the leadership and full-time officials seemed intent on losing
it for us.

On Tuesday the 8th, I awoke in the morning to find an unmarked
brown paper envelope lying on the floor of my hallway. It had apparently
been pushed through my letter-box in the middle of the night. I gingerly
opened it and peered in. There was a bullet inside. I called the police.
They arrived and examined the bullet, pronouncing it to be a live .22
round. There was no death threat accompanying the bullet but the
message was clear. The police took the threat very seriously. They
advised me to safeguard my flat by sealing the letter-box, nailing the
windows permanently closed and drawing the curtains while I was
indoors. They offered to give me a regular police patrol past my flat and
to shadow me as I campaigned round the constituency.

Naturally, I found the bullet particularly unnerving. But death threats
had become part of my life by then, which says a lot about the nature of
the political battle we were engaged in and the viciousness of our
political opponents.

The *Guardian* in its editorial that morning referred to the bizarre
wrangle over the leaflets: ' For Labour to lose Bermondsey, one of its
safest seats in England, would be one of the most formidable electoral
achievements since records began. It still isn't likely; but you've got to
admit they're having a go... The national party and the Bermondsey
party, Mr Foot and the candidate he was never going to swallow, are for
three whole, uncomfortable, unpredictable action-packed weeks
indissolubly stuck with each other.' The events of the next three weeks
were perceived in this light. My fortunes were to become more and more
closely identified with the fortunes, not only of the Labour Party, but of
Foot's leadership as well. Those with an interest in destroying Labour's
credibility as a governing party were to link my possibly narrow majority
with a 'Foot must go' campaign. The knives, already sharpened, were
poised to plunge.

At 9.30 a.m. on Tuesday 8 February, our first press conference of the
campaign finally opened, a day late. It was presided over by Labour's
general secretary. Mortimer ironically began by declaring: 'Peter
Tatchell is the official Labour Party candidate and he has our full

backing.' He then went on to disclaim that I had any responsibility for the decision of the Bermondsey party to use Cambridge Heath Press. This was not true. I had agreed with the campaign committee's decision. Mortimer made his statement to the press as if to preempt anything I might say to the contrary. In response to press questions, I felt unable to contradict his 'absolution' for fear of provoking yet another damaging row and more adverse publicity. It shows how easy it is to feel pressured to compromise and evade the truth for the sake of party unity and electoral victory. Referring to my handling of the incident, the *Financial Times* the next day paid me a back-handed compliment: 'Taking a deep breath, Mr Peter Tatchell squared up to assembled television cameras for his election campaign press conference and after two stalled attempts, and possibly for the first time in his life, fudged the answer to a tricky question. His two minders — Labour's general secretary, Mr Jim Mortimer, and the shadow environment secretary, Mr Gerald Kaufman — relaxed visibly. Mr Tatchell's proclivity for straight answers has been a source of distress and nail-biting anxiety in the Labour Party, prompting many to wonder out loud whether he really is suitable for Parliament.'

Already the storm in the teacup over the Militant-linked Cambridge Heath Press had given valuable ammunition to our opponents and the media. The Militant smear was one they returned to time and time again during the campaign, despite the fact that they knew I had never been a Militant supporter. But they increasingly adopted a new and more sophisticated tack: if I was not actually a member, then I was 'controlled' by Militant. 'He is obviously their puppet,' said O'Grady to the *Standard* on the evening of the cancelled press conference.

In the days immediately after the Cambridge Heath affair, Labour's prospects looked reasonably good. We were getting warm responses from people on the doorsteps. As one woman said, 'I don't give a damn where you get your leaflets printed, just as long as you get into Parliament and get Mrs Thatcher out.' Despite the disastrous start to our campaign, the quality press were confident Labour was going to win. Martin Linton of the *Guardian* noted that voters on the doorsteps were 'surprised to find that Mr Tatchell is quite human. Indeed Mr Tatchell had only one door slammed in his face all morning and found only five or six avowed suporters of his Real Bermondsey Labour rival, Mr John O'Grady, even though he was canvassing in Mr O'Grady's stronghold, around the old Surrey Docks. The official Labour camp were well pleased with the doorstep reaction which was unexpectedly favourable.'

While the *Guardian* tipped a Labour victory, the *Mail* was determined to ensure defeat. After following me canvassing all morning on the 8th and not hearing any sufficiently hostile doorstep responses, the *Mail* reporters went off by themselves for the rest of the day to another part of the constituency in search of some damning quotes. Eventually they found someone who described me as a 'bleeding Australian squatter'. This abuse was dishonestly written up in the *Mail* the next day to appear as though it was a typical voter reaction that had been said to my face while I was out canvassing. Above the article, a photograph of me meeting a middle-aged man was captioned to falsely imply he was unsympathetic, when in fact he had just crossed the road to offer me congratulations and good luck. The *Mail*'s intentions were clear: the truth was subservient to the political objective of ensuring a Labour defeat.

The same day, the 9th, other papers reported on the Real Labour campaign. The *Financial Times* pointed out that O'Grady 'fosters old memories with a picture gallery on the walls of his campaign headquarters — photographs of himself with the former Labour Prime Minister, Mr James Callaghan, and others showing him with the former Labour MP for Bermondsey, Mr Bob Mellish. So impressive are the latter that local wits have dubbed them Ronnie and Reggie, recalling two East End folk heroes. Mr Mellish is helping Mr O'Grady with his campaign and observers are looking to the two of them to set the tone of the election. Mr Mellish began on Monday by calling Mr Tatchell "an ignorant pig" and Mr O'Grady followed up yesterday by calling the Labour candidate "a liar and a hypocrite", though he later retracted.'

Two days later, the *Mirror* was working overtime to foster the notion that there were *two* Labour candidates: 'Only a Labour man can win but which one?' it asked. To encourage its Bermondsey readers to come up with the right answer, the *Mirror* article included a cartoon of me wearing a 'Justice for Muggers' badge.

O'Grady's Gutter Campaign

The O'Grady campaign began in the gutter and never rose above it. His headquarters boasted a press clippings board featuring the worst and most salacious of Fleet Street's smears against me. Just to remind the press of 'that devil', they were gleefully shown these clippings, especially those which focused on my support for gay rights. In his election literature, O'Grady stressed his war record and the fact that he was a 'family man' with children and grandchildren to prove it. Conversely, he was not above referring to my 'bachelor status' and making innuendos about my personal life. Commenting on my refusal to fight in Vietnam, O'Grady said: 'Bermondsey breeds fighters, not dodgers, and our people cannot stomach the fact that the candidate foisted upon them by the local party is reputed to have run away from Australia to avoid being called up into the army.' O'Grady's supporters went much further, branding me as a 'conchie'. To them I was a 'coward' and a 'traitor'.

It was something of a mystery as to who was financing O'Grady's campaign. He claimed that it was entirely funded by individual donations from 'moderate' Labour supporters. But at a morning press conference O'Grady inadvertly let the cat out of the bag when he waved around a letter and £5 donation from a 'typical' supporter. On closer inspection, it was from a Tory voter in Kent.

Private Eye dismissed O'Grady's claims of dependence on personal donations as 'stuff 'n' nonsense'. It alleged that the Real Labour campaign was financed by Nigel Broackes, head of Trafalgar House Investments and chair of the London Docklands Development Corporation. Though Broackes would presumably prefer a pliant pro-LDDC MP representing Bermondsey, he claimed that he did not support any candidate in the campaign and vigorously denied *Private Eye*'s allegations.

Although most commentators did not relish a Tatchell victory, as they became more exposed to the O'Grady and Mellish style of gutter politics they felt an increasing distaste for the Real Labour candidate and his backers — even though at that time O'Grady was seen to have the best chance of defeating me. Some of the press may even have understood better, through this close contact with the Labour old guard, why the broad left in Bermondsey and Southwark had been so intent on removing them from power. Certainly the media's distaste for O'Grady became more noticeable, even in right-wing newspapers, as the campaign rolled on. Perhaps their realisation that O'Grady was not a credible alternative to myself helped to switch press attention to Simon Hughes, the Liberal candidate, in the last week of the campaign. Bermondsey people were not going to buy Mellish and O'Grady, so why not give them a more personable product in order to stop Tatchell?

Every morning throughout the campaign we held press conferences on different areas of Labour policy, though no one would have known this given the way most of our policies were ignored by the media. We particularly emphasised the issues of housing, unemployment, and the role of the LDDC with its plans to build wall-to wall office blocks, luxury flats and yacht marinas in a constituency where so many people lived in appalling housing with few employment or recreational opportunities. O'Grady, the ex-leader of Southwark council, defended his record on housing and his paid position on the board of the LDDC. He called our charges that LDDC's new housing would cost much more than local people could afford to pay 'a monstrous lie'. When defending his decision to serve on the Tory-constituted LDDC board, O'Grady said that although he had opposed its establishment, he had accepted a place on the board because he wanted to be in there helping the people 'rather than standing outside the walls, shouting slogans and waving banners'. The £3,000 salary O'Grady would earn as a board member and the continuing power he would gain from that position obviously had nothing to do with his decision.

At this stage of the campaign, the media were undoubtedly stumped as to which candidate could defeat me. They could not 'sell' the O'Grady-Mellish combo with any enthusiasm. Apart from anything else, O'Grady's television appearances with his mentor, Mellish, did him untold harm. The Liberal, Simon Hughes, was being written off as a certain also-ran at this point. Keith Raffan of the *Express*, writing on 10 February, said: 'Down here in Bermondsey, the Labour Party is defending a 11,576 majority — and the Liberal-SDP Alliance its credibility... At yesterday's Liberal Party press conference Mr Richard Holme, a former party chairman, was opening bat: "The question which you have all identified already, is — who can remove Mr Tatchell?" Profound chaps these Liberals, aren't they? But unfortunately the answer to the question is: "Not them".'

The rest of his article was extremely caustic about how boring and garrulous Simon Hughes was as a candidate. Hughes was far from being the golden boy of the media at this stage. It would take the opinion polls to finally convince them that they had to throw their weight firmly behind this unconvincing candidate in order to stop me.

The victory of any party other than Labour seemed a distant prospect two weeks before the poll. If we were to be defeated, it was obvious that our opponents in all spheres would have to pull out all the stops, and this is precisely what they did. A record of 16 candidates had entered the Bermondsey by-election by the time nominations closed. We did not lack visible opponents to add to the many invisible foes who wanted us to lose, but did not say so publicly. There were four main candidates — myself, O'Grady standing as Real Bermondsey Labour, Simon Hughes for the Liberal/SDP Alliance, and the Conservative Robert Hughes. There were also several candidates of the far right: Alan Baker of the United Democratic party; Dowager Lady Birdwood of the Independent Patriots, who apart from believing in compulsory repatriation for immigrants, thought we should shoot criminals rather than hang them. The New Britain Party put up Michael Keulemans, the National Front stood James Sneath, and for National Labour there was Ann King. There were also two other candidates on the left — Fran Eden from the Revolutionary Communist Party and Bob Gordon of the Communist Party. Gordon and the CP leadership came under considerable criticism from the ranks of their own party for standing against Labour and splitting the left. In the end Gordon received fewer votes than the Communist membership in the constituency. The Communist Party justified standing a candidate against a Labour left-winger on the grounds that they had traditionally done so in Bermondsey. But in the 1981 GLC elections, for the sake of left unity they had stood no one against George Nicholson. An even more flimsy CP pretext was the fact that our introductory election leaflet did not mention unilateral nuclear disarmament. But our other leaflets *did* and I spoke on a CND platform during the campaign.

The RCP supporters were very active during the campaign and followed us everywhere we went, heckling and shouting me down at public meetings and street-corner rallies. Journalists from their newspaper invariably turned up at our press conferences, launching into long RCP election broadcasts badly disguised as questions. They never attacked the Tories or O'Grady. Indeed, the main theme of their campaign was anti-Labour and anti-Tatchell.

The remaining candidates were Bill Giddings (Independent Labour), George Hannah (Ecology), David Wedgewood (Free Trade and Anti-Common Market) and Esmond Bevan (Systems Analysis). Screaming Lord Sutch for the Monster Raving Loony Party provided a touch of madness if any more were needed in the campaign. This record field of 16, including so many bizarre and fringe candidates, helped to reinforce the feeling that the Bermondsey by-election was a freak show and detracted from its seriousness from the outset. The electors were to be faced with a ballot paper that was a record fifteen inches long, inscribed with a confusing list of candidates and parties, including four 'Labour' candidates.

From the beginning, our campaign was severely handicapped by the lack of any election literature. It was nearly a week after the start of the campaign before the reprinted leaflets arrived. They were identical in every respect to the Cambridge Heath ones except for the imprint which read 'Printed by the Victoria House Printing Company'.

Provoking some controversy on the left, our campaign committee took a conscious decision to stress local issues in our election material. This was partly because Bermondsey is a particularly parochial constituency where local issues are of inordinate importance, and partly to counteract O'Grady's claim that, since I wasn't locally 'born and bred', I could not know the problems of Bermondsey. Besides, we felt that in the course of fifteen months of controversy over my candidature, national issues and questions such as extra-parliamentary action had received a lot of publicity. My views on these issues were already well-known. Faced with a by-election, we believed it was time to redress the balance towards the local dimension in our literature, while taking up national policies during doorstep canvassing.

Our leaflets were much more lively than the usual Labour Party fare, with slogans such as 'Shock Thatcher — Vote Tatchell'. Superimposed over a picture of myself with local kids on an earth-mover were the words 'Bulldoze the Tories out of office!' The front page of our election address was headed 'Give the Tories Nightmares — Vote Peter Tatchell Labour'. In the end we were the ones who had the nightmares, but they weren't brought about for lack of eye-catching and imaginative leaflets.

Did the Labour Leadership Want Us to Lose?

By the end of the first week of the election campaign, the suggestion that leading figures in the Labour Party wanted us to lose Bermondsey began to gain ground. Among the first papers to raise this possibility was *Tribune,* the left weekly. Its editorial of 11 February asked: 'Do the Labour Party leadership want to lose Bermondsey? If so, why don't they just come out and say so? They could hardly do more damage if they were openly campaigning for the "independent" Labour candidate, John O'Grady... Even now, with less than two weeks to go to the by-election, Labour's leaders are unable to bring themselves to say anything critical about the record of John O'Grady, Robert Mellish and their friends... Can it be that Messrs Mortimer, Golding, Hughes, Healey and friends feel they have more in common with the style of government practised by O'Grady and Mellish?' This *Tribune* comment was picked up and quoted by other newspapers, notably the *Times* of the 11th under the headline 'Labour Chiefs Trying to Lose'.

Roy Hattersley attended the press conference that day as a supporting front-bench spokesperson. Before we entered to face the press, he warned me to stick to official party policy. With a grin on his face and a self-conscious chortle he said: 'We all have to abide by conference decisions, don't we?' Apart from such snide remarks, Hattersley was pleasant enough to my face. But his real hypocrisy was revealed a few weeks later during the Darlington campaign when he was heard to remark: 'Thank god there are no poofs in this by-election.'

When the *Times* article was quoted to Hattersley he unequivocally backed me and condemned Mellish for committing the 'unforgivable sin' of supporting an opposition candidate. But when Mellish heard this, he accused Hattersley of 'double talk'. Mellish went on to say that after he resigned as MP, he had a meeting with Hattersley and several other 'moderate' Labour MPs where he announced that he would back O'Grady if I was endorsed by the NEC. Mellish claimed that Hattersley had been 'quite gleeful' at the prospect. Later that day Hattersley took the trouble to issue a denial saying that Mellish's outburst was 'rubbish'. Still, remembering the hysterical invective of some right-wing Labour MPs at the time of Foot's statement in the Commons, it was not hard to believe that some of them had rubbed, and were still rubbing, their hands with pleasure at the prospect of a defeat for the left in the person of Peter Tatchell. Certainly, there was plenty of evidence for this view. While we were very grateful for the help received from the national and regional offices of the Labour Party, it was on a negligible scale by comparison to their input into the Peckham and Darlington by-elections. Typically, a hundred full-time Labour Party, trade-union and coop organisers were thrown into other campaigns. But in Bermondsey we had to be content with a mere dozen. Donations to our election fund were derisory. Whereas in Darlington, the party's full organisational machinery was mobilised to draft in thousands of canvassers, we had to make do with the limited numbers we could get, mainly through the left-wing network. The result was that we were only able to canvass 68 per cent of the electors by polling day. Everything about the Bermondsey campaign pointed to halfheartedness and disinterest in winning on the part of the party headquarters.

The theme of a rightward section of the Parliamentary Labour Party looking forward to our defeat reappeared in a *Sunday Express* story on the 13th headed 'Brothers in Hate'. Michael Toner floated the idea that John O'Grady could still win and went on to write: '...and if he does some of the biggest smiles of the night will be on the faces of Labour officials and MPs...' Toner went on to claim: 'Many Labour stalwarts are convinced that Mr Tatchell is not trustworthy enough to be an official Labour candidate. "He's been got at by the militants," claimed one. "John O'Grady will be more loyal than him if he gets in," said another.'

While the *Mail on Sunday* limited itself to comparing me with Damien in *The Omen*, Robin Oakley in the *Mail* the next day took up the *Express* story under the headline 'Fight That Labour Top Brass May Not Really Want To Win'. It posed the question: 'Defeat in a stronghold like Bermondsey would be a humiliation. But would a victory for the brash new left in the shape of Mr Tatchell be any better?'

The theme was now so persistent in the pages of the press and 'off the record' bar talk at Westminster that it clearly had some foundation. The fact that the party hierarchy, or sections of it, might want us to lose Bermondsey was hardly a new thought to us. But to see the idea so freely debated by Fleet Street confirmed our worst fears.

However, there were still no clear signs that the leadership were going to have their wish granted. Martin Linton wrote in the *Guardian* on 14 February: 'Despite a disastrous start to his campaign, the Labour candidate, Mr Peter Tatchell, goes into the second week of the Bermondsey by-election with every reason to be confident that he will win.' He also reported the collapse of the O'Grady campaign; O'Grady had stopped canvassing, claiming that he did not want to disturb the electors. As Linton pointed out, O'Grady seemed to act 'as though the voters only needed to be told the name of the "real" Labour candidate and they would turn out for him'. O'Grady still considered that what had been enough to return Bob Mellish in the last twelve elections would also be enough for him.

That Monday, it had been arranged that I should go to the Commons to be photographed shaking hands with Michael Foot in Parliament Square for the benefit of the press. Foot was friendly and welcoming, but showed a marked reluctance to pose with me and shake my hand for more than the briefest moment. The next day, this was picked up by the press as evidence of the leader's lingering hesitation in supporting me. *Private Eye* also used a photograph of myself with Foot at this meeting on the cover of its issue the next week. The *Eye* depicted Foot asking me: 'You're not a member of the Tendency, are you?' with me replying: 'Of course not, ducky.'

The *Times* on the 15th featured a story headed 'Labour in State of Panic Over Tatchell' which reported Mellish's claim that 'senior party sources had tipped him off that the party was in a state of panic about the chances of Mr Peter Tatchell, its candidate'. Mellish was further quoted as saying: 'I talk to a lot of Labour Party people and you would be surprised at the number of Labour Party people who are praying that John O'Grady will win. And I am talking of a high level.' If further confirmation was needed, Anthony Bevins, the *Times* correspondent, added: 'There is no doubt at Westminster that several Labour figures would like to see Mr Tatchell defeated, if only as a signal to the party's hard left.'

The *Express* the next day reported that O'Grady was beginning to look like a 'no-hoper' and knew it. O'Grady did know it, and as a last desperate measure he sunk to new depths in his campaign. From the back of a horse and trap, which he fondly saw as representing 'good old' Bermondsey, he sang a dirty ditty:

> Tatchell is a poppet, as pretty as can be;
> But he must be slow if he don't know that he won't be your MP.
> Tatchell is an Aussie, he lives in a council flat;
> He wears his trousers back to front because he doesn't know this from that.

The appeal to anti-gay prejudice was plain for everyone to see. There is absolutely no doubt that the O'Grady camp had been whipping up hostility against me on the doorstep because of my homosexuality and the fact that I had been born in Australia. And there is absolutely no doubt that they were meeting with approving prejudice from some voters. However, it was one thing saying on the doorstep that 'we don't want a poof as our MP', it was quite a different thing to be seen on national television singing a low song from a horse and cart. If this was the image that Mellish and O'Grady thought Bermondsey people would identify with, it was a tremendous miscalculation. It spelt the end of their campaign and O'Grady acknowledged a day later that the song had been a mistake. But it was more than an error of judgement. It reflected the Mellish-O'Grady brand of bigoted politics and the patronising contempt they had always had for the Bermondsey electorate. Their dictum was that 'you could run a cocker spaniel in Bermondsey if it had Labour stuck on it'. You couldn't run O'Grady, however, and sink to such depths and hope to win.

As a riposte to the 'poppet' ditty, full-time party officials decided to send O'Grady and Mellish clowns' noses. I was against it on the grounds that the by-election was already enough of a circus and such actions would yet again divert attention away from the issues. But the 'noses' were sent anyway and the press duly blamed me for sending them.

The media could see quite clearly at this point that O'Grady was not going to beat me. They began to look to the Liberal candidate. But there they had a problem. Martin Linton in the *Guardian* of the 16th wrote: 'It is no surprise that the struggle for second place between the two Mr Hugheses has become so sharp. Both are 31 and both are so easily confused on the doorstep that they could have been cloned from the same test-tube.' A Liberal who could not be identified from the no-hope Tory was hardly the stuff of victory! The *Guardian* editorial talked of the Alliance and Conservative parties' 'pursuit of the most enduring fantasies in electoral politics — the projection of likely results from their own canvass returns'. The Liberals at this stage were claiming I had 29 per cent of the definite votes while Hughes had 22 per cent. But the press still did not take seriously the idea that an upset result was in the offing.

The same evening the Labour Party held a very successful public meeting in the Spa Road Library Hall at which Tony Benn, Dennis Skinner, Jo Richardson, Richard Balfe and myself spoke. The undoubted hit of the evening was Dennis Skinner who was in his best knockabout vein. He lambasted Mellish for his performance as Chief Whip. Skinner had refused to agree to pairing with Tory MPs so that they could absent themselves from the Commons to attend to their outside business connections and go to Ascot. He reminded the audience of the parliamentary debate about Value Added Tax. Mellish had been wholly absent from the debate when the Labour side was seeking a reduction in VAT on aids for the disabled. However, he suddenly rushed into the chamber late at night to make an impassioned plea for tax relief on behalf of the horse-racing fraternity. That evening marked the high point in our campaign. From then on it was downhill all the way, as the combined forces of the party leadership, my political opponents and the media colluded to bring about Labour's defeat.

Dirty Tricks By the Liberals and Others

By halfway to polling day, the full viciousness of the personal campaign against me was becoming apparent. The seeds of this viciousness had, of course, been sown many months beforehand by the scares and frights, the stirring up of prejudice by the opposition parties and in the pages of the tabloid press. Now these seeds bore their ugly fruit.

From one end of the constituency to the other, on every subway, bus shelter, railway arch, billboard and tin hoarding there were spray-painted slogans in letters two feet high: 'Keep Tatchell Out', 'Tatchell is a Communist Poof', 'Tatchell is a Red Slag', 'Tatchell is a Nigger-Lover', etc. Some of O'Grady's supporters spread a poisonous web of damaging lies on the doorsteps and through their contacts in tenants' associations, working men's clubs and churches. They set off a train of rumours that I was a squatter with £2,500 rent arrears who only came from Australia two years before the by-election and had previously been in trouble with the police for criminal gangland activities, terrorist offences and sexual assaults on young kids. They started up gossip that I didn't really live in Bermondsey at all; my flat on the Rockingham Estate was just an address of convenience and I really lived in a posh house in Chelsea, discarding my bicycle at night to drive a Rolls-Royce. As if that wasn't enough, they also claimed that if I were elected MP I would stop holding advice surgeries and only help Labour Party members, 'niggers' and 'queers'. That such monstrous fabrications could be believed, or at least sow some doubts in people's minds, says something about the irrational and semi-hysterical atmosphere in which the by-election took place.

After the by-election, of course, the Liberals deplored such personal attacks and smears against me. But during the campaign they were in the thick of them. The first inkling of Liberal tactics came several months beforehand when a copy of their *Focus* newsletter was sent door-to-door featuring a cartoon ridiculing my Australian origins. If it had been about blacks or Jews, that cartoon would have been condemned for the racist appeal to prejudice that it blatantly was. Though I wear the favoured white skin, such attacks against me on account of my Australian background and the constant 'get back to Australia' abuse gave me an acute understanding of what it is like to be on the receiving end of racism. When I sought to publicly expose the stirring up of anti-Australian sentiment, the Liberals' response was to send me a letter threatening legal action.

In the months leading up to the by-election, officers in Southwark's Housing Department repeatedly mislaid my rent rebate renewal applications and failed to inform me of a rent increase for over three months, thereby putting me into arrears and laying me open to press smears along the lines of 'Tatchell Defaults on Rent'. Whenever I appeared on television or radio, these same officers kept a detailed record and later contacted the programmes concerned to check whether I had received an appearance fee, in the hope that they could catch me out and expose me for not declaring such income on my rebate renewal application. Officers in the Housing Department also took an inordinately long time to reply to my enquiries on behalf of local constituents regarding transfers and repairs, etc. Whereas replies to my letters were often subject to a three or four week delay, cases referred by Simon Hughes seemed to be given priority and be processed within three or four days. It made me feel very ill-at-ease knowing that some of these officers were Liberal supporters with a strong antipathy toward myself and the Labour Party. I feared that their actions might have been a deliberate campaign of harassment.

When the by-election finally came, we were not at all surprised by the Liberals' dirty tricks campaign. The first of these, which did us great damage, was an entirely false scare story about rate increases. Under the headline 'Secret Exposed', a Liberal election leaflet revealed: 'Southwark Labour plan rates up 135 per cent — but they won't tell you until after the election.' A graph showed that this would mean an extra £16 per week on the average household's rate bill. In fact, Southwark's Labour council never even contemplated a rate increase anything like 135 per cent, and as expected announced a 26 per cent rise when the council met to fix a new rate soon after the election. To catch votes, the Liberals deliberately publicised the figure of 135 per cent to cynically play on people's fears of major rate increases.

Such references to policies and issues, even misrepresented, were rare in Liberal election literature. Apart from a few mentions of leaking roofs and broken pipes, local and national policies were hardly mentioned by the Liberals. Most of their leaflets were taken up with highly personalised attacks. Right from the outset of the by-election, when asked what the issues were, the Liberal candidate declared that 'Peter Tatchell is the issue'. This was reflected in the Liberals' main campaign slogan: 'Simon Hughes — the only one to beat Tatchell!' It appeared on all their leaflets together with comments like: 'It will be the end of the road for Southwark and Bermondsey if we elect a political joke as our MP. Ordinary decent people in Bermondsey who want to stop Tatchell and the extremists should sink their differences and unite behind the Liberal/SDP Alliance.' The Liberals also made great play of the fact that, as against my Australian origins, their candidate was 'a local man fighting for local people'. It was a clever manipulation of parochial prejudice, but rather dishonest given that Hughes had only moved into the constituency two months before the election.

In the last week of the campaign, any pretence that the Liberals were fighting on the issues gave way totally to opinion polls and tactical voting. Their leaflets ran headlines: 'It's a Two-Horse Race' and 'Latest — Bookies Slash Simon Hughes Odds'. The front pages from newspapers such as the *Standard* were reproduced in big bold letters: 'Tottering Tatchell'. We were more or less powerless to counteract this last-minute flood of Liberal literature. Because we had to put down to election expenses the £400 spent on the confiscated Cambridge Heath leaflets, in the final days we ran out of money for extra leaflets, having reached the legal limit of our election expenditure. Worst of all the Liberal dirty tricks was their crude manipulation of anti-homosexual prejudice for their own electoral advantage. To its credit, the Liberal Party has a very good policy on gay rights. However, in the Bermondsey by-election this policy counted for nothing. Groups of male Liberal canvassers went round stirring up bigotry by wearing lapel stickers emblazoned with the words: 'I've Been Kissed by Peter Tatchell'. On the doorsteps, some Liberal canvassers had the audacity to 'remind' voters that they should not hold against me the fact that I was a 'left-wing extremist, Australian homosexual'. Of course, this disclaimer of prejudice was intended to have the exact opposite effect, which it did. Labour never wanted the bigots' vote and did not get it. The Liberals reaped those mud-stained votes.

Opinion Polls, Tactical Voting and the Liberal Bandwagon

One of the main weapons used against us, which the Liberals took advantage of, were the public opinion polls. The first really damaging one was the NOP poll published in the *Mail* on Friday 18th, six days before the vote. The banner headline 'Tumbling Tatchell' clearly showed what the *Mail* thought about the 'upstart invader from down under', as it had earlier described me. For the first time, the right-wing press could talk of my possible defeat with an element of credibility. The *Mail* linked the poll result with a report of mounting dissatisfaction among Labour MPs with Foot as party leader: 'Last night at a parliamentary party meeting he [Foot] had to listen to criticism from moderate and left-wing Labour MPs alarmed at his failure to make any impact on Mrs Thatcher in the national opinion polls — her current lead ranges from 11 to 21 points. The tidings from Bermondsey will hardly help. NOP shows support there among those who are certain to vote as "Peter Tatchell (Lab) 34 per cent; Simon Hughes (Lib/SDP) 28 per cent; John O'Grady (RBL) 24 per cent; Robert Hughes (Conservative) 11 per cent and others 4 per cent. Among all voters the intentions were Tatchell 37 per cent, Lib/SDP 25 per cent, RBL 24 per cent, Tory 11 per cent.'

For the rest of the by-election period this double focus was to dominate the media. The opinion polls and unceasing rumours of plots to ditch Foot, together with the imminent possibility of his resignation, were directly linked to my chances in Bermondsey and the possibility of a Labour defeat. The effect was very destabilising. Voters, already confused, were being told that something sensational was in the wind, a colossal defeat for Labour that would rock the party to its foundations and cause a change of leadership only a few months before a probable general election. Naturally, it was the pro-Tory papers that focused on the story remorselessly. It was in the interest of their owners and paymasters to make as much trouble for the Labour Party as possible and to engineer a Labour defeat in Bermondsey which could help pave the way for a Tory victory in the subsequent general election. If they could contribute to Labour losing Bermondsey in February, then, with the main opposition party in disarray, the situation would be ripe for Mrs Thatcher to go to the country in the summer. If Foot were forced to resign, the prospect of a bitter leadership battle within the Labour Party only served to further encourage the Tories and their friends in Fleet Street. Certainly the press wanted to stop Tatchell winning, but they had much bigger fish to fry than me.

Other newspapers on Friday 18th raised the possibility of Foot's resignation, linking his decision with the Bermondsey by-election result. The *Star* had a front-page story with the banner headline 'Foot's Party Crisis': 'Panic-stricken Labour MPs turned on Labour leader Michael Foot last night as the party slipped further behind in the ratings.' The polls were being used, not only to create a climate whereby the by-election would slip away from Labour, but also to chase Foot out of the leadership. On the same day *Tribune* led with a story that raised another huge problem the party was about to face — the expulsion of five members of the *Militant* editorial board which was scheduled for the next Wednesday, the eve of poll. The Bermondsey party wrote to the NEC outlining our opposition to expulsions and urging them, whatever decision they planned to take, to postpone it until after the by-election. We felt any decision on the Militant issue just before polling day would stir up controversy, attract massive media attention and undoubtedly damage our electoral prospects the next day. There was absolutely no compelling reason why the NEC should have discussed that particular issue on the eve of the by-election. But they were going to anyway. Our request for a postponement was bluntly turned down. The NEC falsely claimed they had a mandate from annual conference. The expulsions, they said, could not be delayed another day. Was this the attitude of a party leadership that really wanted to win the Bermondsey by-election? Hardly! Compare this behaviour with their attitude a few weeks later when the NEC was due to consider further expulsions on the eve of the Darlington by-election. In response to a request from the local party it agreed to postpone any such considerations until after the poll. That decision exemplified the difference between the NEC's attitude to Bermondsey and to Darlington. In the latter case, they actually wanted to win and were prepared to take steps to see they did.

Tribune had already raised the question of the leadership's will to win Bermondsey the week previously. Now it pointed out the astonishing fact that, 'as the NEC meets to expel Militant, O'Grady is still a party member'. The article went on to reiterate the charge that most of Labour's leadership had yet to disassociate themselves publicly from O'Grady and Mellish. *Tribune* also pointed out that O'Grady was making maximum capital from the fact that he was still a member of the party and would accept the Labour whip if he were elected. What *Tribune* claimed was unfortunately very true. The party leadership's line on the two Bermondsey 'folk heroes' was one of head-shaking sorrow that such good comrades had committed the unforgivable sin of opposing the official Labour candidate. There had been no attack on O'Grady's record as leader of Southwark council and no criticism of their dual role on the LDDC. Such a total absence of any real attack on political opponents lent credence to the idea that O'Grady, if elected, would have been enthusiastically received by the right of the party in Parliament. Indeed, his offer to accept the Labour whip was never rebuffed by Labour's Chief Whip. If the party leadership had weighed in with punchy public criticism of O'Grady and Mellish, then their support would have waned early in the campaign. As it was, the NOP poll on the Friday before election day showed him still with 24 per cent.

Just before the NOP poll result, the *Guardian* was still writing off the campaign by the two Hugheses as a 'clash on who will finish second'. The *Mail* said on the 17th, 'Neither Hughes has much chance of making a big impact on Bermondsey', and the *Sun* still desperately put O'Grady in the running.

Two days later, however, over the final weekend before the vote, the bandwagon against Foot and Tatchell and for Hughes and the Liberals suddenly rolled with a vengeance. The media were intent on picking out Hughes as my main challenger and creating the impression of an unstoppable tide in the Liberals' favour, and conversely dubbing me as a certain loser, even though among all voters I was still 12 points ahead of Hughes and he was only 1 per cent ahead of O'Grady. The *Guardian* editorial on Saturday 19th commented on the effect of the NOP poll: 'One effect of this poll could be to establish in the minds of some previously uncommitted voters the thought that Mr Hughes, rather than the Real Labour candidate, Mr O'Grady, is the true alternative to Mr Tatchell. If that opinion takes root, then a Labour loss in Bermondsey becomes a possibility.' As we now know, the thought did take root and the press made sure that those 'uncommitted voters' were left in no doubt about where they should put their votes to 'Stop Tatchell'.

Other papers that day returned to the theme of Foot's leadership: 'Foot's Fate Now Hangs On Tatchell,' headlined the *Express*. The *Sun* wrote: 'Labour leader Michael Foot faced a storm last night as fears spread that his party could lose the crucial Bermondsey by-election. Panicky Labour MPs were saying that if the polling goes against the party next Thursday Mr Foot's job is on the line and he could be forced to resign. Even Peter Tatchell, the controversial candidate for the South London constituency, said that how he fares will be a pointer to what could happen nationwide in a general election.' While other newspapers continued this line, the *Mail* went straight for the jugular with their story

'Jubilant Liberals Go For The Kill'. That perhaps should have read 'Jubilant *Mail* Goes For The Kill'. The *Times* ran yet another story headed 'Labour Right Wants To Lose Bermondsey'. The article stated: 'Senior figures on Labour's right wing remain so hostile to Mr Tatchell that they admit privately that they would like to see him lose so that the left within the party may be weakened. They see the struggle for control of the party as more important than the loss of a seat.'

The only press coverage I received that was at all encouraging was Tory MP Matthew Parris's article in Saturday's *Times* under the title 'Stop Being Beastly to Tatchell'. He began by asking: 'Am I alone among non-trotskyites in finding the vilification of Mr Peter Tatchell rather offensive? The attacks are always personally pointed rather than ideological... My purpose is not with personalities but to warn that we are succumbing to our national weakness of attributing to individuals conspiracies and plots that should correctly be attributed to deeper and more general forces. Left of Mr Hughes, the Conservative candidate, there is only one candidate who genuinely believes he could change the lives of Bermondsey people — Mr Peter Tatchell; and his own party, in paroxysms of hatred for him, are close to hoping that he will not win.' It is ironic that I had to be defended in print against some of my own party by a Tory, albeit a decent individual like Matthew Parris. All sides of the political spectrum now knew that my own party leadership wanted me to lose this by-election.

While the press were doing their best to undermine us further, hundreds of loyal Labour Party members were flooding into Bermondsey to help our campaign. The support we had throughout the by-election from ordinary members of the party all over the country was heart-warming. Our eventual loss was not due to lack of work on their part. It was the halfheartedness and sabotage of the leadership. Their efforts to sink us were that much more disgraceful when one considers the herculean efforts put in by hundreds of unsung comrades who gave up their holidays and took time off work without pay to campaign for a Labour victory.

That Saturday I also had to contend with the vilest piece of election propaganda that any candidate is ever likely to encounter. The constituency was flooded with 10,000 badly produced and anonymous leaflets bearing the headline 'Which Queen Will You Vote For?' Underneath, next to a sketch of the Queen, was an impression of myself wearing lipstick and pencilled eyebrows with the caption 'Red Pete Tatchell' printed below. This leaflet then went on:

> Peter Tatchell is an outspoken critic of the Queen and Royal Family — he believes that the monarchy should be abolished. The people of Bermondsey have always been loyal to the Crown. Many Bermondsey families lost loved ones during two world wars. They

fought and died to save their country — on the other hand Tatchell
ran away from his home in Australia to avoid fighting for his.
Soldiers from this area also fought in the Falklands — needless to
say Tatchell stabbed our boys in the back by opposing the war.

Tatchell is a traitor to Queen and country.

Don't vote for Tatchell!!

Should you wish to question Mr Tatchell more closely about his
views then why not phone him on... or visit him at his house which
is at...

The leaflet gave my home number and my full address. It bore no
publisher's or printer's imprint as required by law. It was anonymous,
illegal and an incitement to violence. Whoever the culprits were, this
leaflet encapsulated all the prejudice that had been systematically stirred
up against me over many months by the press and our political opponents.
It was they who had created the climate of hatred in which such a leaflet
could be circulated and find a response among a section of the electorate.
They were just as guilty. Within a couple of hours of the leaflet's
distribution, I began to receive a stream of obscene and threatening
phone calls.

We immediately asked the police to investigate who was responsible
and requested a 24-hour police guard outside my flat. The leaflet
contained a clear invitation to 'have a go', and judging from the countless
previous threats and attacks it was highly probable someone would.
Despite this, however, the police turned down my request on the grounds
that they didn't have sufficient manpower.

Here I was, the target of vilification on a scale that few public figures
have had to endure in the middle of a major by-election and the police
could not give me full protection. We were dumbstruck. Our election
agent and the London regional officers of the Labour Party were so
concerned by the leaflet that they advised me to leave my flat until after
the election was over. But I refused. While appreciating their concern
for my safety, I wasn't going to be intimidated by these thugs. To show
fear or weakness would only further encourage them. I stayed put. But on
police advice I boarded up my windows, installed two fire extinguishers,
a fire blanket and a rope ladder to enable me to escape out the back
through my bedroom window in the event of a gun or petrol-bomb
attack.

The *News of the World* led the next day with the headline 'Police Guard
Red Pete', erroneously describing how police were mounting a 24-hour
guard. It then went on to describe the hate leaflets in detail. The article
quoted Hughes and O'Grady as deploring the leaflet while at the same
time reporting the latter's remarks that 'Tatchell is totally unsuitable '
and 'doesn't represent the people'. Underneath the main story was the
subheadline 'Defiant Foot: I'll Fight On'.

Other newspapers dwelt on the same theme. The *Sunday Express* led with the headline on their front page 'Labour Fear Poll Fiasco for Foot'. The article said: 'There is no doubt that most Labour MPs believe they are heading for defeat in the general election if Mr Foot stays on.'

Rumours of 'Dump Foot' and More 'Own Goals'

The *Mail on Sunday* raised the spectre of a June election: 'Labour's dilemma over whether to ditch Michael Foot grew last night as the odds dramatically hardened on a June general election. Mrs Thatcher put Tory party chiefs on alert for a June poll when she met them at a private lunch in London. And that put Labour into a flat spin as they tried to calculate whether they dare to try to install a new leader before they are plunged into an election.' For once, the *Mail on Sunday* had got something right. The 'quality' papers played the same song, more or less. 'Sack Foot Battle Rocks Labour MPs' trumpeted the *Sunday Times*, while the *Sunday Telegraph* had the headline 'New "Foot Must Go" Pressure'. And all this was circulating four days before the voters went to the polls!

The press knew who was the real target of the Labour right. Foot's stand against me in the Commons fifteen months earlier was turning into his own undoing as well. In the press, both his fate and mine were indissolubly linked to the outcome of the by-election. In the last dramatic days of the campaign the mass circulation papers, read by thousands of Bermondsey voters, portrayed a picture of Labour as a deeply divided party in a state of shreds and tatters ready for a putsch against its leader. Unfortunately, it was a picture that bore more than just a passing resemblance to reality. The actions of the national party did very little to win those substantial numbers of Bermondsey voters who were still undecided in the last few days of the campaign. Indeed, they pushed them right into the Liberals' arms. The voters were rightly disgusted by the party in-fighting. They saw that O'Grady was the old type of Labour politician. They had no time for him now. On the other hand, they were fed the image of a notorious demon figure, Red Pete, a conspirator from a foreign land, who disdained Parliament, threatened democracy, and about whom nobody, not even his own party, seemed to have a good word. In such an atmosphere perhaps it was not surprising that so many of the electors went for the safe, conventional figure of Simon Hughes; a vote for nothing-very-much-thank-you, but at least Hughes was not warring with his own party and his leaders actually wanted him to win.

Monday 21st was to bring even worse news and mistakes. The *Mail* led with a story that was a typical mixture of fiction and exaggeration. Its banner headline proclaimed 'Militant Grip on Tatchell'. The article began: 'Members of the ultra-left Militant Tendency — whose leaders this week face expulsion from the Labour Party — have been at the forefront of Peter Tatchell's Bermondsey by-election campaign.' To 'prove' their claim the *Mail* referred to six canvassers out of the hundreds who came to help us. It reported how three of them who had recently written articles in the *Militant* newspaper were among my most active supporters. It is ironic that even though they did help in the campaign, the Militant supporters named in the article were among my most vocal critics in the Bermondsey party. They had never wanted me as candidate, and had been less than fully supportive during the period of my struggle to be endorsed. During the campaign, some Militants seemed more intent on selling copies of their newspaper than getting me elected. When the Bermondsey party's campaign committee issued instructions that no newspapers of any sort be sold on the doorstep, Militant defied the party.

Interestingly, the writer of the *Mail* article, Alan Hall, pretended for the purposes of the piece that he had, of his own accord and presumably without prompting from his editor, decided to help the Tatchell campaign because he was a Labour supporter. He turned up in Chaucer ward, offering his help as a loyal party worker. Over a two-week period, he wormed statements out of unsuspecting Labour canvassers to fit in with the *Mail*'s plan for a Militant scare story in the last week of the campaign. Sure enough, when his article appeared, he gave the entirely false impression that the Bermondsey party had been taken over by Militant and that I was their stooge. He had quotes from Militant supporters saying that Peter Tatchell is 'the only hope for people round here'. 'A true Marxist government is what is needed. That's why Peter is our chance,' another person was quoted as saying. Just for good measure, the *Mail* could not let the opportunity pass without throwing in its 'impartial' observation that 'Tatchell's support for homosexual rights provided a curious dimension to the campaign'. Curious to whom?

Over the weekend, David Fryer, our election agent, made a terrible blunder that further sunk our chances of retrieving a situation which was rapidly running away from us. He admitted to the press that he thought the poll result would be very close, even going to the length of predicting a recount with the Liberal. In a situation like ours, where there was already a strong campaign in support of tactical voting to stop one candidate, it was absolutely suicidal to declare publicly who the main opponent was and to admit that he was close behind us. What Fryer did was to signal to those who wanted to stop me where to put their votes. The *Times* on 21 February highlighted his mistake and added: 'The increased support for Mr Hughes appears mainly to be from would-be followers of Mr John O'Grady.' On television O'Grady said he would not be surprised if Bermondsey people turned to the Liberal. In our eyes this amounted to advising his supporters: 'Look, I've lost. So if you want to stop Tatchell, vote for Hughes.' It was not only the O'Grady supporters who were contemplating switching their votes. The same *Times* article stated: 'Some Conservative supporters are also believed to be planning a tactical switch in favour of the Alliance candidate in an attempt to stop Tatchell.' All the signals were there for tactical voting cutting across all known party allegiances.

At the press conference that same morning, our agent was unfortunately again caught on the hop when the press asked where our promised canvass returns were. We did not have them ready as planned. We had decided to withhold them till the next day while they were double-checked. We could not believe what they were telling us. The press hinted that we were holding back our canvass returns because they were so bad. On the contrary, we were holding them back because they looked so good, in fact, too good to be true. They were completely contrary to the opinion polls and showed a mere 4 per cent positively indicating they would vote Liberal, while we had 42 per cent. O'Grady had 8 per cent. There were, however, 29 per cent doubtfuls. Of course, the election result later revealed these returns to be wildly inaccurate. Yet they were not falsifications on our part as the press alleged and ridiculed. What happened was that people's voting intentions switched in the middle of the campaign. Most of the doubtfuls eventually decided to vote Liberal. Many who had told us they were Labour supporters were so no longer, but apparently felt too embarrassed to admit changing allegiances. At the Monday press conference, without any hard evidence, Fryer rather impetuously speculated to the press that he thought the Liberals were between a thousand and two thousand votes behind us. This was immediately taken up by the *Standard* which spread it across its front page, emphasising what a glaring tactical mistake the agent had made in telling Tatchell-haters how close the Liberals were, thereby confirming the polls and further encouraging voters to switch to Hughes.

Undoubtedly these admissions by our agent did us some harm. But by then the nearness of the Liberal vote to ours had already been fairly well publicised through the opinion polls. These were now having their full impact, and were causing confusion in our ranks and fatalism among Labour voters. The bandwagon was well and truly rolling and there seemed nothing we could do to stop it.

Morale among our own supporters was now low, not only because they realised that defeat was now clearly possible, but because the *Mail* story and our agent's errors had caused dismay and disunity in our ranks. The Militant supporters were very angry about the *Mail* article. They nursed a feeling of betrayal by some comrades in the party who had been quoted in the article as criticising their behaviour. That was always one of the greatest dangers of the press vilification; the causing of disunity among our own ranks. The lies and distortions did sow the seeds of doubt and distrust among former comrades and unmistakably weakened our fight.

Michael Foot came to speak in Bermondsey that Monday night to a public meeting at the London College of Printing. He was given a very enthusiastic reception by the packed audience. Naturally, the press photographers and television cameras were anxious to record the event for posterity. Here was Michael Foot sharing an election platform with the person he said would 'never be' an endorsed candidate of the Labour Party. Foot, as is his wont, threw aside his prepared speech and launched into an impassioned attack on the gutter tactics of the press and our opponents. He called the campaign a disgrace to British politics and added: 'I urge you to vote Labour on Thursday, not only in the interests of our party, but in the name of decent politics here in Britain. I ask you to repudiate all the slurs, slanders and smears ... We are not going to have our politics dictated by a smear and scare campaign.'

Foot went on to say that I had been chosen as the Labour Party candidate by the same process as Bob Mellish thirty-six years beforehand. He continued: 'I was not in favour of an immediate by-election here in Bermondsey... I thought it should be delayed because it might be an election in which the Tories and some of their hangers-on, in the normal fashion, would try to push aside the real issues and fight on smears and scares. It was for that reason that I tried to persuade the parties concerned, Peter Tatchell and Bob Mellish, that it would be in the best interests of Bermondsey, and of the Labour Party as a whole, that we should not have a by-election. Peter Tatchell kept his word. Bob Mellish broke his. That was why we have an election.'

Clearly, that explanation of events confirmed the theory of plots and pacts. Nevertheless, Foot's speech was heartening in its intensity and its public accusation of Mellish, his former colleague. But by that stage it was too late to stem the tide that was flowing so strongly against us. That evening, before he came to the Bermondsey meeting, the Tribune group of MPs had given Foot a rousing reception when he addressed them. They could not stomach the prospect of Foot being ousted and Healey taking over the reins. Perhaps it was the strength of their support that gave Foot such conviction and fervour when he spoke up for me later that evening.

On the Tuesday before the election there were more 'own goals' that we could have done without. The Troops Out Movement had requested a £50,000 grant from the Labour-controlled Greater London Council to monitor the operation of the Prevention of Terrorism Act. It was due to be considered by the Police Committee that afternoon. Here was another godsend of an issue to hammer us with. Naturally, there was a wholly political slant to the revelation. As the *Financial Times* reported, it was Shirley Williams who brought the attention of the media to the proposed grant, calling it 'the worst abuse yet of London ratepayers' money'. The Labour shadow cabinet had decided to oppose the renewal of the Act, but official party policy did not support the Troops Out Movement. Foot irately phoned Ken Livingstone, leader of the GLC, to rebuke him for allowing this proposal to come before the committee. He insisted that it be refused. The same *Financial Times* article ended with the comment that such a revelation about the use of public funds in contravention of party policy could only damage 'the already vulnerable Labour candidate Mr Peter Tatchell'. How all things seemed to be conspiring against us!

I was asked my attitude to the grant at the Tuesday morning press conference. I answered that as it was only a proposal at that stage, I would not comment on it until a decision was taken. The next day, after the grant had been turned down, I expressed my agreement with the decision. While strongly opposing the PTA, I felt that the monitoring of the Act would have more public credibility if it were done by an independent civil liberties group rather than an obviously politically-partial movement such as Troops Out. The row between Foot and Livingstone over such an inflammatory issue as Ireland, just two days before the election, hardly helped our campaign. Nor did the *South London Press* poll result on that same Tuesday, which under a front-page headline 'Alliance Ahead' gave Hughes a 9-point lead with 34 per cent and showed myself trailing with 25 per cent.

Grassroots Community Socialism

Professor Laurie Taylor of York University in the *Times* of 22 February introduced the rather dubious concept of 'Tatchell Man'. In fact the ideas he referred to are far from exclusive to Peter Tatchell. They are shared by a large cross-section of Labour members and even quite a few MPs. Taylor claimed that I had latched onto the need for a type of politics that 'avoided the woolly anarchism of the love generation and the hard-line authoritarianism of the revolutionary sects. Down-to-earth organisation without dogma. There was a model close at hand in social work, especially in community work: the practical involvement in the problems (or better still the "struggles") of ordinary people, in housing, education, childcare, medical provision.' After fairly gently knocking my chances of becoming Bermondsey's MP, Taylor went on to say: 'But Tatchellism — or radical post-materialism, to give it a title for the textbooks — has still got plenty of promise, quite enough to frighten a good many sitting MPs. Its claim to be a new kind of community politics may have some holes, but it's certainly more grass-roots, much closer to the housing and educational problems of the people it tries to represent, than either the old-time working–class Labour barons or the polite and slightly distant style of the lecturers and lawyers who've rolled into the Parliamentary Labour Party over the last two decades. It's also thoroughly pragmatic. Anyone can be its friend. Tatchell's own list includes feminism, environmental conservation, racial equality, disarmament, gay rights

and Third World Development. These are the groups which will involve
"millions of people in politics", creating that extra-parliamentary
pressure which has caused Tatchell so much bother with those who
unfairly wished to nail him as an instant revolutionary.'

In some ways this article misrepresents my politics and trivialises the
issues, but it does also raise important questions about the nature of new
left Labour politics and the new breed of Labour 'anti-politician' which
some observers saw myself as representing. More accurately than
Taylor's presentation, my view is that the transformation of capitalism
has got to be built upon a grassroots community-based vision of socialism,
created from the local base upwards with real popular involvement
rather than imposed from above as in the 'command socialism' of Eastern
Europe or the more benign Fabian version.

Grassroots community socialism seeks to link up with people's
everyday life and common experience to involve them in struggles to
defend their own interests, decide their own future and run their own
lives. In this process, the structure of power and wealth and the resistance
of the establishment to change is revealed to the participants. Political
consciousness is expanded. People become increasingly aware that what
they previously perceived as purely personal and local problems are
shared by many others elsewhere as well and are symptomatic of the
deeper-seated structural inequalities in society. Hence the need for
radical social change. The focal point around which grassroots
community socialism organises is not so exclusively the workplace, but
increasingly the state bureaucracy. People are nowadays experiencing
their main form of oppression less predominantly at work, particularly at
a time of high unemployment. Instead, as the numbers on welfare grow,
people suffer more than ever as dependants on social security — as
unemployed, pensioners and single parents who have to batle through
masses of red tape to receive meagre benefits which are no better than the
poverty line. Many others, even those in work, also increasingly
experience major hardship as council tenants afflicted by an upward
spiral of rent and rate increases and a downward spiral of repairs which in
some inner-city area can take months, if not years to get done. More and
more, the state bureaucracy is 'the enemy' and principal focus of people's
grievances. Whether it is the social security system or the housing
department, this bureaucracy is popularly perceived to be insensitive,
impersonal and incompetent. And often it is. Hence the need to defend
the rights of the people against the inflexibility and excesses of
officialdom, and the tendency of Labour's new left to look to forms of
autonomy and decentralisation including workers' cooperatives,
industrial democracy, tenants' participation, locally-based housing
management and the democratisation and humanisation of vast
anonymous public institutions such as the Department of Health and

Social Security and the National Health Service. This, more than anything else that Taylor's article mentions, is distinctive of the new grassroots community socialism approach which myself and many others are seeking to evolve.

Violence, Expulsions and Defeat

In the last few days of the by-election campaign, the atmosphere of hatred and irrationality reached fever pitch. It was an almost fascist-like mass hysteria, more reminiscent of Germany in the 1930s or McCarthyite America than British politics as we know it. Pilloried as a communist, foreigner, draft-dodger, traitor, homosexual and nigger-lover, I had to run a daily gauntlet of threats and obscene abuse, as did so many of our Labour canvassers. Such was the climate of fear and violence that people displaying 'Vote Tatchell Labour' posters had their windows smashed, and many others were threatened that if they didn't take them down they too would get a brick through their window in the middle of the night. No wonder there were so few Labour posters up! The case of a Labour canvasser who came down from Manchester illustrates the depth of hatred to which the campaign had sunk. On each of his first two days out canvassing, he was attacked twice simply for knocking on doors asking people to vote Labour. On the second night, when he returned to the home of relatives where he was staying, his cousin told him that he would have to leave because the neighbours were ostracising the family after discovering he was canvassing for 'that red poof' in Bermondsey.

As more and more incidents like this occurred, there was a growing feeling, even among people not politically sympathetic to Labour, that media lies and slurs were substantially responsible for the mud-slinging and thuggery which marred the campaign. An all-party group of MPs were moved to table a motion on 22 February expressing 'disgust at sections of the press, television and radio in their treatment of the Southwark-Bermondsey by-election and their character assassination and smear tactics'.

On Tuesday evening, 22 February, Thames Television announced the result of a poll that Opinion Research Centre had carried out for them. It showed that Hughes and I were running neck and neck at 30 per cent each, with the tide moving in his favour. From this point, Hughes was forecast the 'winner' and I was marked down as the 'loser'. In a period of six weeks from the *Mail*'s NOP poll in early January, I had lost a lead of nearly 30 per cent over my nearest rival. In the space of five days after the *Mail*'s second NOP poll on 18 February, I had lost another 7 per cent. Hughes was now confidently tipped by nearly everyone to win the seat. The succession of polls tagged the Labour cause with a sense of hopelessness and helped to create a tide in favour of the Liberals that was unstoppable. In normal circumstances that tide would certainly not have flowed so rapidly, but such had been the campaign of vilification against me that many decent people who would never have thought of voting Liberal had been convinced I was the monster figure that had to be stopped. Simon Hughes is an average Liberal candidate with all the political deficiencies this implies. He had made no impact when he stood in the 1981 GLC election in Bermondsey. But suddenly he was on the crest of a wave of general approval that had almost nothing to do with whatever personal qualities he may possess or with the attractiveness of the Liberal/SDP Alliance as a party. His bandwagon had everything to do with the hate campaign that had been stirred up for fifteen months and the polls that followed in its wake.

The day before the election, the papers played up the result of the Thames ORC poll just in case any Bermondsey voters had missed the television news the previous evening. Typical of the morning's headlines was the *Guardian*: 'Liberals Ready to Take Labour Masada'. The scene was set for the debacle.

There was however one final nail in the coffin of our hopes which had still to be hammered in. The NEC of the Labour Party were meeting that Wednesday afternoon to discuss the expulsion of the *Militant* editorial board. This was the meeting that the Bermondsey party had argued would prove a disastrous embarrassment on the eve of the election. By that time, Labour's cause was almost certainly lost. But if there was any remaining doubt, then the television news that night set the seal on it with pictures of those five party members trooping into Labour's Walworth Road headquarters and reappearing a couple of hours later having been expelled. By a vote of 19 to 9 the NEC agreed their expulsion. The motion to expel was put by right-winger John Golding. Foot and Healey both voted for the motion. The five were not allowed to reply at any length to the charges and no substantial evidence was offered. On television, one of the five, Peter Taffe, rightly denounced the NEC hearing as a 'kangaroo court'. What an image of the Labour Party to present to the public on the eve of a vital by-election! No political party seriously interested in winning an election would have allowed those expulsions to take place at that time. And I was expected to be the standard-bearer for this party at the polls the next day!

On Wednesday evening, the television news announced the results of the latest poll, conducted for the *Sun* by telephone, the results of which were to be published in that newspaper the next morning as voting began. This poll showed Hughes romping home with 42 per cent of the vote. Although the newscasters added the rider that many experts doubted the accuracy of telephone polls, the damage was already done. It was firmly established in people's minds that, not only was Hughes going to win, but he was going to win by a huge margin. The polls had done their immeasurable damage right to the very end. They had marked me as a no-hoper and created an atmosphere of despair and defeatism among Labour supporters.

The day of the by-election I put a brave face on it, as I had to, if only to encourage the hundreds of helpers who were attempting to get out the Labour vote. But I knew in my heart that we stood little chance. The Liberals were cock-a-hoop, and from what Labour workers were gleaning from people coming out of the polls, a considerable number of Tories as well as O'Grady supporters were switching their vote to Hughes in a determined attempt to stop me. The word-of-mouth signal round Bermondsey from the O'Grady camp was that all was lost and their supporters should tactically vote Liberal to keep me out. Such was the antagonism of the Real Labourites that they preferred the seat to fall into Liberal hands rather than I should win it.

By the end of the campaign, the Liberals were almost as tainted in their vote-catching techniques as the Real Labour canvassers. It was sad that they should stoop to such levels when they had always boasted that they were the party of conscience, of libertarianism, personal freedom and choice. That tradition had certainly not imprinted itself on those Liberal supporters in Bermondsey who derided me as an 'Australian draft-dodging poof' right to the end. It is ironic that, although I took all the abuse about the gay issue and not being 'Bermondsey born and bred', Bob Mellish had originally been an 'outsider', and so had Simon Hughes, while both were also enthusiastic supporters of gay rights.

Defeat was staring us in the face by 4 p.m. We had the consolation, however, that we had fought a clean campaign on a genuinely socialist programme. I was given strength in those dark hours until the official declaration by the immense loyalty and support of my comrades in the Bermondsey party and many well-wishers from all over the country.

The result came at about two on Friday morning. It was a major setback for Labour:

> Simon Hughes (Liberal/SDP Alliance) 17,017
> Peter Tatchell (Labour) 7,698
> John O'Grady (Real Bermondsey Labour) 2,243
> Robert Hughes (Conservative) 1,631

The National Front candidate polled 426 votes, but none of the other candidates reached three figures. O'Grady and the Conservative lost their deposits. However, O'Grady had served his purpose. By running against me he had destroyed old Labour loyalties, split the Labour vote and secured our defeat. Mellish left Bermondsey as he intended, inflicting as much damage on Labour as he could. He is now associated in Labour Party history with other traitors such as Reg Prentice, George Brown and Richard Marsh. In doing what he did, however, he destroyed forever the myth of 'good old Bob Mellish'. Even people who were not well-disposed to me found his behaviour and crude insults absolutely loathsome. His dubious political career ended ignominiously and without a shred of integrity or honesty attached to it.

Hughes, in his long 'Simon says' victory speech, very belatedly condemned the campaign of personal abuse. Although I felt sad at Labour's loss, the adversity we had been through for so many months produced its own energy and defiance. Even in defeat, as I stood on the platform at the count, I felt no regret for advocating the radical socialist policies I believed in. And no regret for confronting prejudice. I was very proud of all our comrades who had fought the good fight and fought it honestly. I was full of admiration on election night for their courage in defying the thuggery and intimidation which had shadowed the campaign. As I stood on the stage delivering the runner-up's speech, I could say with conviction that we had lost with honour. The Bermondsey by-election brought out the very best in the Labour movement — an idealism and determination to swim against an unprecedented torrent of abuse and smears. When the going got rough, we didn't scatter. We stuck together and stuck by our principles. That, surely, is what solidarity and comradeship are all about. In the midst of the gloom, it was immensely encouraging that there were over 7,500 real socialists in Bermondsey whose commitment to Labour was put to the ultimate test and who stuck by us in spite of everything. Not since the war had the people of Bermondsey been asked to vote for socialist policies or a socialist candidate. Perhaps, then, it was hardly surprising that we did not win a majority on our first try for nearly forty years. I concluded my speech with a rallying cry to party members around the country: 'We may have lost a battle, but we haven't lost the war. Don't mourn, organise for a Labour victory in the general election.'

The machinations of the party leadership had helped us lose Bermondsey, and the appalling result helped to prepare for the massacre which followed in the general election. The right wing of the Labour Party had gambled for very high stakes. As a result, the whole party paid a very high price. Such a foolish gamble must never be allowed to happen in the Labour Party again.

Chapter Six

Aftermath, Reflections and The Future

Our defeat on 24 February 1983 was not the first time Labour had experienced setbacks in Bermondsey. In 1923 and 1931, the 'turkey and coal' votes defeated Dr Salter and Ben Smith. In my election, however, Labour's opponents and their allies in Fleet Street didn't hand out turkeys or sacks of coal. Their modern-day equivalent was the lie and the smear. They felt compelled to resort to such methods because Bermondsey was no ordinary by-election. It had acquired a symbolic significance as a battle for Labour's soul, so much so that the result was headlines not only in Britain, but in many other countries as well. In West Germany, where parallels were drawn between aspects of my politics and those of the Greens, the result was the top news story on the day after the poll.

Press Reaction, Letters and More Threats

Here in Britain, that morning of 25 February, the news headlines were more often 'Tatchell Defeated' than 'Liberals Victorious', as if to emphasise that the main aim of our opponents all along was to ensure my defeat, rather than the success of any particular other candidate. The *Guardian* that day took a dissenting view from the majority of the media, which put the blame for Labour's defeat squarely on my own shoulders as an 'unsuitable' and 'extremist' candidate. Its correspondent David McKie wrote: 'The BBC team who polled voters as they left the booths noted that far more of those switching from Labour to Liberal cited the strife-torn state of the Labour Party as their reason for moving than specifically mentioned Mr Tatchell.'

Certainly the appalling state of the Labour Party and Foot's lack of popular appeal were factors in our defeat. The *Standard*, under a front page headline 'Massacre', that evening summed up most commentators' views with its sub-heading 'Tatchell Beaten — Foot Fighting for Survival'. Below, just to add to the humiliation, they dredged up a picture from their files of me blowing my nose to make it look as though I was in tears on the day after the poll.

The next day the 'Foot must go' chorus reached a new crescendo in the tabloids with rumours of new plots to oust him as leader and install Healey in his place. The *Guardian* reported unnamed Labour front-benchers talking about 'knives being sharpened in the dark — what we need is a contract killer'. Others referred to Foot 'gambling' his future on the outcome of the Darlington by-election in March. Even after achieving its goal of a Labour defeat, the *Sun* could not resist a full-page editorial overflowing with spite and malice which described me as 'a travesty of a candidate'. 'Who needed this little pipsqueak whose undignified posturing rendered him unworthy to be a candidate for the most obscure parish council, let alone Parliament?'

Of course the Liberals claimed Bermondsey as a great triumph for their party and its policies. But given that they had hardly mentioned policies, while ours were hardly ever mentioned by the press, this was rather an extravagant claim. Both the Liberals and their SDP partners boasted that Bermondsey was 'a historic turning-point in British politics'. Henceforth, they said, the Labour Party was finished and the Alliance was on its way to forming the next government. But even many hard-bitten anti-Labour pundits could not be so generous. In the main, they saw Bermondsey as a 'one-off' aberration given the extraordinary machinations and smears leading up to the poll.

The Liberals have had many such false dawns since the war; their 'amazing' by-election victory in Orpington in the sixties is a memorable example. Bermondsey was claimed to be even more significant than that, because it was not only the Liberals who had won this 'historic victory', but the SDP/Liberal *Alliance*, and they had captured a rock-solid, Labour-heartland, working-class seat to boot! David Owen, Bill Rogers, Roy Jenkins and Shirley Williams (who was present at the Bermondsey count beaming vindictively at the humiliation of the party she had stabbed in the back), were all quoted in the immediate aftermath of Bermondsey as saying that the Alliance was now the legitimate alternative governing party to the Tories. Four months later, Rodgers and Williams failed to get themselves elected to Parliament in the general election and the SDP ended up with six seats altogether. The Liberals fared slightly better with 17, but such results were ludicrously feeble when all their crowing and boasting after Bermondsey is remembered. The Alliance failed to dislodge Labour from its working-class strongholds in the general election, the very thing Bermondsey was meant to presage. The Alliance's best showing was in challenging the Tories in Tory-held seats, which says a lot about the nature and appeal of Liberal/SDP politics.

The Sunday papers were full of in-depth analysis, with some, such as the *Sunday Times*, reporting on the delight of right-wing and soft left Labour MPs at my humiliation and how it would strengthen their position in the party.

But the popular press just had to dig the knife in one last time. The *Sunday Mirror* pictured me beside the headline 'What a Freak'. The Labour press had its own inquest. In summing up the 'Bermondsey Disaster', *Labour Weekly* said: 'The candidate had laid himself open to attack... He was unemployed, a champion of gay rights, Australian, a supporter of extra-parliamentary activity and opposed to MPs' present salaries. Peter Tatchell's trouble was that he said so.' Others in the Labour movement were less charitable. On BBC Radio 4's *Any Questions* programme on 25 February, Frank Chapple, leader of the electricians' union, sneered: 'What we didn't need in the House of Commons was a gay draft-dodger from Australia, and we don't need them in the Labour Party either.' On the same programme, Jean Rook, that bastion of journalistic prejudice and ignorance, joined with Chapple in expressing low insults about my sexuality, implying that I had got my just deserts. She quite falsely claimed that I had rammed gay rights down voters' throats at every opportunity, when in fact it had been the press that focused so remorselessly on my gayness. Perhaps this is another example how the media after a while begin to believe their own lies. Rook and Chapple — could any two people deserve each other more?

Undaunted and undeterred by defeat, in the days immediately after the by-election we carried on our local campaigning as per usual. The very day after the poll, I held my Labour Party constituents' advice surgery, and the day after that a group of us toured local shopping centres to thank the electors who voted for us.

As I stood with my comrades in our local marketplace, The Blue, on that Saturday morning, two days after the biggest electoral defeat the Labour Party had experienced for many years, I was very moved by the number of ordinary Bermondsey people who spontaneously came up to shake my hand, wish me well, and say how sad they were at the result and how disgusted they were by the muck that had been thrown at me. Those many direct and sincere expressions of affection and support by ordinary Bermondsey people helped to remind me that by no means had all of them been taken over by propaganda and prejudice. There was still a basic human decency in the community, a common core of humane and tolerant values that we could build on in the future. Even the hard-bitten reporters who were still accompanying me that Saturday morning reflected that not everyone saw me as the monster from the Rockingham Estate. We even began to wonder where all the Liberal voters were!

In the weeks after the election, as we resumed our door-to-door visits and attended local campaign meetings on the continuing fight to save St Olave's Hospital, we were repeatedly struck by some of the responses we received from local people. Not infrequently, long-time Labour supporters would confess to voting Liberal. Typically, one old woman said to me: 'I'm sorry, Mr Tatchell, I didn't vote for you. I don't know why. It's just that the papers and everyone else were against you. They all said you were bad. I guess I just got swept along with the tide. Like all the rest round here I voted for that Hughes chap.' Comments like that just go to show the irrational atmosphere of the campaign and the effect of the polls and smears in creating a Liberal bandwagon. It was most encouraging how even six months after the by-election, when I was no longer the candidate and had faded out of the news, many local people still looked to me for help with their housing problems. Despite everything that had been said against me, among a sizeable section of the electorate there was still enormous trust and faith. It made me feel an even greater sense of gratitude to those whose loyalty to Labour really was 'through thick and thin'. Having also felt much gratitude to Labour's early pioneers who had been such an inspiration to me through our difficult struggle, I went to Southwark Park a few days after the election to pay homage at the Tree of Heaven (Ailanthus Grandulosa) dedicated to Ada Salter in memory of her devotion to the socialist cause and the working-class people of Bermondsey. My spirits were uplifted.

In the month or so after the by-election, I was deluged with over 2,500 letters from well-wishers all over the country. Most of them reflected the widespread public revulsion at the hate campaign directed against me. It was deeply heart-warming to read such kind letters of solidarity which cut across party political allegiances. A Liberal from Surrey wrote that he hadn't helped Hughes in the campaign 'because from all I had read and seen, you were fighting on the issues. I would have been equally happy if you had won'. Another Alliance supporter in Manchester complained, 'I wish the media had let me know what you stood for instead of shrouding you in trash,' while a Liberal voter in Edgbaston found it 'a frightening fact that the Tory press had decided that it was their duty to make and not report the news'. From Bury St Edmunds, a Liberal member of thirty years' standing confessed that Hughes won 'a hollow victory given the abuse you were subjected to', and in Ayr, another Liberal supporter suggested that 'our candidate would never have won if it hadn't been for the dirtiest smear campaign in political history'.

Even Tories were not slow to express their disgust. One of their members in Jarrow wrote: 'While naturally I am politically opposed to you, I am indeed sorry that your election was fought and lost on a slur campaign. Such campaigns only serve to damage our democratic political set-up.' Another Tory from Central London, admitting to being 'as right-wing a Conservative as you would ever wish not to meet', expressed his hope 'that you stand your ground in Bermondsey... and make it to the House of Commons'. An army major from Belgravia, describing himself as 'a Conservative of three generations', confided that he was 'very anxious that you would win' because the by-election 'was the most disgusting event I have ever known'. Yet another Tory who canvassed for their candidate in Bermondsey wrote to 'deplore the shameful and sick campaign against you'.

But it wasn't just Labour's opponents who sent messages of support. From Nottingham a nineteen-year-old unemployed youth wrote: 'I thought that you might like to know that some good has come from your struggle — you have inspired me to join the Labour Party when otherwise I would have continued to sit back and let others fight for that which I believe in.' An older man urged me: 'Don't be downcast at what has happened in this election. As an ex-Bermondsey boy who fought in the old days for our beloved Dr Salter, what has happened to you, they did to us. But believe me, we triumphed in the end.'

Then there were the many letters from people not involved in politics at all, often simply addressed to 'Peter Tatchell, Bermondsey' or 'The Rebel on the Rockingham Estate, South London'. A woman from Reading wrote: 'My mother, an old Irish Catholic, lit a candle for you at church. All of us, suffering the same brand of cynical politics, were praying for you.' Another began: 'I don't know how to start this letter as I have never written to a stranger before. But I had to write to you. I was horrified at the treatment you got; all because you wanted to stand for the Labour Party.'

And just to show how far and wide the Bermondsey saga spread, a sympathiser from Chicago wrote: 'If more people had the respect for their fellow men like you, there would be peace in the world... may God watch over you.'

All these letters were deeply moving and gave me a tremendous sense of reassurance and optimism. They rekindled my faith in basic human decency and made every burden we had shouldered seem worthwhile. Of course, not all the post-election letters were so uplifting. Still lots of hateful ones flooded in: 'I expect you are feeling particularly gay today following the very satisfactory and quite proper result of the Bermondsey election... the people of Bermondsey showed their disgust towards you — a filthy homosexual. At least you won't be able to corrupt the youth of the area or spread physical disease through your demonstration of buggery — the unnatural and indecent act between two dirty males seeking an erotic exercise. Trestrail is possibly available or Blunt — a little old perhaps for your energetic thrusts.' It is amazing how self-deluding some individuals can be about the nature of their own feelings and desires. Such relish, such salivating over acts that they believe, on their conscious level, they detest!

In addition to this hate mail, more direct abuse and attacks continued almost daily, even after the general election four months later. The virulent bigotry which was stirred up by the campaign was not something that could be turned off like a tap. It kept pouring out in hundreds of incidents months later. There were further attempts by car drivers to run me down. A bottle was hurled at me from a passing vehicle as I waited at a local bus stop. The keyhole of my flat was jammed with wire and nails. Swastikas were plastered over my windows. While out bicycling I was stoned on several occasions and once had a fistful of coins thrown at my face from a passing car. There were plenty of verbal threats too, as I carried on campaigning or even just went to the local shops: 'Didn't you get the message from the voters? You'd better pack your bags and get out of this area before it's too late.' All this has made me virtually resigned to living my life looking over my shoulder and answering my phone or front door with apprehension.

Reflecting on what most people acknowledged to be the dirtiest election since the war, it was amazing that we got 7,698 votes. The reasons for our defeat go much deeper than the by-election period itself. They began thirty years beforehand with the demise of the Bermondsey Labour Party as an active campaigning political organisation. Under Mellish and O'Grady, complacency and apathy set in as even the pretence of arguing for socialist ideas was abandoned. There was declining consultation and accountability, both to local party members and to the wider electorate. Southwark's Labour council became a fount of backward and unimaginative policies which created a gigantic and sclerotic bureaucracy, notorious for its inefficiency. Long before the Bermondsey by-election, Labour's hold had begun to slip as more and more local people became frustrated and disillusioned with the Mellish-O'Grady style of 'city boss Labourism'.

Between the 1970 and 1979 general elections, Mellish's share of the vote dropped dramatically from nearly 80 per cent to 63 per cent. By playing the anti-Labour council card, the opposition parties were further able to cut down Labour's share of the vote to 48 per cent in the 1982 borough council elections. That represented a 30 per cent drop in Labour support even before the by-election began. For eighteen months before the poll, as we began to revitalise the Bermondsey party and win growing local support for Labour, the area's two most influential political figures, Mellish and O'Grady, maintained constant public attacks on myself and the local party to undermine our success.

But it was denunciation by the leader of the Labour Party, Michael Foot, and non-endorsement by the NEC, which did us even greater damage. Their repudiation lent real credibility to our opponents' claim that I was a dangerous extremist who was unfit to be an MP. Thereafter, the opposition could always point to the fact that I had been disowned by my own party. In blocking my candidature, the leadership of the Labour Party were effectively saying: 'We don't want Peter Tatchell as an MP. He is not one of us. He doesn't belong in our party.'

The actions of Michael Foot and the NEC, more than anything else, opened the door to the campaign of vilification and gave Fleet Street the signal that I was fair game. For over a year there was tremendous controversy surrounded by constant publicity as the Bermondsey party battled to win my eventual endorsement. This battle and the general fight against the right-wing witchhunt not only presented a public image of a disunited and warring party, for fifteen months it diverted our energies away from external campaigning on the doorstep into an internal struggle to defend party democracy and the rights of constituency parties. Throughout the period of my non-endorsement, there was the non-stop 'drip effect' of a hostile media, culminating in nine major fabricated stories clearly intent on discrediting my eventual candidacy. As *Labour Weekly* pointed out, by the time the by-election campaign officially began, I started top of the handicap 'like a horse with his legs tied together. But despite this Tatchell managed to show ahead'. Not for long, however. On the very first day of the campaign, the party leadership confiscated our leaflets and cancelled our opening press conference. In the three weeks thereafter, the half-baked organisational support given by national Labour headquarters meant that in one ward we only completed a 40 per cent canvass. We were pitted against the combined opposition of fifteen anti-Labour candidates, most of whom sang the same simple tune: 'Stop Tatchell'. For every one canvasser we sent out fifteen others followed urging electors: 'Don't vote Labour'. Yet amazingly, after the first two weeks we still stuck doggedly in front.

From the outset, the more partisan sections of the press virtually ignored the issues and policies, preferring to concentrate on slurs and scares. But in the last week they went all out for character assassination and rumours of plots to ditch Foot as Labour leader. In the closing stages the opinion polls and tactical voting also came to rescue our trailing opponents, dramatically influencing the result of the election they purported to predict. Our agent's blundering admission that the Liberals were close behind us only served to confirm the polls and accelerate the switch of votes. To cap it all and crown our campaign, on the eve of the poll the NEC expelled five party members in a blaze of media publicity. Yes, with such odds stacked against us for so long and with so many 'own goals', it was truly amazing that we got as many votes as we did!

After Bermondsey came Darlington. The Labour candidate there, Ossie O'Brien, was a 'safe' married man who projected a traditional Labour image. After we won that by-election the right claimed it was 'proof' that the party would only win with 'moderate' policies and candidates. But there really was no comparison at all between Bermondsey and Darlington. To begin with, O'Brien was never denounced by the party leader or subjected to months of media distortion and innuendo. In fact, a sense of guilt among sections of the press corps at what they had done to me in Bermondsey helped ensure that O'Brien received relatively sympathetic coverage. Whereas Fleet Street largely ignored or ridiculed my knowledge of local issues, for O'Brien the same local familiarity was a great plus in the eyes of the media which made him their favoured candidate and eased him to victory.

Reforming the Media

The behaviour of the press during the Bermondsey campaign raises a whole series of questions which are fairly fundamental to the conduct of elections in a free society. Our claim to democracy is premised on the fact that anyone can put themselves up as a candidate. But surely the existence of democracy requires the additional rider that the views and policies of those candidates must be presented in a roughly equal and impartial manner by the media so the electors can make an objective and rational judgement? That certainly did not happen in Bermondsey. The readers of the popular press were given a jaundiced view and little opportunity to hear what I actually stood for. Indeed, when I picked up a newspaper I often saw a picture of myself that I did not recognise. The Peter Tatchell of the tabloid press was not me. Much of the media abused its immense power to control the news and manipulate information with the politically-motivated intent of discrediting my candidature. It was not a grand state-controlled conspiracy such as we associate with Eastern Europe or the Latin American dictatorships, but its effect was the same in undermining the free and open debate of ideas which is at the heart of the democratic electoral process.

In the fifteen months leading up to the by-election there were numerous false stories in the papers. Though the Bermondsey party made eight official complaints to the Press Council, by the time of the by-election this body had not taken action on a single one of those gross misrepresentations. It was a total and utter waste of time. Perhaps we should not have been surprised. The Press Council is financed by the newspaper industry and dominated by its representatives. Typically, of the 534 complaints to the Council in 1976, only 34 were upheld. Between 1977 and 1980, 75 per cent of all complaints to the Press Council were 'withdrawn'. The commonly cited reason was the complainants' frustration at the Council's bureaucratic procedures and delays. Some of our correspondence with the offending newspaper editors was nevertheless instructive. In response to complaints to the *Sun* about their 'Gay Olympics' and 'Middle-Class Past' inventions, Richard Parrack, the editorial manager, wrote, 'You make this allegation without any supporting evidence', as if the burden was on us to prove that the *Sun* stories were false! Following our objection to the *News of the World* retouching a photograph of myself which then portrayed me in an effeminate maner, Henry Douglas, their legal manager, replied by way of justification that the picture was 'transmitted by wire to Manchester. As not uncommonly happens in wiring, the colour tone was somewhat bleached and some of the features blurred. In an attempt to compensate for this, some retouching was done in Manchester'. He then contradictorily asserted, 'I would not suggest that the retouching was faultless,' but 'we do not agree that we have made misrepresentations'. Less than faultless retouching would seem by definition, misrepresentation. But not in Fleet Street!

Many times we were tempted to sue the papers concerned. But there is no legal aid for libel and it is a very expensive business. Besides, a number of papers warned me off issuing writs by stating that their defence would be along the lines of the Vanessa Redgrave case, i.e. although the articles about me were untrue, they were not defamatory because my extremist views place in me in such low public esteem that I have no reputation left to defame. Of course, I was not the first, and certainly not the last, to suffer at the hands of the yellow press. It is a great tribute to the determination and courage of people like Tony Benn, Ken Livingstone and Ted Knight that they have withstood the denigration of Fleet Street for so many years.

Out of my personal experience, I am more convinced than ever that we need proper safeguards against abuse of media power. To begin with, it seems absolutely wrong that a handful of mainly multinational companies should control roughly three-quarters of all British newspapers and periodicals. In six of nine national newspapers, ultimate control rests with a single individual, family or their trustees. Such a monopoly over the sources of news and information cannot be healthy for democracy. In the Bermondsey by-election, there was not a single Fleet Street newspaper which supported myself and the Labour Party, and in the general election, only one of the nine national dailies urged its readers to vote Labour.

At the very minimum, there seems a good case for diversifying and decentralising the mass media by breaking up the big monopolies and placing legal restrictions on the number of media outlets any one individual or corporation can own. It may reasonably be argued that there is no place at all for the private ownership of the means of communication where the rich and the powerful can buy political influence and manipulate news and information for partisan purposes as occurred in Bermondsey. As an alternative, ownership could instead be better vested in the hands of workers' and subscribers' cooperatives to give press and broadcasting greater independence from big business interests. It also seems very important to encourage a more diversified press and a wider range of choice, especially pertaining to minority interests and views which are largely unrepresented at present. Ways of achieving this could include a newsprint subsidy weighted in favour of smaller circulation publications, and an advertising revenue pool to collect a proportion of all advertising and redistribute it from the bigger and financially viable press and broadcasting outlets to the smaller independents. But at the end of the day, the diversification of the media is pointless if wholesalers and retailers refuse to handle minority publications. We therefore need a system like the French whereby distributors and sales outlets have a legal obligation to supply, display and sell any lawful publication offered to them.

Even this, however, does not solve the problem of the media fabrications and smears we experienced in Bermondsey. To its credit, the National Union of Journalists has a very good voluntary code of conduct which requires impartiality and objectivity and opposes inflammatory reporting that stereotypes and ridicules minorities. It is supposed to be binding on all union members. But in the by-election this code of conduct might just as well have never existed. The president of the NUJ, the late Jonathan Hammond, wrote in the *Guardian* on 8 March 1983:

> The NUJ has no political affiliation, so has no view on the result of the by-election. It does, however, have a very strong code of conduct and policy on unwarranted intrusions of privacy, both of which were consistently violated in Mr Tatchell's case. The personal abuse, vilification and lies to which he was subjected by several Fleet Street newspapers and journalists were appalling. I cannot remember any individual in recent times being subjected to such unfair and relentless pressures by the media. What was particularly disgraceful and unforgivable was the hounding of him and his colleagues at his place of work, the North Lambeth Day Centre, so much so that he had to leave his job. Mr Tatchell behaved with great personal dignity in the face of considerable provocation. The fact that some of this provocation was provided by NUJ members is not something of which the union can be proud.

With the union powerless to enforce its own ethics, is it not time that something akin to the NUJ code of conduct was incorporated into statute law, with very substantial penalties of up to £100,000 fines and six months imprisonment for offending editors and journalists? Direct recourse to the courts would be a far more effective way of dealing with misrepresentation, prejudice and harassment than seeking to reform the toothless Press Council.

Legal action can, of course, take a very long time, and would not have been swift enough to correct the falsehoods which appeared during the Bermondsey by-election campaign before polling day on the 24th. This requires 'right of reply' legislation. In the case of inaccurate reporting, press and broadcasting would be required to put the record straight within three days, giving equal space and prominence to their apology and correction.

Finally, the libel laws need to be reformed so that they cease to be the prerogative of the rich to protect their often dubious reputations by preventing the investigation and reporting of facts through the issuing of 'gagging' writs. Such a reform is in the interest of a free press with the right to investigate and report the unfettered truth. There also needs to be legal aid for libel, and libel law needs to be revised so as to end the absurd situation whereby reporting the truth without being able to prove it can sometimes be libellous, whereas fabricated stories may not necessarily be so. For example, there were other figures in the Bermondsey by-election who were also homosexual. But if the *Sun* had named them, those people could have sued the paper for libel. However, I could not sue the *Sun* for its Gay Olympics story, even though it was a falsehood. If I had taken the *Sun* to court, the first question their lawyers would have put to me in the witness box would have been: 'Are you a homosexual?' Since I am, I would have answered: 'Yes.' Next, they would have asked: 'Are you ashamed of your homosexuality?' My truthful reply would have been: 'No.' Then their lawyers would have enquired: 'Do you think the Gay Olympics was a reasonable and legitimate sporting event?' After hearing me reply that it was, the *Sun*'s lawyers would then have argued that since I was not ashamed of my homosexuality and thought the Gay Olympics to be perfectly legitimate and reasonable, what they had written might have been untrue, but it was not defamation of my character.

It is entirely unjust for the media to be able to persistently denigrate someone so their public standing is damaged and then claim as their defence that the person concerned is held in such low public esteem that it is not possible to defame them. That was precisely the argument used against Vanessa Redgrave and threatened against myself. The 'no reputation left to defame' defence in libel cases has got to be abolished.

Why I Stuck by Gay Rights

In the wake of the Bermondsey by-election, there was a lot of debate and criticism within the gay movement of the way I handled my own sexuality during the campaign. The *Gay News* editorial on 3 March described Bermondsey as 'the most homophobic by-election of our times' and the 'most long-drawn-out pillorying of a homosexual since the 1950s'. The editorial strongly criticised me for not fully coming out as gay and suggested that this 'closetry' on my part had exacerbated the vilification. Other critics likewise claimed that if I had declared my homosexuality from the beginning, that would have been the end of it, leaving the press with nothing else to print. If only that were true! The reality is that sections of Fleet Street were determined to 'get' me, and the admission of my gayness would have merely given them carte blanche to run a succession of 'kiss and tell' gossip stories about my private life day after day, which would have totally dominated the election campaign to the exclusion of Labour policies. Aside from the unique and exceptional circumstances that characterised the Bermondsey by-election, it is certainly important that homosexuals in public life are open about their sexuality. Keeping one's gayness secret and private only serves to reinforce the view that homosexuality is something negative and shameful that has to be hidden away.

Coming out not only lifts the burden of a double life and fear of blackmail, it creates positive images of homosexuals in society which can only help lessen the anxiety felt by many isolated and guilt-ridden young gay men and women as they come to terms with their sexuality for the first time. It was always my intention that as soon as the furore surrounding the by-election died down, I would publicly declare my sexuality. Indeed, if I had been elected to the House of Commons, I had hoped to persuade as many gay MPs as possible to sign a joint statement declaring their support for gay rights as gay MPs. As it is, many of them resist coming out because they fear isolation and vulnerability to exactly the kind of gay-baiting which I experienced. However, the safety in numbers afforded by a collective coming-out would make it more difficult for the gutter press to single out individuals and pick them off one by one. After the initial shock was over, a public assertion by a group of homosexual MPs would radically alter the atmosphere, making it much more favourable for gay MPs and candidates in the future.

One of the most distasteful and hypocritical aspects of the post-election debate within the gay movement was provided by the Gay Liberals and Gay Social-Democrats. In a crude attempt to score cheap party political points, they attacked Labour's handling of the gay issue, accusing us of 'dragging gay rights through the mud', and continued their smear campaign by putting it about that I had reneged on my support for gay rights and had even adopted an anti-gay stance during the by-election campaign. Such behaviour had nothing to do with promoting homosexual equality and everything to do with their own party political interests. It was an example of the Alliance's extraordinary hypocrisy, given their manipulation of homophobia during the by-election and the fact that not a single gay Liberal or Social-Democrat MP has yet come out. This latter fact is, of course, conveniently ignored by the media. Their persistent focus on my sexuality during the campaign was a supreme example of double standards and politically-motivated intent. After all, there are already many homosexual MPs in all parties, and there always have been. I have heard journalists themselves estimate there to be over one hundred gay MPs in the present Parliament, many of them pressured into marriage to ensure an unreproachable public image. Their sexuality does not in any way diminish their ability to be good MPs.

Some of them have held the highest offices in government and enjoy wide public respect. Sadly, among some of the electorate this respect might be considerably less if their sexuality became public knowledge. If anything adversely affects the competence of these gay MPs, it is not their sexuality, but their fear of exposure and ridicule and the double life and obsessive secrecy which they consequently observe.

So what made me different from all those other gay MPs and candidates whose sexuality the press ignores? Well, most of them are part of the establishment and the establishment does protect its own. Providing they maintain a degree of discretion, by 'gentleman's agreement' they are shielded from the glare of publicity by their establishment colleagues in Fleet Street. Such 'protection' is not, however, extended to left-wing socialists such as myself who challenge Westminster's cosy club. The fact that I was a radical Labour candidate fighting a crucial by-election in the run-up to the general election made my personal life 'fair game' for the pro-Tory press. But what Fleet Street really objected to was my socialism rather than my homosexuality. They merely played on my gayness to discredit my left-wing politics. This was the real target of their smears. My sexuality was merely the means to the end. If I had been a Tory, Liberal or SDP candidate, there would have been no innuendo about my private life at all.

In the weeks after the by-election there was one question more than any other which journalists put to me: 'In retrospect don't you regret making such an issue of gay rights?' My answer was always: 'No, I don't.' For far too long the oppression of homosexual women and men has been kept off the political agenda. It has never been seen as more than a peripheral fringe issue, in much the same way as racial and women's equality were relegated to the sidelines twenty years ago. As recently as the early 1970s, even sections of the left were still echoing the Stalin era in condemning homosexuality as a 'bourgeois perversion' — a vice of the middle class with fascist associations — which would 'disappear' under socialism. The more benevolent left simply dismissed gay rights as 'not a priority'. It was always something that would have to wait until 'after the revolution'. But, of course, the revolution never came and gay people were still suffering.

To confront the denial of our human rights, the modern gay movement was founded in Britain in 1970. It was not welcomed as an ally of the Labour movement, let alone as part of it. As well as battling the right and their friends in the medical and psychiatric professions, which at the time still described homosexuality as an illness and mental disorder, the gay movement had to confront the prejudice of socialists as well. In 1971, on the 'Kill the Bill' demonstration against the Industrial Relations Act, a contingent of gay workers were attacked by fellow trade-unionists. Homosexuals were also assaulted a year later when they joined the

Bloody Sunday protest against the murder in Londonderry of thirteen civil rights demonstrators by the British Army. A few years ago, when a number of gay people were beaten up at the Labour Party Young Socialists summer camp, the LPYS leadership did nothing to condemn the incident or rebuke the queer-bashers. Perhaps this condonement by silence was to be expected given Militant's control of the LPYS and its notorious antipathy to the gay rights struggle. Militant, with its appeal to macho workerism, now stands alone on the British left in not having a commitment to homosexual equality. Nor is it likely to have one in the foreseeable future. The Militant majority in the LPYS have successfully kept debates on gay rights off the agenda at the Young Socialists annual conference for the last eight years, preferring to have rehash debates on abolishing the monarchy instead.

On the other side of the spectrum, Labour's right wing also has a lamentable record of neglect and discrimination. A couple of years ago, the Labour-controlled Barking council sacked a lesbian employee, Susan Shell, purely and simply on the grounds of her sexuality. In Coventry, Labour representatives refused to hire out premises for the 1983 Gayfest, and the Manchester Gay Advice Centre only had its grant temporarily renewed after massive protests forced the hands of reluctant Labour councillors.

The neglect of homosexual rights by the Labour movement is all the more inexcusable when one considers that it *is* a class issue. Not only are most gay people working-class, they suffer disproportionately on account of it. Working-class homosexuals are more likely to lose their jobs, be queer-bashed and get arrested and convicted for minor homosexual offences. Middle-class gays, however, are more likely to know their rights and have a good solicitor, and to live and work in environments where their sexual orientation is better tolerated.

For all the failings of the Labour movement, progress is being made. More and more unions now recognise an obligation to protect their gay members against unfair dismissal. When Judith Williams was sacked from her social work job by Care Concern in 1982, NALGO promptly took up the fight on her behalf. Several other unions and the Labour Party are now pledged to extend employment protection legislation to make it illegal to sack a worker on the grounds of his or her sexual orientation. New left-controlled Labour councils have already adopted anti-discrimination clauses covering employment, housing and the provision of council services to gay people. To the outrage of the Tories and papers such as the *Standard* and *Sun*, a gay community centre and switchboard advice services have been funded through grants from the GLC. And why not? Homosexuals pay rates and taxes too. We have every right to expect that at least a small proportion of our money is used for our own benefit. As it is, what we contribute to the exchequer is often used to finance our own oppression. Gay people's rates help fund the police to harass us. By paying licence fees we support the BBC which virtually excludes the interests of gay viewers from its programming and denigrates homosexual men in mocking prejudicial comedies such as *Are You Being Served?* As for lesbians, the BBC seems to believe, or wish, that they don't exist.

Though the 1967 Act was supposed to legalise homosexuality, since then the number of gay men convicted for importuning and gross indecency has vastly increased in defiance of the whole spirit and intent of legalisation. However, similar activity among heterosexuals is rarely grounds for prosecution. In the case of importuning under Section 32 of the 1956 Sexual Offences Act, convictions can be obtained on the basis that the offending gay man was loitering and chatted up, or even merely persistently glanced at, other men. The police do not have to produce a victim or complainant in court, nor do they have to prove that a member of the public witnesed, let alone was offended by, the act of importuning. Indeed, most importuning cases are brought to court purely on police evidence. To get their evidence, many police forces use agents provocateurs (i.e. policemen disguised as homosexuals) to entice and entrap gay men into committing minor sexual offences in public places such as toilets, railway stations and parks. Having been encouraged by the police to commit offences they otherwise would not have committed, these homosexuals are then arrested and become part of the police's success in crime detection! In some cases, police still see homosexuals as a soft touch to boost their arrest figures. They know many gay men fear exposure, and even innocent people have been pressured by the police to plead guilty so as to get their case over and done with and avoid unwanted publicity.

Despite the 1967 law reform, homosexuality is still completely illegal in the armed forces and merchant navy, also for or with men under the age of twenty-one. With monotonous regularity, soldiers and merchant seamen with impeccable records are drummed out of the services. In a more tragic instance three years ago, a young gay army private was driven to suicide by remorseless bullying and ridicule.

Not long ago, a twenty-two-year-old man whose love for an eighteen-year-old was unmasked by the police was sentenced to two years imprisonment — in the 1980s! Such judicial medievalism is only rivalled by the case of a judge in the late 1970s who gave a man a twelve-month suspended sentence for killing his wife after discovering that she was having a lesbian affair. Justifying his leniency, the judge said the husband had faced a terrible provocation! Likewise, in divorce cases, many judges are markedly reluctant to grant the custody of children to lesbian mothers, even when these are best placed to provide them with a loving home and the husband is evidently unsuitable.

Immigration and nationality law is another area where gay people still suffer discrimination. Without any official recognition of long-term gay relationships,the foreign partners of British homosexuals are denied the right to enter and settle in the UK with their lovers.

Twelve years after the first Gay Pride March, there remains an enormous battle to be fought and won by Britain's three million gay men and women. That, perhaps, explains why I consciously chose not to flinch from a forthright defence of gay rights during the Bermondsey by-election. Since then, with the re-election of the Conservative government, this battle becomes ever more urgent. Mrs Thatcher's pledge to return to Victorian values means a return to Victorian oppression for homosexuals. After all, it was only just over a hundred years ago that homosexuals were still hung in England. Thatcher's vision of the 1980s is based on making a virtue of a return to laissez-faire capitalism, authoritarian government and puritan morality. It poses a grave danger to the rights of gay people, not so much through the enactment of new restrictive legislation, as through the creation of a climate of intolerance and backlash which results in more police prosecutions, more queer-bashing and more sackings of gay workers.

The biggest backlash of all is likely to be on the issue of so-called 'gay diseases' such as Acquired Immune Deficiency Syndrome, otherwise known as AIDS. Far from being a gay disease, gay people are merely its principal victims. Increasing numbers of heterosexuals are now also being confirmed as AIDS sufferers. Nevertheless, Christian and right-wing fanatics will no doubt scapegoat the gay community, hailing AIDS as divine retribution on sinners and decadence and branding homosexuality a danger to the health of the nation, as has already occurred in the United States. Although to date only a small number of people in Britain have been diagnosed as suffering from AIDS, in the USA there have been over 2,000 confirmed cases, including hundreds of deaths.

Our government has ignored all the warnings from across the Atlantic. So far, it has set aside pitifully little government money for research. One can't help feeling that if AIDS had affected new-born infants or expectant mothers, by now there would have been a national appeal and a new charity sponsored by the great and the good to pump millions into finding a cure.

Standing Down as Candidate and Labour's Future

Within twenty-four hours of the Bermondsey by-election result, I was swamped by pressure from local party members to stand down as parliamentary candidate. Initially, out of a sense of accountability, I felt obliged to accede to such overwhelming pressure. But later, after reflection, I secured the agreement of the party that there should be full consultation with the membership in the ward branches. For several weeks, this discussion took place at the grassroots. In the end not one single branch wanted me to remain as the candidate. It was quite decisive. The number of individuals in the entire party who urged me to stay on was less than a dozen. I had no choice but to do the honourable thing and bow to the wishes of local party members. With very few exceptions, their attitude was not born out of any sense of personal malice. It was based on the feeling that the falsehoods and bigotry surrounding the by-election had taken such a strong hold in the minds of many Bermondsey electors that they could not be erased in the foreseeable future. Furthermore, in the general election as with the by-election, it would be impossible for me to receive a fair and objective hearing in the popular press.

Local members believed that the Liberals had to be ousted as soon as possible, before they got a foothold in the constituency, and that I was the candidate least likely to be able to do this. The number one priority was to win the seat back for Labour at the next election, and another candidate was felt to stand a better chance of success. In my view, that was a perfectly legitimate position to argue, particularly since there was speculation at the time of a close-run general election and Labour would need every seat it could get. However, while I agreed that winning the seat back was important, at what price?

Post-Bermondsey there was a lot of talk within the Labour Party about the need for more 'suitable' and less 'vulnerable' candidates. More 'suitable' to whom? Doesn't that argument effectively mean more 'suitable' to the yellow press and more in conformity with popular prejudices? People who questioned my appropriateness should have first reflected on the history of the Bermondsey Labour Party. If ever there was an 'unsuitable' candidate, it was Dr Salter. A Quaker, teetotal pacifist and militant republican, he used to go around during elections promising to tax beer and tobacco. They were bad for people's health, he argued, and the money raised could be used to finance a National Health Service. These ideas were not at all popular to begin with among the dockers and working men's clubs of Bermondsey. Neither was his championing of home rule for Ireland and independence for the colonies. Taking in a black conscientious objector to lodge with him after the first world war created quite a local stir as well. But the response of Salter and the Bermondsey party was not to renege on their principles. They stuck by their guns and for many years Salter never got more than 2,000 votes in a parliamentary election. In the end, however, Labour did win a majority in 1922. Those Labour voters were not simply registering an anti-Tory vote or expressing the half-hearted attitude 'We'll give the other lot a try'. Through determined effort over fourteen years, the Bermondsey party had won local people to a real and positive socialist commitment which was to last almost another sixty.

Looking at the House of Commons today, its composition is very unrepresentative of the wider society. Most of its members are drawn from a narrow cross-section of the population. There are precious few women MPs and not a single black face is to be seen. Within the Parliamentary Labour Party there are already too many clones from the Labour candidate factory: moderate, middle-class, middle-aged, married, macho and male. Do we need any more? If, in the after-shock from Bermondsey, we merely restrict ourselves to reproduce that safe, traditional stereotype of Labour candidate, we will never get an adequate representation of working-class, women and black MPs — let alone any who are openly gay. Instead of overcoming prejudices, we will end up reinforcing them by conducting our parliamentary selection conferences within the parameters of 'acceptable' candidates as defined by the media and opposing parties. Allowing others to dictate Labour's choice of candidates is only one step away from allowing them to determine our policies as well. If we permit ourselves to be bullied and intimidated down that road, we will be colluding with the transformation of Labour into a 'second eleven' for the SDP.

As it turned out, the Bermondsey party was wrong in its reasoning. A very good candidate was chosen to replace me, John Tilley, the former Labour MP for neighbouring Lambeth Central. Though he was able to stand on his excellent record in Parliament and an untarnished heterosexual image as a husband and father, in the general election he did no better than I had four months earlier in the midst of all the smears and 'own goals'.

In the general election, the Liberals slightly increased their vote to 17,185. Though Tilley pushed the Labour vote up by nearly 4,500 to 12,021 it was really no improvement. Firstly, he had the influx of an extra ward with over 5,000 votes as a result of boundary changes. Secondly, the Labour vote was not split by an Independent candidate such as O'Grady who had taken 2,243 votes in February. Despite this, of the extra seven thousand votes which could have come to Labour, we got only 4,500 of them. Thirdly, all the Conservatives, up to 3,000 of them, who had tactically voted Liberal to stop me in the by-election, switched back to the Tory candidate in June. Presumably, a significant number of O'Grady supporters who tactically voted Liberal to stop me also switched back to Labour. Thus, in increasing their vote despite this big loss of tactical voters, the Liberals actually substantially improved their support in the general election. Given these factors, if anything the June result was even worse for Labour than the by-election and only served to reinforce the dubiousness of reneging on principles.

In years to come, the Bermondsey by-election and the general election which followed in its wake may well be seen as a watershed for the future of the left and the whole Labour Party. We suffered a terrible defeat, but in the process important issues such as extra-parliamentary action and gay rights which rarely get a public hearing were debated and some, albeit painful, lessons were learnt. One of those enduring lessons is that the Labour Party cannot witchhunt its own members and then expect to win elections. Another is that we lost support, not because our policies were too radical, but because we had not argued long and hard enough for them. If the Labour leadership had previously established a strong record of defending gay rights, perhaps when the by-election came the bigotry stirred up might have found a less receptive audience and our opponents might have been deprived of an ugly weapon which they so readily and effectively used to Labour's cost. It is this historic evasion by Labour of awkward questions for short-term electoral advantage that was ultimately our undoing in Bermondsey and, indeed, in the general election as well.

Even before the Bermondsey defeat, it seemed unlikely that Labour would win the imminent general election and form a new socialist government to rescue people from the oppression of Thatcherism. After the Bermondsey loss, despite victory in Darlington, the writing was on the wall. So where is the hope and optimism for Labour's future? It depends, in part, on us avoiding Labour's all too common tendency to set up scapegoats which can explain away setbacks. There is no simple, single cause for the two debacles of 1983. The right are wrong when they ascribe defeat to unsuitable candidates and extremist policies. The left are equally mistaken to put down our losses purely to the witchhunt, media bias, opinion polls, sabotage by Healey and Callaghan and betrayal by the last Labour government. These certainly were contributing factors, but the reasons why Labour faltered are much more varied and complex. Labour's rot goes much deeper and began much longer ago. In places like Bermondsey, up and down the country, Labour has decayed and atrophied. It has ceased to be the dynamic locally-based political force which built up support for the municipal socialism of the 1920s and 30s and paved the way for 1945. These local roots on the housing estates and in the workplaces have gradually withered and wilted since the war. For over a generation, we have taken many of our supporters for granted. Too often we have relied on the traditional loyalty of Labour voters and depended on a negative anti-Tory vote, rather than making the effort to win positive support for a clear socialist alternative. We are now paying the price of this complacency as measured by rising electoral absenteeism in working-class constituencies and Labour's long-term declining share of the vote.

This decline cannot be reversed simply by changing the leaders or the policies of the party, as some on both left and right seem to believe. It requires a much more fundamental restructuring of Labour as an outward-going and campaigning socialist organisation with strong local roots in the everyday lives, experiences and struggles of people in each and every constituency. Instead of concentrating almost exclusively on the formalities and institutions of parliamentary power, and viewing the party as primarily an election machine, in future we have got to put much more effort into the preliminary task which is to 'agitate, educate and organise' — to win the battle of ideas so that next time around, not only will Labour be voted into government, but we will have an unambiguous popular mandate for far-reaching socialist reforms. There are those who will complain that this sounds like a long hard slog. It is. As the failures of the Wilson and Callaghan years show, there are no short cuts to socialism, no easy routes. When Labour wins elections through fudge and compromise, it may end up forming a government, but at the end of the day it has neither the mandate nor the power to do anything very substantial. The net result is increased cynicism as more people cease to believe that Labour offers any hope of significantly changing things for the better.

Unless we learn the lessons of the rise and fall of Labour in Bermondsey over the 75 years from 1908 to 1983, in time other constituencies and other elections will go the same way and Labour's historic demise will continue. On the other hand, the next few years in opposition give us the opportunity to honestly and critically examine Labour's malaise in all its facets and all its rotten boroughs. We have the chance to reverse the decline through a wholesale revitalisation of the party's leadership, policies and organisation. Starting at the local constituency base, we have to construct alliances with other progressive movements hitherto outside mainstream Labourism and build a new majority coalition which, under Labour's banner, can unite all oppressed classes, peoples and minorities. Labour has to re-assert itself as the broad church of the left, the natural focus for all radical ideas and movements. If the shock at the scale of our defeats in 1983 can impel us to achieve this and turn ourselves outward as a campaigning party, then some good will have come from our losses. The victory of socialism has been long delayed. It rests in our hands to ensure that it is not denied.

Peter Tatchell
Secretary, Southwark and Bermondsey Labour Party
Rockingham Estate
September 1983

heretic books ℔

Heretic Books is a publishing imprint of the independent left. As our name implies, many of our authors are people who have swum against the tide and suffered severe persecution for doing so. The first few Heretic authors include three who have spent long terms in prison: Rudolf Bahro, sentenced in East Germany for his critique of 'actually existing socialism', Pat Arrowsmith, imprisoned ten times for her activities in the peace movement, and Alan Reeve, whom the British Home Secretary refused to release from Broadmoor for explicitly political reasons. We'd particularly like to recommend what these writers have to say.

Alan Reeve
Notes From a Waiting-Room   £3.50   US $6.50

After a violent upbringing, Alan Reeve killed a fellow teenager and was detained in Broadmoor, Britain's most notorious psychiatric prison. Though he soon overcame his mental problems, sought to live as decent a life as possible in this total institution, and reached postgraduate level in studies with the Open University, he also fought for prisoners' rights and gay liberation, and became a revolutionary Marxist. Fifteen years later the authorities still refused to release him unless he renounced his political convictions. While on the run, before his recapture in Amsterdam in August 1982, he wrote this autobiography, a brilliant exposure of a vicious system.

Pat Arrowsmith
Jericho   £3.95   US $7.50

A novel of the peace movement, set in the late 1950s and centring on the story of a peace camp outside a nuclear weapons factory. Yet surprisingly contemporary again today, not just with the resurgence of similar issues and struggles, but also in its depiction of the tensions within the movement between women and men, heterosexual and gay, pacifists and socialists.

Rudolf Bahro
Socialism and Survival

paper £3.50   US $ 6.50
cased £6.95   US $12.95

Widely reviewed and debated since its publication in October 1982, this volume of essays by one of Europe's leading radical thinkers argues that the liberatory goals of socialism can be promoted in the industrialised countries today only through the green movement. A book whose influence is sure to grow as the dialectic between red and green finally gets under way in the English-speaking world.

Other Heretic Books include:

Erik Dammann
Revolution in the Affluent Society

£4.95   US $8.95★

A concrete and practical project to tackle the inequality between North and South, stemming from the work of the Future in Our Hands movement in Norway.

John Collier
The Dynamic of Socialism

£5.95   US $10.95

A bold attempt to analyse the 'law of motion' of post-capitalist society, by a veteran socialist and one of the few foreigners to participate in Mao Zedong's Cultural Revolution.

Jan Myrdal and Gun Kessle
India Waits

paper £6.95   US $10.95★
cased £15.00   US $25.00

Beneath the pretensions of the 'world's largest democracy' lies a turmoil of conflicts moving ever closer to revolutionary explosion. Written with a deep understanding of India's past, this book offers a panoramic vision of this great country, and an invaluable guide to the storms now impending.

Louis Mackay and David Fernbach (eds)
Nuclear-Free Defence

£3.95   US $7.50

A symposium with 23 leading figures in the British peace movement, including Frank Allaun MP, Pat Arrowsmith, Joan Maynard MP, Peter Tatchell, Stuart Christie, Ronald Higgins. This book debates alternatives to **nuclear** strategy that range from pragmatic to utopian, and contains a **wealth of ideas** whose relevance is by no means limited to Britain.

Die Grünen
Manifesto of the German Green Party £1.50 US $2.95

The election address which won the German Greens representation in parliament in the Federal elections of 1983.

Amrit Wilson
The Leaves of Resistance £2.50 US $4.50

A study that connects the plight of the plantation workers in Sri Lanka, and the oppression of the Tamil minority, with the country's integration into the imperialist world economy.

Kit Mouat
Fighting For Our Lives £2.50 US $4.50
Cancer sufferers who have come together in the Cancer Contact group discuss their struggle for control over their bodies and for an informed choice about the therapies available to them.

★Titles marked with an asterisk are published in North America by Lake View Press, P O Box 25421, Chicago, IL 60625, USA. Our other books can be ordered in North America from Carrier Pigeon, 40 Plympton St, Boston, MA 02118, USA.

Elsewhere in the world, order all titles from Heretic Books, P O Box 247, London N15 6RW. For personal mail order, please add 10% for postage.